Highway to dystopia

About spaceship Earth, Climate Change and more

2nd edition

Written by
Mathijs Beckers

For Huub and Loek

"Everyone is an impressionist painting. Up close, lots of different colours that don't always make sense, but take a step back and you see the whole picture, the whole person."

- Carolyn Richards -

Foreword

This book is something from nothing.

My name is Mathijs Beckers and I am very angry about our lack of reason and science during our cultural, political, and economic endeavors. Dogma is pushing us in all the wrong directions, not only in a religious sense but also in an economic, political, and technological sense.

I am also very disappointed at the movements that are trying to discredit the science of Anthropogenic Climate Change and equally disappointed at the movements that try to convince people that we can avert catastrophes through the implementation of non-solutions. We all have access to Science books, we all have calculators and I expect everyone to read and do some math before taking hold of the reigns and steering us into a cul-de-sac with oblivion sitting at the end.

I hope we will both be much wiser when we reach the end of this book.

I am incredibly fortunate because I was born in the Netherlands. And this means that excellent education, good medical care, the freedom to play, food a plenty, great TV-shows, and true documentaries about science and history were available to me. Later, I also had access to free and unimpeded internet access and the chance to learn something about this wonderful world and the cosmos around us.

Other people aren't as fortunate because they live in a constant state of oppression and repression, and they have no access to the immense vaults of free information, they are being told how to live and what to think. Many people are barred from free inquiry, they live in a continuing and seemingly unending dystopia. They live in a world in which the worth of a person is determined by scriptural horse crap, or by supreme leaders with an absolute and iron grip, or by groups that spread fear in the hearts of the people, or by imperialistic regimes that occupy foreign lands with massive amounts of military power.

Consider the futures of all the children of our world, keep in mind that they deserve a chance to experience this world in all its magnificence.

It is up to us to make a difference. Let's free ourselves from these evils, let's see what we can learn and do to progress humanity in a more optimistic and just future, full of discovery and enjoyment and wonder. A future in which human potential will be maximized for each individual.

In my quest to understand the fundamental questions to the problems of our age, I've tried to be as inquisitive and understanding as I could possibly be. During my life, I've hung some skeletons in my closet. I have lived a far from perfect life. Having been depressed for fourteen years has led me through some very dark and daunting times. However, there's a second, third, fourth and even a fifth chance for everyone. There's always something else one can do. I chose to dedicate my life to try to understand the fundamental questions of our age, and I want to share this process with you.

I'm ill-equipped to do so, but I'm going to try nevertheless. I will not certify that everything I've written is true. You will have to find that out for yourself. I am always prepared to re-examine my reasoning, and so should you! If you think I've made a critical error or have said something that isn't true, please provide your evidence and explain why you think that I am wrong. I will change my views and my texts in accordance with the evidence.

I've made some unsubstantiated claims that come from my gut, from looking at the evidence and understanding some of it, but sometimes not all of it. it is my responsibility to my children to write this book, even if I will not see the catastrophic effects on Earth in my lifetime my two boys will. I want my readers to question what I have written, to become engaged in finding out for themselves what is true and what is not true based on evidence, and I hope that you, as inquisitive and intelligent readers, will try to understand what is happening to and on our beautiful planet.

Don't take anything at face value, be skeptical. Do not let yourself be fooled by politics, religion, doctrines or dogmas. Be very skeptical about them and challenge them. Let truth, understanding, knowledge and reason be your guides. Not just for you and your family, but for the sake of humanity, nature, and the Earth. Rationality can and will guide us out of this mess, but we have to start soon because time is running out.

I envy those who witnessed the dawn of the space age. In a sense, we're still in it, but the great, inspirational, first endeavors into space now lie in the past. space budgets are being cut. People of my age, gen Y, are now called the people from the climate change age. Instead of living in an age of optimism about human potential, we're being challenged by the troubles of our planet, which we've caused ourselves, economically and culturally and politically. We need many bright people that acquire knowledge through empiric principles rather than through doctrinal beliefs because they will be able to lead humanity out of this mess.

I'm not a proponent of tolerance. Tolerance can be patronizing and, in some instances, even harmful. Questionable practices, questionable beliefs, idiosyncrasies, scripturally justified foolishness, misogyny, hatred of same sex lovers, or even atrocities cannot be tolerated. Instead, they need to be challenged. We cannot accept people telling freethinkers and skeptics that their form of discourse is offensive. You take offense to something I've said? Here's one for my freedom of speech: Well so fucking what!?! (Thank you Stephen Fry)

I am a Freedom of Speech Absolutist (the one thing where absolutism is allowed if you ask me), you must be able to say whatever the hell you want to say.

Some theocracies have passed laws against offensive remarks and blasphemy (which is often considered to be the same). This is an impediment of the freedom of speech and freedom of thought. The true victims of these regimes are the repressed people who cannot express their thoughts and use their critical faculties. We must fight all these things by using wisdom and skepticism. Critical thinking and freedom of speech must be allowed, no matter how offensive it might be. No idea is sacrosanct, not even religion, religious beliefs and especially not religious dogma. And don't go about trying to shut someone up by telling him or her that you're offended, or even hurt by what they've told you.

The success of civilization, in my opinion, should not be measured by the success of individuals or their acquisition of fame, wealth and power. Instead, let's value the sum of happiness, gathered knowledge, prosperity, harmony, freedom and love.

We are able to shape our own destiny. We can engage in a pursuit of knowledge, a pursuit of excellence, understanding, and wisdom, and we must rely on science and its child – technology – if we are to have a justifiable sense of optimism.

We must avert, or at least moderate, a real and looming Arctic Methane Apocalypse and an equally serious Ocean acidification disaster. In order to do this, we must change the ways we think and act – but will we?

We spend billions on weapons and waging war and on searching for environment-damaging fossil fuels while ignoring poverty, disease and other problems we could easily solve. Don't we care about the children of tomorrow? The animals? The amazing discoveries yet to come?

Science, evidence, reason, knowledge, and understanding are beautiful things, please use them if you have the capacity to do so. I will remain on the fringes, I am only a bystander, a spectator, I love watching people engage in science, call me a science voyeur if you will.

There are absolutist and ideological and psychopathic and religious tyrants who want to stifle and even nullify human progress by destroying our true heritage, the accumulated wealth of knowledge.

We must never submit to these miscreants, we have to uphold the amazing gifts bestowed upon us by great individuals like Galileo, Pythagoras, Curie, Socrates, Descartes, Copernicus, Marx, Faraday, Plato, Euclid, Newton, Hubble, Pasteur, Aristotle, Carnot, Einstein, Eratosthenes, Paine, Darwin, Feynman, Planck, Russell, Keynes, Tesla, Hawking and many more.

The knowledge and methods and principles provided by these individuals is essential to progress. Without them, we would be clueless. It is time for us to remove the shackles of power and greed, and start working on a better future for all life on Earth.

Humanity can be a beautiful flower, it is, however, dormant and waiting for the correct conditions to flourish. Will it ever show its true beauty? That is up to us because we make up our own meaning. Let's make the most out of it by making Earth a place that is better and more hospitable for all living creatures.

We are all from Earth, and our petty differences do not count. just imagine our planet without strife over borders, ideologies, doctrines, power and commodities. I am an Earthling. We are all Earthlings. We share this Earth. We breathe the same air, and we watch the same stars with awe and wonder. I admit, I paraphrased JFK and Carl Sagan there.

I want to be optimistic. I want to dream about tomorrow.

Shall we take the next exit and leave this highway to dystopia? We've got far more interesting places to go. Let's embark on this quest and find out what we can learn.

Contents

From a cosmological viewpoint   1

From a biological viewpoint   10

The wonders of science   17

ACC – the sounding alarm bells   27

ACC – Ecosystem collapse   37

Diminishing Water supplies   47

Dystopian analogies   56

Obliteration humanity   68

Power, greed, dishonesty and false commitments   90

Homo Stupiditous   109

Women of the world   117

Forests and more   131

The Energy Challenges of Humanity   138

The harm of the extraction economy   145

Speculating about transportation and energy changes   161

Questioning renewable technologies   173

The nuclear stigma   188

Energy decision making   210

The new "Global Manhattan Project"   222

Retrospect & conclusions   240

Appendix I   255

   Reading, listening and viewing recommendations   255

Appendix II   266

   Organizations   266

Appendix III   269

   References & Backgrounds   269

From a cosmological viewpoint

"A mote of dust suspended in a sunbeam" a small portion of a wonderful phrase coined by Carl Sagan. We live on a pale blue dot, a tiny speck of dust in an immeasurable Universe.

Imagine the Hubble Telescope flying around in the Andromeda Galaxy, 2,5 million light years away, taking a snapshot of our Galaxy, the Milky Way. Even with the best possible resolution, we would not be able to see the Earth on that picture among the 400 billion stars that call the Milky Way their home. Our beautiful Earth would not even be a pixel in this amazing picture would-be-taken by the Hubble Telescope so far away.

The Hubble telescope, fortunately, remains relatively close to Earth and keeps peering into deep space and delivers us the most magnificent pictures of distant galaxies, nebulas, and stars. There is a YouTube video out there of a stupefying photograph of the Andromeda Galaxy, made by the Hubble Telescope, it's absolutely awesome!

One light year is the distance a photon of light will travel at the speed of light in a year. A light year is about $9,46 \times 10^{15}$ (9,46 trillion) meters or roughly 5,8 trillion miles, a figure that boggles the mind. If we continue this exercise by comparing our solar system to the galaxy we live in, we will discover that we're microscopically small. And if we compare our galaxy to the universe, we're nothing but a speck of dust in an immeasurable universe filled with beauty of a majestic sort.

Because space is so vast, it is almost incomprehensible. The observable universe has a diameter of 28 billion light years and it is expanding at an accelerating rate. The galaxies and stars we've observed at the outer edges of space, our cosmic horizon if you will, are now much farther away than when we first saw them. Does this mean that we cannot see the entire universe? Yes, that is precisely what it means. We can assert with a high degree of probability that the entire universe has a larger diameter than the observable one.

Our Universe probably began with a "big bang" roughly 13.7 billion years ago. What set it off is unclear. We do not know why the big bang occurred. It is hypothesized that time, gravity, the weak and the strong force got created right after the big bang.

Not long after the big bang some of the most basic elements were created: Hydrogen isotopes, Helium isotopes, Lithium and small amounts Beryllium. This process is called Big Bang Nucleo-synthesis or Primordial Nucleosynthesis. As the universe cooled, dense clouds of hydrogen and helium gas formed. and once these clouds had the right density and internal pressure, thermonuclear fusion began creating the first stars about 200 million years after the big bang.

In these first stars, new elements were formed through Nucleo-synthesis. Through the fusion of hydrogen atoms and helium atoms into the heavier elements, all of the naturally occurring elements on the periodic table were created. Later came the heavy, man-made elements, thanks to nuclear research on Earth.

When the first dying stars ran out of hydrogen and helium, leaving nothing but iron and some other heavy elements in the core, they exploded, dispersing all the newly formed elements into the universe. This cosmic evolution eventually led to the formation of galaxies, nebulas, stars, terrestrial (rocky) and gaseous planets, dwarf planets, and asteroids.

These stars ending in supernovae are really awe inspiring. Before they die, they shine with the intensity of millions of stars. They shine so bright they seem as bright as the center of galaxies. And as they explode, an amazing amount of energy and materials gets released into the surrounding universe in a colorful cosmic display of power. These supernovae have seeded the universe with the atoms necessary for life. A supernova precipitated the birth of our solar system, we can exist because another big star died. "*We are made out of star stuff.*" as Carl Sagan said and later repeated by Lawrence Krauss and Neil deGrasse Tyson.

These are some of the fundamental questions occupying our minds: Where did energy and matter come from? What was there before the big bang? How does the universe work? People with incredibly powerful brains are working on these issues and trying to find the answers.

We once believed that the universe was infinite and that the gravity of all the stars and the planets kept everything together. However, scientists have recently discovered that the Universe is actually expanding – or inflating. Does this mean that some of the stars and planets are moving apart at the speed of light, or even faster? It does not, scientists have concluded that it is the space between the stars that is expanding.

This would also explain how the universe could expand within seconds from the size of marble or even smaller into a universe that is thousands, millions or even billions of light-years across.

Early humans were fascinated by the motions of the moon and the sun, the stars and the constellations and the occasional "shooting star". Later we discovered the beauty of other planets, planetoids, comets, meteors and asteroids, other galaxies, supernovae and quasars, and nebulas.

The beautiful eagle nebula, which contains the "pillars of creation", has been photographed in great detail by the Hubble Telescope. The pillars of creation are so named because in these pillars of gas and dust new stars are formed.

The universe is a wondrous and mystifying display for us to observe. The immense beauty of the cosmos is there to behold, to try and make sense of it by being part of the great scientific journey of cosmology is inspiring.

Earth is situated somewhere in the backwaters of the Universe. We are like a speck of dust and this speck of dust plus the sun and the moon would be all we know were it not for people like Sir Isaac Newton, Johannes Kepler, Galileo, Copernicus and people like Edwin Hubble, Konstantin Tsiolkovsky, Wernher von Braun, Robbert Goddard and more recently Arnold Penzius, Robert Wilson, Carl Sagan, Isaac Asimov and Stephen Hawking and Neil deGrasse Tyson.

These people had vision, they wanted to look up to the skies and imagine what was up there. Not only did they imagine beautiful things, they scientifically researched and innovated the view and knowledge of the human race upward. From early rudimentary inventions such as models of our solar system to more sophisticated ones like telescopes, rockets, satellites, space stations and even planetary rovers. We have to thank these people, and the thousands of people who engaged on these endeavors with them, for the little yet incredibly valuable knowledge about our cosmos which we have gained ever since.

Let's save a special place of honor for Yuri Gagarin, Alan Shepard, Gus Grissom, Gherman Titov and John Glenn. The astronauts who captivated our imaginations. Envision the scene that Neil

Armstrong and Buzz Aldrin saw when they landed on the moon on July 24th, 1969. No man had ever seen the Earth from the Moon up until then. One can only imagine what the crew of the Apollo 11 mission felt during those 21 hours on the moon as pioneers for the human race. Eventually, 12 people visited the moon, but for some reason, we stopped doing it. Only a couple of hundred people have joined the ranks of the great pioneers, the people who went up into the frontier of the unknown, into space.

There are stars in the universe that are much bigger than our sun, which is the largest sphere in our solar system. Try to imagine how tiny the sun is compared to the (arguably) largest star humanity has discovered so far. It is called UY Scuti and it is 9500 light years away, and although it is a billion times larger than our sun, it is insignificant in the vastness of space, as are we.

Nevertheless, what we have on our Earth is precious and we need to employ intelligence, science, reason, understanding and wisdom if we want our grandchildren to enjoy and love the planet that nurtures us – the planet that we have unwittingly despoiled and must now struggle to restore.

Earth is our spaceship, it placidly zooms through space around the sun. We all breathe the air that is created by photosynthetic life forms. We share the Earth with countless of other beings. We call this place home. We have not yet discovered another planet which has life as well. We know of no other planet that could sustain us, which is why the earth is quite literally precious.

The Earth and the Sun are about 4,6 billion years old. Our solar system formed with the most dense elements near the center, and the less dense materials further away from the sun. Our wonderful star bathes the Earth with the energy it needs to be a life-sustaining planet.

The energy which gets emitted by the sun is generated by Thermonuclear Fusion of hydrogen. It is estimated that the sun has enough hydrogen for this process to last for another 4 or 5 billion years. When the sun runs out of hydrogen, it will become what Astronomers and Cosmologists call a red giant. Growing large enough to engulf the earth, where life will already have ended.

We humans are having a terrible effect on spaceship Earth, and maintenance is severely lacking. If you compared the Earth to a car, it would be severely dented and scratched, the interior would be worn out and the engine would be running on only three cylinders instead of four. The Earth is becoming less able to sustain life, partly because our ecosystem is damaged by the pursuit of riches and wealth. Massive amounts of evidence are being presented to us on a daily basis by observing scientists from all over the world.

Some of the observations are made by satellites that gather data on emission quantities, soil moisture levels, ice sheet data, oceanic temperatures, deforestation rates plus plankton and algae declines. These observations reveal that the earth's biosphere is not only degrading, but it will also soon become worse unless we drastically reduce the burning of fossil fuels and biomass for creating electricity, for heating and for transportation while simultaneously doing whatever it takes to hold the earth's human population at or below present levels.

Humans seem to be unaware that catastrophic climate events, present and coming, can be caused by us. The massive release of arctic methane, the rising temperature of the seas and the oceans, the acidification of the oceans and the consequential decline in carbon capturing life forms like algae and phytoplankton should ring bells of alarm, but even the dying coral reefs, the shrinking global fresh water supplies, crop failures and rising sea levels fail to capture the attention of many people who simply don't know how bad things are becoming – or just don't care.

Even if we could avert these catastrophes, we would not be in the clear. An asteroid is said to have led to the extinction of the dinosaurs 64 million years ago, and there are comets in our Solar System, which could do the same. Apophis, a planetoid that comes quite near the Earth, could become a so-called impactor. If it hits the Earth, mass extinctions would be inevitable.

For evidence of prior impacts, consider the geology of the terrestrial (rocky) planets in our solar system: the Earth, Mars, Venus, and Mercury or the moons of our giant gaseous neighbors, which are strewn with thousands of impact marks from meteors and asteroids. All these planets and moons have been bombarded with asteroids. Mars in its current form is the product of a planet-sized impactor hitting it. There is also the broadly accepted hypothesis that the Moon is a result of a young and primordial Earth being hit with a planetary sized body or protoplanet the size of Mars called Theia.

Fortunately, the biggest impact yet to happen is not due for a long time. The Andromeda Galaxy, the Milky Way's closest neighbor, is on a direct collision course with the Milky Way. One can only speculate what kind of influence that event will have on our solar system if it still exists in its current form. The collision could be cataclysmic, it could be a strange sort of tombola of stars and planets swirling around each other seemingly erratically, who knows what will happen, these questions will be answered by brilliant astrophysicists.

Cosmology has led to new knowledge and understanding, not just of our Earth but also about its place and significance in the universe. we must use this knowledge to create a more sustainable and durable society – a society geared toward achieving greatness, not in a destructive and antagonistic sense, but through progress in scientific, cultural and technological ways. All this knowledge is readily available via libraries, the internet or television, yet we fail to reduce our practices that damage the one thing that keeps us alive, the wonderful spaceship called Earth.

My *infatuation* with cosmology began with a fascination for science fiction. I am a big fan of Star Wars and Star Trek. I used to imagine flying in a spaceship like the Millennium Falcon or the Enterprise. When I was a boy, I was always watching the night sky, and when I started recognizing constellations and stars, my love for Cosmology was born. It grew steadily with the endeavors of humankind, especially seeing the wondrous pictures made by the Hubble Telescope. The universe is even more beautiful than I first imagined, the colorful pictures of other planets, nebula's and spiraling galaxies are amazing.

I recently stumbled upon a breathtaking, one hour video made by an astronaut while on a spacewalk around the International Space Station. anyone who watches this video will become more aware of the immense beauty of our planet. You can find it on the sciencealert.com website.

Our future lies in space. Not only on the moon or on mars, but also on Europa, Ganymede, Callisto, Engaladus, Triton, Titan, Mimas, and Pluto. Mars will be our next stop, of that I am quite sure. humans need a diversion from its self-destructive path. We need a sense of optimism that will have grown once we've been on Mars. Imagine a human civilization extended into space with a permanent presence. Space stations around all the planets making observations, constant travel between Earth, the moon, mars and the other planets and moons. Imagine the first humans arriving at Pluto, the small dwarf-planet right on the outer edges of our solar system. To go there, to look for what is out there is – for me – the ultimate trek to engage in.

Highway to Dystopia

Imagine cracking the code for faster modes of travel or becoming able to reach or even surpass light-speed – or making the trip to the next solar system in a matter of years! Reaching Proxima Centauri would be a staggering achievement. having done that, we can go anywhere, but it will take the full measure of human ingenuity to get it done. Will it be a hyperdrive? A warp drive? Will it be a way of shrinking and expanding space? Will it be a rocket or a booster powered by nuclear fusion? We do not know, we will have to find out, and we will only do so if we set out to do the research and to do the testing and to go out pioneering and discover great things.

"If we knew what it was we were doing, it would not be called research, would it?" – Albert Einstein.

We need to keep reaching out into the future to inspire youths with wonderful discoveries and engage with them in the love for science. Nothing is going to last forever. Within the context of deep time, our existence, our being here is meaningless. It will end. This sounds nihilistic, but we can make this brief flash of human existence grand and meaningful as we make up our own meaning.

We could and should rise to a higher form of civilization that is more in tune with nature. It all starts with us. Be the future physicist, cosmologist, the planetary scientist, geologist, biologist, be the future rocket scientist or the space engineer. To do the things that improve our knowledge and understanding is to step into the footsteps of the great and visionary pioneers of cosmology and physics. We must reach for the planets and the stars and all the other wonderful, magnificent and majestic manifestations beyond our Earth's horizons. Let's keep discovering new and wonderful things. We don't have to linger on in meaninglessness like some people would want us to. We can go out there and discover many new things while Earth, our spaceship, will remain our home, until its very end.

From a biological viewpoint

I love to take longs walks in the parks where I live. One day I walked through a park with a sandy flat, some shrubs, small plants, lots of insects and little ponds. I am always amazed at the multitude of different animals and insects that live there. I saw a buzzard flying around looking for prey and a flock of startled ducks flying off into the distance. On a path I came across a small adder, a European snake, sunbathing on the sand with its head raised slightly, and in a nearby pond, several startled frogs dove to safety when I approached. I spend much time visiting these parks and watching all these animals.

From very small and simple origins complex life has evolved over millions of generations. For billions of years, life has roamed the surface of the Earth, gradually creating the diversity that exists today. 98% of all species that ever lived have gone extinct, but our beautiful planet still teems with an incredible versatility of life.

There is a great variance of life on our world of small creatures and large creatures, of plants, trees, flowers, insects, fish, reptiles, mammals, marsupials and birds. Creatures and views in all hues. The green of the trees and the plants, the gray of the rock and the blue of the sky and the sea. The colors of our world are amazing, consider a bright red parrot or a striped Zebra. Or a peacock with its brightly colored feathers spread to impress the females of its species. This is an appeal to the recognition of beauty. We live on a wonderful planet, a great display of immense beauty that we need to cherish and protect. For it is here only on a temporal notice. Before you know it, it is gone like so many species have gone before us.

We have to find out more about the wonders of nature, and we need the time to do so. The exploration in biology is far from over, it has only just begun. Great pioneers of biology have set foot in completely new and unknown areas of knowledge.

I am talking of course about Charles Darwin and his theory of Evolution, which he meticulously described in "the Origin of Species". The theory of Evolution is the basis for all biological knowledge and biological scientific research. People often fail to grasp the meaning of the word theory. A theory is an explanation on how something works which is substantiated by large amounts of evidence and facts. It is not the "theory" that is used in police detective stories, which are often personal opinions based on hunches and gut feelings. Watering down biology because there are some people who seem to think that evolution conflicts with their religion is absurd. If we yield, our world will become a poorer, more ignorant place. In fact those who reject evolution are doing themselves and their children a tremendous disservice. Call it the devolutionary process. I do not know who started this delusional movement, but giving equal time to pseudoscientific subjects like creationism or "intelligent design" under the guise of fairness is mad. These people want to push us into a neo dark-age.

We're not going to call the thousands upon thousands of biologists and geneticists and paleontologists to tell them that their work has been in vain, we're not mad, the creationists are.

All life on Earth is connected, and biologists envision these connections with an evolutionary tree of life, which can be found in every biology book and on the internet, simply Google it. The tree of life shows how all species are connected to each other and have evolved from one species into another over billions of years. The tree of life shows just how closely related we are to Chimpanzees, Bonobos, Gorillas and more distant but beautiful Orangutans. Before all these species with which we share much kinship lived a plethora of beautiful apes.

Lucy for instance has become a household name, she is member of a species, Australopithecus Afarensis, ancestral to several of the hominids. Her species lived about 3,2 to 2,9 million years ago. From her species bloomed a whole set of different hominids that went extinct, best known are the Neanderthals and Homo Erectus. We even have pictures and sculptures of how Lucy probably looked. Many people might mistake Lucy for a small gorilla or chimpanzee if she were to appear today, but she is not the common ancestor of Homo Sapiens, Chimpanzees, Gorillas, and the incredibly intelligent Bonobos. That species lived longer ago, it is now believed to be about 7 to 10 million years ago. And we, Homo Sapiens, are all that is left from this branch of human life.

There are many odd relationships in the animal kingdom. What if I told you that trees and plants are distant cousins of the humans, or that bacterium and tigers are related? Or that all life bloomed from a single point of conception a few billion years ago.

Although it's hard to believe, whales are related to hippos and even more surprisingly, we know that the Elephant is related to the Rock Hyrax, a small furry animal that looks like a rodent. Close relatives of the Elephants also include Elephant Shrews (small insect eaters), Aardvarks and even Sea Cows – and we know this because of the molecular evidence found in DNA and certain morphological similarities. This gradual divergence which occurred over millions of years led to a great diversity in just a small part of the tree of life. Their common ancestors probably became separated causing some to adapt to new circumstances in a process that leads to what scientists call speciation.

Highway to Dystopia

The relationship between hippos and whales is addressed by a YouTube video called "Evolution of Whales animation": it shows how Pakicetus, a land animal, evolved from living on land to becoming semi-aquatic before becoming the fully aquatic ancestor of the many species of whales we know today. The common ancestor of whales and hippos must have become segregated, and each adapted to different circumstances over long periods of time. It is believed that this segregation, or split if you will, occurred gradually about 55 million years ago. Natural selection has been the catalyst in this process. Animals with characteristics better suited to the changing environment survived and propagated. After thousands of generations, significant change could be noticed.

There's a fair amount of predictability in nature, and if you study nature carefully, you can predict what is happening. For instance, if you pull back a rotting piece of bark, you will find certain insects, if you go to the plains of the Africa, you are bound to see predators trying to catch their prey. Scientists not only study living animals and plants they also examine anatomical evidence, evidence in the fossil record, and evidence in DNA. Animals that are seemingly different in size and lifestyle might be closely related to each other. It is all due to the adaptation to different circumstances over periods of deep time and many generations that lead to these great differences.

The secrets unlocked by molecular Biology have given us new insights in the evolutionary pathways of many species all around the world giving us peeks into their ancestry. Biology has been "digitalized", and genes contain information that explains the unknowns of the tree of life, allowing us to see similarities that no one had seen before.

This great variety, this wondrous tree of life in all its magnificence is there, and we have the chance to explore it. To dig into the Earth and look for new species to complete this tree. Look at it as a big puzzle and look for pieces missing. Unfortunately, evolution is a gradual process over many thousands of generations, so all you will find are intermediate species, evolution carries through from generation to generation. That famed missing link people have been searching for is really just another intermediate, because each individual is an intermediate in the long, slow, gradual flow of evolution. We can, however, page through the fractured history of the tree of life as we look for evidence of earlier species. This is the job of Paleontologists. Biologists are also seeking for new unseen animals which dwell in places where man has not yet been, or have been but did not look well enough. It is a journey filled with wonder, pushing into the frontiers of the unknown. The search for new discoveries in Biology is never over.

The beauty of nature is everywhere and is evident if you open your mind and eyes for it. To look for beauty in nature is to see beauty in nature. Whether it is a butterfly, a snail, a toad, a deer, a beautifully colored bird or some sort of marsupial like the incredibly cute lead beater possum, beauty is everywhere, even in places where you might not expect it. But because beauty is subjective, not everyone uses the same standards of beauty. I, however, see great beauty and elegance in all life, even in fungi and insects, lizards and in the trees, and even in the weeds.

Life is everywhere, it is all interconnected, whether by distant relation, in deep time or by some dependence on one and other. The process of natural selection and adaptation have gradually formed this omnipresent beauty of life.

To see the beauty in nature is to look at nature not only in a way of esthetics but one must also understand how it manifests itself. The dance of life and the struggle for life. Reproduction, feeding, hunting, and fleeing are the basics of life. Try to extend the notion that every living organism is related to every other living organism on Earth: Bacteria, Viruses, microscopic life forms, insects, fish, mammals, marsupials, birds, fungi, plants, trees, crops, etc. All of these diverge from one single point, one single organism at the point of *Abiogenesis.*

Extinctions are the evidence of an unsuccessful struggle for survival. Survival of the fittest, the smartest, strongest, most elusive, fastest and the best adaptable. Gene survival is the key to evolution, but as our climate changes too rapidly, we are pushing the limits of adaptation, and we could easily cause another mass extinction.

Did you know that modern day birds descendants of the Dinosaurs? People often think that all the dinosaurs went extinct, but this is not entirely true, although most of the dinosaurs died off in a mass extinction some 65 million years ago. some species likely closely related Archaeopteryx or micro raptors, survived and gradually evolved into birds. The birds we see today are the descendants of the dinosaurs that were able to adapt to the circumstances during and right after the mass extinction event about 65 million years ago.

Biologists, Paleontologists, Physicists, and chemists are seeking the answers to how nature works and how life began. Our ignorance, when not willful, spurs on the search for knowledge. There's still a lot we do not know which means that there is still a lot to learn. A fine prospect, we never cease to learn. One of the questions that keep us occupied is about the origin of life. Did life start on Earth? Did it come from another planet like Mars, on a comet?

We don't know, and that's why we conjure up all sorts of ideas to explain how life on Earth began four billion years ago. some people try to convince us that it happened by some kind of magic, by invoking celestial and omnipotent men. Scientists, however, say that we must seek answers in evidence and observations. Our theories and hypotheses in the quest for truth and knowledge must be substantiated.

It's a fact that we come from the stars. all of the atoms in our bodies were created by stars with thermonuclear fusion i.e. nucleosynthesis of hydrogen and helium and were then dispersed into the universe when these stars exploded and died.

This fact leads to the probability of life on other planets since the materials needed for the existence of life are ubiquitous. Given the multiple billions of galaxies, each with billions of stars, many of which would probably have life-friendly planets, the seemingly unlikely could easily happen. It is a majestic idea that the elements that constitute life on Earth might have come from other parts of the Milky Way and could have led to genesis on other planets as well.

Life on Earth is fragile. If the temperature of the oceans rises just a couple of degrees, it could mean the end for algae, plankton, and coral reefs. All this life is tied together in one big ecosystem, the biosphere. If one species suffers, other species will suffer as well.

Oddly enough, the most important species are at the bottom of the pyramid – plankton and algae constitute the foundation of life. As the basic source of sustenance for all marine life and a major source of oxygen, they are indispensable. And yet we pollute the oceans in which they live. don't we even care? Are we even aware? Do we realize that the harm we do them will eventually be done to ourselves?

It is time humanity starts to become more aware of its effects on the Earth and all of its wondrous inhabitants, big animals or small and seemingly unimportant organisms, regardless.

The wonders of science

In 1831, The HMS Beagle embarked upon a trip around the world. Setting out from Southampton, the Beagle crossed the Atlantic towards South America and The Falkland Islands. After rounding cape horn, the ship stopped at the Galapagos Islands, Australia, and South Africa before returning to England. Bringing an end to five long and adventurous years at sea.

What was so special about this particular trip? On this voyage, the HMS Beagle carried Charles Darwin across the seas and oceans of our world. Darwin, who was well schooled, had a fascination for biology and geology, so he collected samples of hundreds of different species of plants and animals while also searching for fossils.

Before Charles Darwin devised his theory of evolution, life had always been mysterious. We could only imagine how life on Earth started, with almost everyone believing that life must have been zapped into being by some divine spark. and then Charles Darwin revolutionized Biology with his book "*Charles Darwin, On the Origin of Species, by means of natural selection*", in which he described the process of evolution.

Evolution doesn't explain how life started, but it does describe how the diversity of life came to be. in so doing, Darwin gave humanity an incredible gift: he opened a new dimension of the unknown, with the hope of even more knowledge yet to be found. If this is not a wonderful contribution to the human endeavor, nothing is!

In appreciation, Charles Darwin was buried in Westminster Abbey – not far from one of the greatest mathematicians and physicists the world has known: Sir Isaac Newton. The apple that fell from the tree, the famous anecdote of the way how Sir Isaac Newton started thinking about the theory of gravitation. "*why should that apple always descend perpendicularly to the ground*" Newton would have thought according to William Stukeley. Newton "co-invented" calculus and devised the most fundamental natural laws in physics: the theory of universal gravitation and the three laws of motion, which he described in "*Principia, the mathematical principles of natural philosophy*".

Those who use math or physics rely on the work of Sir Isaac Newton, one of the brightest and most eccentric people to ever populate the halls of science.

A century later came Michael Faraday, the inquisitive inventor of primitive electromagnetic motors and dynamos. Without his generators, we'd be back to living like we did back in the 1850s.

Although Thomas Edison is more widely known, his competitor, Nicola Tesla, was an incredibly intelligent man whose name, incidentally, graces the Tesla motor car, a beautiful and revolutionary vehicle manufactured by Elon Musk.

Tesla, who invented alternating current, developed plans for the transmission of electricity without the use of cables and advised on ways to best transport electricity, was a true pioneer in technological advances. He first created designs and experiments in his mind, and then built them. Unfortunately, Tesla was swept aside for lack of funds. One can only imagine what wonders he'd have created if he'd gotten the support required to fulfill them.

Highway to Dystopia

Sustainable powered, controlled flight, the dream of Icarus and of men for centuries, became possible when the Wright brothers took to the air in 1903 by making a flight no longer than the wingspan of a Boeing 747 – a flight that will be remembered forever. The Wright brothers, who were bicycle builders, knew that people riding bikes had to lean to one side to change direction, and by studying birds they thought they could alter their course by changing the shape of their wings. They also methodically studied the glider's movements and did wind tunnel tests. Although the Wrights first glider could bend its wings, it lacked a rudder – a defect that was quickly remedied. as a consequence, their 1902 glider had twistable wings that could roll the airplane, a rudder for steering and an elevator to allow the plane to safely climb and descend.

In 1903, Wilbur and Orville added an engine, arguably creating the first aircraft to have three axis controls and an engine that made it possible to achieve controlled, sustainable flight. That flight occurred at Kill Devil Hills in North Carolina on December 17. 1903 when Orville Wright flew the 1903 "glider" for a distance of 120 feet (37 meters) in 12 seconds. then came the Wright Flyer II and III, and on October 5, 1905, Wilbur Wright flew 24 miles (39 km) in 39 minutes.

During the 20TH century, aviation progressed from biplanes to high-speed monoplanes, from piston engines to turboprops, and from short hops to flying the Atlantic, not to mention jet engines, breaking the sound barrier and flights into space.

Three axis control is now a staple: Aircraft, submarines, robots, space shuttles, space stations and satellites use it. This incredible journey that was initiated by Wilbur and Orville Wright has allowed us to fly the oceans, the skies and the vastness of space. Their 1903 glider and other flyers were true wonders of science.

Professor Stephen Hawking, A physicist, and cosmologist of great genius and persistence, has been trying to figure out how the universe works and how the big bang came to be. He lectures students all over the world about the nature of time and space.

Gravitational collapse of stars leads to the creation of black holes with singularities at their center. Hawking is convinced that the universe must have been a singularity that spontaneously evolved into the Big Bang, the beginning of the universe, coming into existence without a prime mover or cause.

He discovered that Black Holes must be emitting particles like a hot object loses heat, which means that black holes must evaporate particles. In the past, we've thought that black holes suck everything into themselves and that nothing can escape from them, but Hawking deduced that there are emissions that do escape. We call these emissions "Hawking radiation". If the people at CERN can create tiny black holes in the Large Hadron Collider, we might then be able to observe Hawking Radiation. I would love to be a spectator in the room where they would make the discovery, it's probably going to be a pivotal moment and would probably warrant a Nobel Prize.

Hawking's book "A Brief History of Time" has become one of the best-selling science books ever published.

We have to thank the people who have taken care of him. Since 1985, Hawking has been diagnosed with amyotrophic lateral sclerosis (better known as ALS). He uses a computer to communicate with other people. If he would be asked for a role in a movie, he could easily be one of the most iconic evil antagonists ever to play in a James Bond movie! (something he alluded to in the Dutch Panorama magazine)

His precious being amongst us has enriched our species tremendously. His dedication to helping people to think about the universe and to make new discoveries is great. His contributions to science are fundamental. His attributions to humanity in a literary and scientific sense are mind boggling and magnificent!

Highway to Dystopia

Lawrence Krauss has written a book called "A Universe from nothing". I have trouble to wrap my head around the concept "nothing". Krauss tries to explain how the Universe began. It's on my bucket list to ask him about the nature of nothing and have a really cool conversation about cosmology and the wonders we've discovered. The idea that a cube of space, stripped of all the material in it, still has energy is something that keeps my mind occupied at times. Hearing him talk about particle physics and the Origins Project always gets me excited.

To inspire people to engage in science or to develop a love for science is to be an inspiring person. One of the scientific wonders is not the science itself, but how it is shared with laymen like [maybe] you and me. This requires someone like Carl Sagan, whose books and science programs were awesome. His eloquence, broad vision, and depth of knowledge made him the perfect commentator on science issues. It was a joy to hear him speak in his prosaic manner.

His precious documentaries and talks are still available to us, I express my sincerest hope that future generations will take note of his wisdom and the knowledge he shared with us.

From the wonderful achievements of some of the pioneers in science we now move on to institutions and groups of people who have expanded our knowledge of the universe and our scientific understanding.

The Manhattan project spawned a wonder in science, a terrible wonder. A wonder that has ensnared the human race in constant fear. Thousands of engineers and scientists worked on the Manhattan Project, and in their quest to unlock the nuclear force, they discovered Nuclear Energy and Nuclear Bombs.

in New Mexico, at the Trinity site, they unleashed the first nuclear bomb – and about 2500 nuclear bombs have been detonated since then. Achieving nuclear fission is a scientific wonder, but achieving

21

the *controlled* nuclear reaction that we use to generate electricity is an even greater achievement. Without a fundamental understanding of the structure of atoms, this would not have been possible, Besides giving us CO_2-free energy, the Manhattan project led us to new medical treatments and innovations in space exploration.

The Large Hadron Collider is one of the most impressive, current scientific enterprises. It has been built by thousands of scientists, mainly physicists, and engineers. They have converged on this project from all over the world to make this wondrous and extremely complex piece of equipment possible. The search for the most basic particles, to understand the nature of the atoms and what keeps them together and gives mass to these particles is the quest in which people are engaged at CERN. They built this stupefying machine, to make sense of an infinitesimally small and yet fundamental piece of the universe.

The National American Space Agency has been the cradle of many efforts to enrich our understanding about space flight, space science, and planetary science. Some projects were spurred by political antagonism, i.e. or race with the Russians to get to the moon. I hope that NASA will not get stifled by political movements that lack proper scientific understanding. People that push a short-sighted ideological agenda might just as well muck us down in mundane efforts of non-discovery and willful ignorance.

Greatness lies just over the horizon, we'd only achieve it if we are willing to go over it.

with NASA, we have ventured into space with (nuclear powered) robots and probes designed to scan the earth and probe our solar system. They went into space, they did measurements never done before, they gather data continuously, they continuously improve on their observational and measurement techniques, they look at our planet and try to make more sense of it, they look at the stars in order to try to understand the universe, and they've sent satellites and rovers to other planets and moons to try to explore them.

To try and understand how planets work is to engage in complex voyages, full of math, physics, geology, chemistry and the development of intricate technologies.

The Cassini-Huygens mission inspired me to start following the unmanned treks into space. Cassini-Huygens traveled to Saturn to take photos of its many moons and rings and to examine its atmosphere. It even landed a probe named Huygens on titan.

The Huygens probe is named for the brilliant Dutch astronomer Christiaan Huygens, who discovered Titan in 1655. The Cassini Orbiter is named after Giovanni Cassini, an Italian Astronomer, who also lived in the 17th century.

Voyager I, the first man-made probe to leave our solar system, now ventures through interstellar space. Its original mission was to examine and photograph Saturn and Jupiter and their moons.

These deep-space satellites were made possible by the use of plutonium-powered Radioisotope Thermoelectric Generators or RTG's. The RTG of the Voyager I is expected to work until 2025. In the meantime, it will transmit back to Earth whatever observations it makes.

One wonders if we will ever be able to take a closer look at Alpha and Proxima Centauri. Though they are our nearest stars, they are 4 light years away. Entering those systems in person or with probes, would mean that we would have unlocked the secrets of interstellar travel.

A great array of satellites have been making observations of the Earth, our Solar system and the Universe. The apex of all these space adventures has been reached quite recently by the Plutonium powered New Horizons space craft that completed a flyby with Pluto. Pluto and Plutonium finally united by science! From the beautiful pictures taken by the Hubble telescope to the great tour of Voyager I and the trek of the New Horizons craft, our presence in space has to keep growing, for there our future lies.

Putting men on the moon is one of the most incredible things we've ever done. Apollo 11 lifted off from the Earth on July 16th, 1969. The herculean Saturn V rocket, 111 meters long, launched Buzz Aldrin, Neil Armstrong, and Michael Collins on an incredible voyage to the moon. Four days later, in one of the most inspiring moments in human history, Neil Armstrong set foot on the moon and later described Africa, parts of Europe and the Middle East from the moon, exclaiming at our beautiful orb, suspended in an immensely dark backdrop riddled with billions of stars. What a magnificent, impressive wonder of achievement that was.

Our voyage through the wonders of science hasn't reached its end, nor will it ever. One example is the attempt to recreate conditions of the Sun. ITER or "International Thermonuclear Experimental Reactor" will have a Tokomak Reactor Core in which hydrogen isotopes will be fused together to produce energy. Fusing atoms together is impossible without extreme heat and pressure, but how sustainable can this process be? Can we do this over a prolonged period of time? Do we have the materials required to do it? How stable will it be? Can we actually get more energy from it than we use to get it going?

ITER is supposed to be a proof of concept. We can do Fusion, but we don't know how to do it in ways that can fuel the world's energy needs *yet*.

Scientists and research institutes and universities from all over the world are engaged in finding answers to fundamental questions in many different fields of science. These endeavors have been with us for thousands of years, the human capacity for wonder and critical thought spurred people like Plato, Eratosthenes, Socrates, Newton, Darwin, Russell, Tesla and Hawking and many others on to engage in the search for truth and knowledge. Whether you are interested in Biology, Cosmology, Geology, Chemistry or Physics, there are always unanswered questions. To engage in the search for answers to fundamental questions is exciting. Science is not all about making new discoveries in big forward leaps, science is also dedicated to the small observations, the baby steps, the lifelong commitments in the search for what is true. And your precious time could also be invested in something that could possibly and would probably be falsified, it is all part of the scientific endeavor.

with the tools of science, we've erected incredible buildings and discovered many beautiful things. Consider the Pyramids, the Taj Mahal, the Pantheon, the Chinese Wall, Stonehenge, the Parthenon, the Brooklyn Bridge, the Hundertwasser building, Mont Saint Michel, Sagrada Familia and the magnificence of the lost cities of Mohenjo-Daro Vijayanangar, Ani, Thebes, Persepolis, Ephesus, Angkor, Cichén Itzá, and Machu Picchu. These are just a few of the wonders we have built.

The ongoing endeavors of humanity have culminated in a huge amount of beautiful architectural marvels and incredible technological advances.

We began with the shaping of rocks, the fashioning of spears, the bow and arrow, the first homes, the first wheels, self-sustaining arches, aqueducts, plumbing, public bath houses, castles, great cities, boats, ocean-going ships, trains, airplanes, jet engines, light bulbs, telephones, television, space rockets, great barriers to protect countries from the sea like the Dutch North Sea works, The Thames Barrier, communications satellites, computers and smart phones, etc.. Without science, none of this would be possible.

Progress in technology is ever ongoing, no significant technological advance is possible without a basic understanding about the elemental science behind it. Without it, we would not have had all the technologies we have today, knowledge and the scientific method will help humanity progress.

Joint efforts like the International Space Station, The LHC, and ITER show that if we pool our resources and efforts and gather our scientists and engineers, amazing things can be done.

Just think of all the stupendous things we have discovered and deduced, think about string theory, quantum mechanics, the four elemental forces of nature, the mass-energy equivalence equation, the theory of general relativity, Newton's three laws of motion, the theory of Evolution, Hawking radiation, Pythagorean theorem, the law of Archimedes, Boyle's law, you name it, we've discovered many beautiful, practical, interesting and awe-inspiring things.

We should never quit exploring for that is forsaking our nature, let's go look for the next wonders in science.

ACC – the sounding alarm bells

Although some people reject Anthropogenic Climate Change, the scientific community is in a broad agreement that "ACC" is a fact. Scientists have known for more than a hundred years that if you increase the levels of greenhouse gases, temperatures will rise. The science behind it is clear.

We have a massive body of evidence to prove anthropogenic climate change, thus, it is rendered nigh indisputable. The issues we need to iron out is how exactly the temperature reacts, what patterns influence it, and how we can build models to predict the climate more accurately. This is something we can do to a certain degree, however, there is still chance involved, the models are often too conservative or too overdone and thus fall prey to people who want to discredit the science behind ACC.

To make predictions is to see whether your claims stick, to test the predictions we only have to "sit down", measure the temperature all over the globe and statistically analyze them. Temperature is one of the things that is quite hard to measure overall, especially on a worldly context. Effects that are easily measurable, however, show definite signs of runaway behavior.

What would you say if I told you that some states – like Florida – have ordered state employees to avoid using the words Climate Change or Global Warming? To put it bluntly, this is incredibly stupid and dangerous.

Our planet needs the energy from the sun in order to sustain life. when the mix of radiation (light, x-ray, infra red, ultraviolet, etc.) strikes snow or ice, very little of it changes to low energy, long wave (infrared) radiation that can be trapped by greenhouse gases when it radiates back toward space, not being trapped in the atmosphere, this is called the Albedo-effect. However, if it falls on land or bare seas or worse yet, black rooftops or asphalt, the conversion to "heat" radiation is more complete, and when the greenhouse gases block it from escaping into space, our planet warms more rapidly. in addition, as more greenhouse gases are added to the atmosphere, even less heat can escape, and the warming increases.

That said, greenhouse gases are required to trap heat in the atmosphere. If we didn't have any greenhouse gases in the atmosphere, it would be a lot colder on the Earth. As a matter of fact, the temperature would fall below freezing point causing the earth to become a giant freezing ball instead of lush planet full of life. The most significant greenhouse gases are Water vapor (H_2O), Carbon Dioxide (CO_2), Methane (CH_4) and Ozone (O_3).

In 1859, John Tyndall discovered how heat gets trapped in the atmosphere. He measured this through a dark tube filled with gas, the conception of absorption spectroscopy. He was the first physicist to prove the greenhouse effect by measuring the heat absorption capacities of nitrogen, oxygen, water vapor, carbon dioxide, ozone, and methane.

A few decades later Svante Arrhenius investigated the influence of greenhouse gases in the atmosphere. He published a paper in 1896 in which he shared how he measured how Carbon Dioxide contributes to the greenhouse effect. He also speculated that anthropogenic emissions of carbon dioxide would change the earth's climate.

The influence of greenhouse gases has been known for more than a hundred years, yet there are a lot of fools claiming all sorts of things that aren't true, and try to keep the debate ongoing, despite the science being clear. The science is just as clear as the Theory of evolution being true, or the round-earth hypothesis being true.

One could say that greenhouse gases are the earth's thermostat. too little, and we freeze, but too much – and we *boil*.

The accelerated melting of glaciers and circumpolar icepacks is confirmed by direct observations and by satellites like the GRACE satellite – an acronym for the Gravity Recovery and Climate Experiment. these satellites are so accurate that they can detect even slight differences in the ice thickness. There are a multitude of sophisticated satellites in orbit, some of them have acronymic names like SORCE, SMAP, and OSTM. These satellites record the Earth's surface, the seas and the oceans, the land, clouds, particulates, temperatures, soil moisture levels, solar radiation levels and more. It's these kinds of observations, made by satellites and other measurement equipment that help us form a clear view of what is happening on our Earth. It is through some of the observations of these satellites that we can predict the formation of hurricanes and other weather patterns.

In addition, all across our world, scientists are evaluating changes in glacial melt cycles, tree growth, animal and fish health issues, weather patterns, drought- & fire statistics, crop growth ratings and more.

At this moment, the level of atmospheric CO_2 is at a historic high of 400 Parts Per Million (ppm). Throughout recorded history the Earth's greenhouse gas levels have not been this high and when the levels were higher the Earth was an inhospitable place. If we look at the history which has been recorded and put into chart models, we can clearly see that currently the amount of CO_2 in the atmosphere has vastly exceeded the historical patterns of the last 400 millennia. Levels of CO_2 have been as low as 180PPM during the ice ages and as high as 300PPM between the ice ages – also called Interglacial Periods. Current CO2 levels fluctuate around the 400PPM-mark. We are out of bounds and as a result we see a steady incline of the average temperatures, and as a result of that, we see our climate becoming more unstable.

Carbon dioxide is essential for healthy trees, plants, and basic aquatic organisms. Trees and plants are a major source of oxygen and food – as are phytoplankton – the tiny organisms that form the base of life in the oceans. These organisms turn CO2 into Biomass and Oxygen. Some have argued that more Carbon Dioxide in the air means that there is more food for plants. But one has to consider that in order for plants to be able to do photosynthesis, they need water. With the increased overall temperature and a steady decrease in precipitation, the world is getting dryer. With the ongoing depletion of aquifers, water for plants is becoming increasingly more scarce, which means that the photosynthetic processes are reduced. At one point plant life will die off, negating this supposed perk of CO2-Fertilization.

A logical outcome of increased temperatures is ice melt. If the amount of melting exceeds the amount of ice growth, you will see that the volume of ice starts declining. The problematic side of this is that there's a vast amount of water on the land in the form of glaciers and snow. The largest bodies of ice and snow are on Antarctica and Greenland. The higher the elevation and/or the latitude the more glaciers and snow ice you are bound to find. At least now you will, try again in a couple of decades.

The arctic system is showing clear signs of runaway behavior. The facts are almost irrefutable, the Arctic is about to become a sea without any substantial ice cover in the summer. When this exactly will happen, we do not know. But it is feared that it will happen within this decade. By 2030, the Arctic will probably have little or no ice in the summer, and the implications of an ice–free Arctic are enormous. The Arctic region spreads over the Arctic Sea, Denmark i.e. Greenland, Canada, the United States i.e. Alaska, Norway, Finland, Sweden, Iceland, and Russia.

Each of these countries have clear problems caused by global warming, one of which is the accelerated calving of glaciers. Imagine these colossal blocks of ice sliding into the ocean, raising giant waves, then drifting away. As the surface of the glacier melts, the water burrows a hole to the bottom of the glacier, eroding it not only from the top but also from within, which makes it less stable. the water acts like a lubricant and lifts the glacier very slightly yet enough to make the glacier slide down slope at a faster than normal rate.

Antarctica's glaciers are also experiencing accelerated melting and calving, with some being as large as Rhode island. Major glaciers on Antarctica are on the verge of sliding into an unstoppable collapse: the Totten Glacier, the Amundsen Glacier, and the Thwaites Glacier. An immense amount of ice that took tens of thousands of years to form is about to get discharged into the seas around the Antarctic in a matter of years. Vast mountains of ice, hundreds of meters high and several hundreds of meters wide are calving into the sea. These calving events are well documented and you can view them on websites like YouTube.

At this moment, the world is Deglaciating rapidly. All over the Earth, glaciers are discharging ice and water into the oceans and there is enough ice on the land to raise the oceans hundreds of feet.

Once the ice and snow is gone, darker surfaces will be exposed. Snow and Ice reflect sunlight and serve as a cooling mechanism. The decrease in solar reflection will increase energy absorption. Dark surfaces absorb more sunlight and this will accelerate global warming.

It is estimated that by 2100 all of the Canadian and US glaciers will have declined by about 60 to 70% and the Sierra Nevada snow pack already is all but gone.

When the Arctic Sea is no longer covered with ice, the water will absorb massive amounts of solar energy and warm up, which will create another serious problem because subsea permafrost contains vast quantities of methane. The warming of the Arctic Sea will cause subsea permafrost to thaw and when the permafrost thaws, huge amounts of methane will be released.

The effect on the Tundra by a warmer open seacoast is another problem. The open sea will have an influence on the air above it, warming it. Once this air moves over the tundra, it starts warming the Tundra as well thus thawing the tundra permafrost, releasing yet more methane and capturing more heat. Rotting vegetation will also be a factor in the methane release. Once the permafrost is gone, this vegetation will decompose. If there is no oxygen present during this decomposition process it means that methane is produced, If there is oxygen present, microorganisms decomposing rotting vegetation release carbon dioxide.

In the Yamal Region of Siberia, methane has begun to burst out of the ground, creating large craters that leak more methane. if all of the subsea and tundra-covered methane is released, the effect could be catastrophic because methane is at least 20 times more potent than co2 as a greenhouse gas. People worry about the prospect of the Earth's atmosphere rising by two degrees, but releasing this much methane could worsen climate change enough to make it debatable if humanity could survive. Please watch "Arctic Death Spiral and the Methane Time Bomb" which can be found on YouTube. It summarizes perfectly what is bound to happen if we keep heading on this disastrous course.

The melting of the ice will cause the sea levels to rise. The seas will not rise by the melting of arctic sea ice since that ice is already displacing water, but by ice discharging from land masses such as Greenland and Antarctica and the glaciers of the great mountain ranges.

If all the earth's ice and snow melts, sea levels will rise about 200 feet or 60 meters, which is enough to obscure half of the statue of liberty. Coast lines will shift far inland. Many of the world's largest cities will be destroyed, and about one billion people will become refugees. There's about five million cubic miles of ice on the Earth and this amount is decreasing. It is not unthinkable that the sea level will rise several feet within the next couple of decades. And even a sea-level rise of say a foot will cause many problems.

The heating of the oceans should worry everyone, primarily because it could cause the extinction of small photosynthetic organisms like phytoplankton, algae, diatoms, etc.. these organisms convert sunlight, water, and carbon dioxide into biomass and simultaneously produce oxygen, so they are vital to the existence of life on Earth. However, these organisms reproduce best in cold water so a warmer ocean could cause the extinction of these quintessential organisms – and much life Earth.

As if we haven't been scared enough, we also need to become serious about the acidification of the oceans, which is caused by excess atmospheric CO2 being absorbed by the oceans. CO2 combines with water to form carbonic acid – H_2CO_3 – which "breaks down" into HCO_3^- and H^+ ions. Another reaction is involved which creates CO_3^{2-} and H^+ ions, adding two H^+ ions per CO2 and H2O molecule. It's the increase in H ions that makes the water acidic, which can damage the shells of many mollusks, crustaceans and all ocean life that relies on even the thinnest of shells for protection. Carbonate molecules in the shells of shellfish become sequestered when they die and sink to the bottom of the ocean, a means to sequester CO2.

The ocean's PH level, which is a measure of how acidic or basic it is, has been 8.2 for millions of years, but it has now fallen to 8.1. The critical threshold for shell-forming organisms is 8.0, which means that we are dangerously close.

Some people claim that volcanic and tectonic activity have a higher influence on ocean acidification, but those processes have been occurring for millions of years with no change in ocean PH. Today, thousands of scientists agree that the changes in climate are being caused by humans, but the international panel on climate change (IPCC) did us a disservice by making a more conservative arctic sea ice melt prediction than has actually occurred, largely because they have a laborious process that causes them to reach a conclusion late in the game. Because temperatures, acidification, and melt processes are increasing exponentially, they are outrunning the IPPC's capacity to provide useable advice.

We are now on the verge of raising the amount of CO_2 way above sustainable levels, we are already 50 PPM above sustainable bounds and the feedbacks of this transgression are en route through the pipeline of time. scientists have estimated that we cannot burn more than one Trillion metric tons of carbon if we do not want the average temperature on the Earth to rise for more than two degrees, but we have already burned half of that since the beginning of the industrial age. By carbon we mean anything that contains carbon atoms (C) which can be burned for energy i.e. heat and electricity, these are predominantly oil, coal, gas and biomass. If we continue on our current rate, we will reach the ceiling of one trillion tons well before 2050. Add the possible release of sequestered methane gas, add the breakdown of biomass due to increased droughts and it becomes obvious that we are in serious trouble.

All these processes create exponential curves upward and downward when created as graphs. Temperature, CO_2 concentrations, Ice Melt, Acidification, droughts and diminishing water supplies all show exponential curves or steadily increasing or diminishing trends. And all these processes amplify each other, creating positive feedbacks. It is feared by some that these processes are already beyond the point of no return.

A rapid increase of methane emissions from the arctic would most probably lead to famine and yet more increasing methane and carbon dioxide levels from die-off and rotting processes. That's why we need to start mitigating anthropogenic greenhouse gas emissions aggressively. We need to stop destabilizing the carbon cycle and start developing carbon dioxide capturing and sequestering mechanisms, preferably natural ones, but also look at geo-engineering as a last resort.

We cannot assert with absolute certainty that temperature will rise only two degrees if we stay within the bounds of burning one trillion tons of carbon. There might be unknown positive feedbacks. These are feedbacks that extend the natural cycle of greenhouse gases, helping the cycle spin out of control and out of bounds. Leading to an increasing uncertainty of our future.

Many people don't realize that climate, nature, and the Earth are connected in one big system. Some of these natural systems have a buffering mechanisms, and can take some abuse. However once a tipping point is reached, even those mechanisms become useless. they will not show a gentle and gradual change, no, they will tip into new states once criticality is reached. We can expect some of these rapid changes to show themselves on short notice. The influence of humanity is an external factor in the natural carbon cycle that has been relatively stable for millions of years. But since the beginning of the industrial age, when we began increasing emissions we've been putting the biosphere at risk.

I don't think we are too late to stave off mass extinctions. However, reversing the damage will need not just decades, but hundreds of years. We need to stop breaking the thing that keeps us alive.

The oceans have a giant volume and can store lots of energy. This means that the Oceans cause a lag between the emission of greenhouse gases and their effects. First the Ocean stores excess energy and at some point this will lead to increased amplitudes in weather patterns, causing more severe extremes.

One other thing we have to consider is that there's also a thing that is within the natural bounds of the Earth's cycle: Ice Ages. I can't predict when we are due for the next one, but if things settle down again, the Earth's cycle gets back to business as usual, we will be facing a new Ice Age at some point in the distant future. How are we going to cope with that? I don't think we should engineer our way out of it, I think we should adapt civilization to those circumstances,

It is time that we become smarter about planetary sciences, learn more about it, make more observations and try to truly understand what is happening and adapt.

I don't ask you to take my word for it, I don't want you to accept any of what I've written at face value. I want you to be skeptical about my claims as well as the claims of influential deniers, I ask you to look at the data, and look at the evidence especially provided on websites (like NASA's climate change page).

The main questions are: are the positive feedbacks already set in motion? Is there anything we can do? What must we do? Or are we too late?

ACC – Ecosystem collapse

Pandas, tigers, orangutans, seals and polar bears are animals used by conservationists to signify the harm done on the animal kingdom by humans. At this moment, more than 2000 species of animals and more than 2000 species of plants are categorized as critically endangered and the list is growing.

I consider the woes of the animals on our planet. Why are these species in great peril and what are the factors that lead to this situation? We could address this problem from a simplistic viewpoint because it is quite clear that we are doing this. But what would we learn from it?

Let's begin at the bottom of the food pyramid, the foundation of practically all life on Earth. Plankton, diatoms, and Algae constitute the base of all life in the oceans. They are a vital part in the management of CO_2 levels in both the air and the oceans. some of These small organisms use photosynthesis to turn CO_2 and sunlight into Oxygen and Biomass, the building blocks of life. About one-third of all CO_2 emitted by civilization is being absorbed by the world's oceans.

There are about 5000 different species of plankton. Phytoplankton use photosynthesis to be and to create biomass. Zooplankton and other plankton, krill and other micro organisms in term feed on phytoplankton as well. The ocean is filled with all sorts of micro organisms, you could look at the ocean as a large bowl of nutritious soup.

Many species of fish, small, medium and large feed on plankton. Great mammals such as whales feed on plankton as well. Great whales with baleen plates exclusively feed on micro organisms. Their baleen plates function as sieves, allowing only the microscopically small organisms into their digestive systems. The whale shark is also a filter feeding organism. Due to the abundance of microorganisms in the oceans and the seas, there are many species of filter feeders. Why go after the food if you swim through a soup of it? Certain forms of corals, anemones and sponges feed on plankton as well.

Studies have shown that these organisms i.e. diatoms, plankton, and algae are ill-equipped to cope with rising temperatures and acidification. As described earlier, the oceans are warming up, due to an increase of dark surface, especially in the arctic regions. This increase in warmth in the oceans has a negative effect on these micro organisms.

Higher atmospheric levels of CO_2 increases the acidity of the oceans, which hinders shell formation, and it can even dissolve shells if the pH of the water gets low enough excess acidity can also damage and kill coral reefs, leaving behind their bleached *skeletons*.

Without plankton, the seas and oceans would be dead. Simplified the oceanic food chain looks like this from the bottom up: Phytoplankton are eaten by zooplankton which get eaten by predatory zooplankton which get eaten by filter feeders which get eaten predatory fish. We are pushing the limits, as plankton dwindles, so will the rest of all marine life.

Consider Sardines, a small predatory fish. The amount of species that depend on the sardines for nourishment is quite substantial:

Highway to Dystopia

Sharks, Dolphins, Salmon, Tuna, Halibut, Sea Lions, Seals, Squids, all sorts of birds and of course the Humans. Sardines eat zooplankton, which means that they are still quite low in the food chain. What is more, sardines are one of the prime marine sources of proteins for human consumption. Sardine numbers have been dwindling a lot lately, mainly due to overfishing. The Sardine population could collapse either because of overfishing or because their source of food collapses as well. Remember that they feed on zooplankton. The marine life pyramid as we know it is about to collapse if we do not act.

From the bone-chilling perils of the seas we crawl onto the land, as our distant ancestors once did. We will find great peril and suffering on the face of the Earth as well. We humans have precipitated a lot of problems on our biosphere. Even though extinctions and mass extinctions have happened before, we are now catalyzing another mass-extinction process and sometimes we are even speeding it up, seemingly willfully.

We'll start by having a look at the indirect destruction of our biosphere, let's take a look at the forests for instance. Many trees are now at risk of being destroyed by forest fires, dying from droughts or being killed by beetles. In the western states of the US several pine species are in trouble because of the warming climate. Normally insects like the Mountain Pine Beetle would remain manageable due to the natural cycle of warm and colder weather. The Mountain Pine Beetle is an insect that feeds of the bark of trees. Due to the longer warm periods and less severe winters, the Mountain Pine Beetles survival rate increases. A search on the Internet will provide pictures of entire mountain sides riddled with dead trees that didn't survive Mountain Pine Beetle infestations.

With the ensuing droughts all over the world, many forests fall prey to wildfires, destroying millions of acres of woods and releasing tons of CO_2. Wildfires, beetles, and diseases kill the trees and destroy the natural forest habitats. The warming of the atmosphere and lessening of the precipitation is making forests vulnerable. Millions of acres of forest are lost each year, in the Northern Hemisphere alone. Forests in Canada and Russia are diminishing significantly. In the southern hemisphere, huge tracts of forests have been clear-cut for lumber and farming and mining.

Insects like the monarch butterfly are also suffering from our adverse effects on the biosphere. Monarch Butterfly populations are declining significantly. James Hansen uses the Monarch Butterfly to underline what effects our activities have on nature.

Our use of pesticides and herbicides is causing trouble for many species of insects. Pesticides are used to get rid of plant-eating insects such as grasshoppers, caterpillars, beetles, and aphids. Also certain unwanted weeds are being removed with herbicides, thus destroying the source of food for certain species of insects. One of which is the larvae of the monarch butterfly, which feeds on milkweeds. Farmers, however, dislike milkweeds, so we use herbicides to get rid of them. What are the larvae going to eat if we strip the lands of these milkweeds? Exactly, the diminishing of a food source will cause a species to start dwindling.

Pesticides are indiscriminate, they kill whatever insect they come in contact with. Pollinators are insects that feed on the nectar provided by plants and subsequently carry pollen from one plant to another, thus fertilizing them. Pollinators are also in grave danger these are insects like bees, bumblebees, and wasps. It was believed that extensive use of pesticides in the Netherlands, for instance, caused a steady decline in bee populations, a dangerous development. Pollinators are required for certain forms of food to grow, especially certain types of fruits like apples and pears for instance. I like to call bees the alpha-pollinator, they pollinate about 70 of the roughly 100 essential sources of food for human consumption, mainly fruits, and vegetables. Without bees, we will be unable to sustain a civilization.

Honeybees are in trouble, not just in the Netherlands but all over the world. In a sense, they are the plankton of the extra-marine world. They are the essential movers of our own vital nutritious soup on land. The well being of bees is directly tied to climate, they have difficulty coping with long and harsh winters on one side and hot summers with severe droughts on the other side. A very hot summer with severe drought means famine in crop and plant life, the essential source of nutrition for the bees. On top of all that, we are using poison to kill bugs. It is quite puzzling to see us being so careless with these essential species. Insecticides, Fungicides, and Herbicides are wreaking havoc on a vital part of the biosphere. I am optimistic about our ability to save the bees from extinction, I am however skeptical about us having the willpower to do so. People always tend to go for maximizing crop yields for the highest possible profits, forsaking the "cides" would be analogous to giving profit away and that's a hard thing to do. However it is also important to look at this issue critically, we've got 7 billion mouths to feed. So much more research on this issue is needed because the jury is still out on this issue.

Finally, I have to address the willful extermination of species, the effect our greed has on the well-being and existence of certain animals.

Many years ago homo sapiens discovered the Dodo, a big flightless bird living on a remote island in the middle of the Indian Ocean. The doom of the Dodo arrived with us, we appeared and the dodo went away. Not in a good sense, they went extinct, thanks to us... The story is of course that we hunted and ate them, for which there is evidence by the way. Other causes might be that the rats that came with us ate their eggs or that some kind of poisonous snake ate them. Whatever it was, the demise of the Dodo is exemplary of the destructive influence of our species.

The Golden Toad has also gone extinct. The only place where they were found was the Monteverde Cloud Forest Reserve in Costa Rica. These toads fell victim to the warming climate when the breeding pools required for them to reproduce dried up before the toads could get there. Also, the rise of toxic fungi and pollution are contributing factors of toads going extinct. about one-third of all the amphibians in the world are in trouble, as revealed by their declining numbers. Most fall victim to extremes of long cold periods, droughts, changing habitats and pollution. Amphibians are also very vulnerable to certain infestations such as fungi.

It is said that a staggering five hundred thousand rhinoceroses roamed the Earth around the year 1900. Widespread horn poaching has led the Rhinos population to drop to about 29.000 today, a stupefying demise. There are five main species of rhinos, the white tip, the black, the greater one–horned, the Sumatran and the Javan rhinos. The Javan rhino species has disappeared almost completely, the Sumatran rhino is on the brink of extinction and the other rhino species aren't doing well either. All the rhinos are now protected, yet the poaching continues. There are about 20.000 white and 5.000 black rhinos left in the wild. The northern white rhino – Ceratotherium simum cottoni – is on the brink of extinction, only five [edit: four] of them remain, two females live in captivity, one female, and only one male remain in the wild. The male rhino is being guarded continuously, look it up, there are pictures of it with armed people closely guarding it.

Just to give an impression of how widespread the poaching problem is, in South Africa alone 386 rhino poaching arrests were made in 2014, the year before 343 arrests were made and in 2012 267. This signifies just how important it is to actively protect these animals if we wouldn't protect them actively. They are bound to go extinct before the next decade is over.

One hundred thousand tigers lived on the face of the planet around the year 1900, but only 3000 to 3500 remain. The area in which tigers lived spanned from eastern Turkey to the most eastern parts of Russia and several of the large island of Indonesia. There are a couple of subspecies of the tiger, three of which have gone extinct. The Bali, Javan, and Caspian tigers have gone extinct in the 20th century. The remaining species are the Bengal, Indochinese, Malayan, Siberian, South China, and Sumatran tigers.

India, Nepal, China, Russia, Indochina and South East Asia are some of the areas where Tigers still live in the wild. Their numbers have been diminishing steadily over the last couple of decades. Increased deforestation has led to the steady decline of their habitats. Their space to live in is becoming smaller, places to hide themselves are becoming scarcer and they are forced to move outside their habitats and into "human territory". Once they get in touch with civilization, there is no way to tell what will happen. Will they be scared away? Will they be captured? Or will they be shot and killed under the guise of them being a threat to humans? Hunting tigers and their potential prey have been drivers behind the steady demise of the tiger, also illegal poaching continues.

The existence of these majestic animals is nearing the precipitous cliffs of extinction, once they go over the edge, they are gone forever – extinction is forever.

"The person of the forest", Malay for Orangutan. An incredibly beautiful ruddy great ape with incredibly long arms lives in the rainforests of South East Asia. They can only be found in certain areas of Sumatra and Borneo. Just as the tigers, the Orangutans are running out of living space. Their habitat is being destroyed for the cultivation of Palm Oil Plantations. There are very few Orangutans left, these primates are dependent on their habitat for survival.

Logging and other activities destroying their habitats must stop, for this wondrous creature to survive in the wild.

They have been mentioned before, the most intelligent, gracious, empathic and beautiful of or close cousins, the peaceful Bonobos. Bonobos live in the Congo and have barely survived the wars in the Angola, Congo, and Ruanda region. Bonobos have been hunted for their meat. Widespread poaching has driven them near the brink of extinction. Today approximately 30 to 50.000 Bonobos live in the Congo. These mammalian primates are closely related to humans and it is paramount that we leave them alone and stop hunting them. Can you imagine that humans are eating creatures that are closely related to us? Not a single species of animals on the world is so closely related to us as the Bonobos.

Fortunately, there are also some hopeful stories as well. Let's have a brief look at the story of the whales. Whales are aquatic mammals, sharing a common ancestor with the Water horse aka the Hippo. There are many species of whales: Blue Whales, Bowhead's, Fin Whales, Humpback Whales, Sperm Whales (we call them Potvis...), Orca's, Vaquitas, and Dolphins. These ocean-dwelling mammals are gracious and magnificent creatures. Some of them swim slowly and gently while others clearly have a more predatory way of moving around. Orcas and Dolphins, in particular, shoot through the water like torpedoes, hunting all sorts of fish and other mammals.

We have almost caused the complete demise of several species of whale by aggressive and massive hunting that began in the early 1800's and continued well into the 20th century. With some nations still whaling commercially despite it being forbidden, hunting down and killing over a thousand whales per year. Whales are also vulnerable to becoming entangled in fishing nets, close encounters with ships and ingestion of spilled oil.

Luckily many regions of the seas are now off limits to whale hunting, giving whale populations a chance to flourish again. The whales are still not into the clear, however. As stated earlier, plankton, of which krill is the predominant food source for the whales, are having a difficult time coping with the rising of the sea temperatures and the possible acidification of the oceans. I hope it is not too late and that we can still alter this possible destructive course of events. If not, we will be dragging all these beautiful creatures into the deep cold abyss of death with us.

What is more, people remain a destructive force in the animal kingdom. Poaching elephants and rhino's for their tusks and horns, shooting bears and other animals for trophies, the hunting of whales just for economic gain are reprehensible acts and need to stop. We are destroying the most amazing and beautiful places of the Earth, the Amazon, the Everglades, the redwoods, the Sequoya woods, the 140 million-year-old Borneo tropical rain forest, Coral reefs, the Arctic, you name it...

The earth has seen many mass extinctions: the Cretaceous-Tertiary mass extinction, the Triassic-Jurassic mass extinction, the Permian mass extinction, the late Devonian mass extinction and the Ordovician-Silurian mass extinction. The unique thing about the looming Holocene-Anthropocene mass extinction is that for the first time, "intelligent" life forms can see it coming and have a chance to reduce its severity if they make drastic reforms. The worst that could happen within a few decades is the extinction of the microscopic oceanic photosynthetic life forms, it would be the beginning of a new set of domino's that would fall down.

This happened before about 252 million years ago. The acidity levels of the oceans and seas were so high that 90% of all marine life and 66% of all land-based life on Earth went extinct. We know this, this is factual knowledge, none of it is in dispute... This past mass extinction event, the Permian extinction, provides an example of what we are creating by our overproduction of greenhouse gases with which we disturb the carbon cycle.

For more on this topic see: "*Ocean acidification and the Permo-Triassic mass extinction*" which can be found on sciencemag.org.

Although we talk about inalienable rights and defend them, whenever our way of life is threatened, our way of life... What about the lives of all the beautiful creatures that share the earth with us? Do they have inalienable rights too? When will we outgrow this self-centeredness? The Earth is not ours alone...

The extinction of species are difficult matters, hard to comprehend. Delving into the known issues of the animal kingdom is a voyage of many sad tales. Some species have become so endangered that we seriously have to consider that they might not be around anymore in a couple of decades. This is something that saddens me deeply.

The sixth mass extinction is happening as we speak, it is being caused by us, by humans, by our "civilization". We will be held accountable and responsible in the end. We continue to venture on this destructive course. We seem to be careless, we seem to lack empathy and are foolish enough to disregard the possible and dire outcomes of our behavior. Power, greed, and negligence seem to be the arbiters on matters of life and death, of existence and the right to be.

Our children and grandchildren will pay a huge price for our indifference and our pursuit of profits at any cost. Our hexing influence has caused a lot of damage. The earth will make us understand what we have done.

All these beautiful animals and plants and trees are in great peril and have no other place to go...

Highway to Dystopia

Diminishing Water supplies

Fresh water is the source of all life on land, without it the land would become dry and barren, crops, plants, and trees would be unable to grow and many animals would die.

All over the world, people are withdrawing fresh water from glacial areas, rivers and from groundwater supplies more rapidly than it is being replenished. At this moment, many of these supplies are running out of water at alarmingly high rates. Not only do we draw water from these sources faster than they are being replenished we also have to face the consequences of the warming of our climate and the steady decline in precipitation, a factor that is worsening these issues.

A growing world population is putting increasing pressure on our water supplies. 750 million people do not have direct access to potable water and this number is expected to grow exponentially and at least double in the coming decade. Many people don't worry that their water supply will dry up, but in time, they will. Just look at California. There, as everywhere else, we use water for irrigation, farming, energy production, manufacturing and domestic use.

We withdraw water from fresh water resources. These sources are all tied into the hydrological system. Precipitation that isn't absorbed by the earth or captured in snow-packs or in glaciers either evaporates or runs downhill towards the oceans. During this run off process, water gets used by plants and animals. In the case of plants and trees, the water not used for photosynthesis returns to the atmosphere. We call this process evapotranspiration, which creates clouds, especially in the heavily forested areas like the rainforests. These clouds eventually release their water in the form of snow, hail, sleet or rain as the hydrological cycle continues.

However, problems can arise when we tap into the hydrological cycle excessively, if we do so we unbalance it. The more water we draw in contrast to the replenishment rate, the faster our fresh water resources will diminish. Cutting forests also influences the hydrological cycle, and we have already reduced the world's forests by 40%. By doing this, we have upset the apple cart in terms of precipitation. It is starting to become apparent that we're tweaking the natural cycles, but not in an optimization process, this is a process of disruption.

We also pollute. Our thirst for fossil fuels contributes to the pollution of rivers, lakes and groundwater reserves and the seas. Manufacturing processes also produce harmful substances like benzene, mercury and arsenic that often end up in our water supplies. Despite strict rules and regulations, vital sources of fresh water are being contaminated with hazardous substances. And it is high time that humanity starts figuring out how to stop this because these sources of fresh water are indispensable and vital to our long-term survival.

The Ogallala Aquifer is one of the most important sources for fresh water in the United States. It is a vital source for water for the great plains. Almost all human activities depend on the reserves of fresh water in the Ogallala aquifer. Crop and cattle raising are the biggest users of Ogallala fresh water. Excessive irrigation is lowering its water table farther every year. When – not if – the Ogallala aquifer runs dry, food production in the great plains will evaporate.

Diminishing Water supplies

The biggest food producing area in the world depends on a water supply which is being strained and stressed tremendously. It is not unthinkable that the US will suffer from a mega draught NASA says.

Aquifer depletion occurs when there is a negative imbalance between water drawn and replenishment rates. Replenishment comes mainly from precipitation. Water is drawn from aquifers by river run off, plant life or by human extraction activities at wells.

We humans have the ability to extract huge amounts of water that exceed nature's ability to replace what we use – and waste. NASA has several climate models that predict a decrease in the precipitation patterns for the great plains, which could cause a return of the dust bowl years endured in the early 20TH century.

In order for the aquifers to recharge, we will need to find alternatives. Instead of building oil pipelines, one could imagine using pipelines to transport desalinated water for irrigation and other needs. A spill in one of these pipelines would have no detrimental effect in contrast to oil spilling from pipelines like Keystone or the one in the Black Sea. We will need to decide how much water needs to be desalinated, where it needs go, how it is to be allotted and how it can be accomplished – because desalination is a power hungry, expensive process.

Fossil aquifers do not replenish since there is no precipitation to feed them. Saudi Arabia has one of these fossil aquifers and has used its fresh water supply for grain cultivation. It is unfortunate but these activities were unsustainable since this aquifer did not get any replenishment and is in the process of running dry, almost 80% of its fresh water has been used. The desalination of sea water is too costly to use for irrigation and so the Saudi's have stopped the cultivation of grain since there is almost no more water for them to use and their aquifer will deplete quite soon. It shows that we have to think about our water uses before we start pumping it up. Simply sticking a pipe in the ground and sucking stuff up has proven to be one of the dumbest things we humans do.

All over the world glaciers are shrinking, another seemingly unstoppable trend. Glaciers on Antarctica, in the Himalayas, the Andes, the Alps, the Southern Alps of New Zealand, Norway, Iceland, the Rocky Mountains, and Greenland are diminishing. The decline in glacier mass can be explained by looking at balance between the buildup and the decline of ice and snow ice. The decline in ice and snow ice is directly tied to the decline in precipitation and the rising of average temperatures i.e. the shortening of freezing periods and the lengthening of thawing periods.

The internet has a lot of photographic galleries of before and after photo's taken from the same spot after a couple of decades, I suggest you look them up, in some cases the amount of glacier decline is stupefying.

Consider the shrinking Sierra Nevada snowpack that is the source of fresh water for about a third of the people in California. The Sierra Nevada snow pack depends on snow fall in the winter to replenish. The replenishment rate of the Sierra Nevada Snowpack has declined significantly. Glaciers and snow packs are an important source for fresh water and the decline in glacial volume and snow cover is troublesome. These are sources of fresh water that diminish even if we do not draw any water from them, water simply gets discharged in the thawing season. The only way they replenish is by new snowfall and lower average temperatures are needed to limit the amount of runoff.

Other basins of fresh water necessary to keep California from drying up are diminishing as well. It is reported by the government of California that these sources have fallen far below average and keep losing more water. The fresh water resources of California will be put to the test in the summer of 2015 due to an El Nino.

Diminishing Water supplies

Even more heat and less precipitation will put the resources under a tremendous amount of stress. Fortunately, El Ninos also can bring alleviation to California as they sometimes bring more moisture. This, however, doesn't mean that an El Nino is good by any means. It has effects all over the globe.

The great draught in the west of the United States has been ongoing for a long time now. California is one of the most drought-stricken areas in the United States. And NASA scientists have even predicted that California probably will run out of fresh water within a few years. Bi-weekly reports of the Californian Government paint a similarly grim picture. All of the fresh water basin levels have fallen significantly below average.

With California as dry as a cork, its governor is proposing that water usage be cut by a quarter, so how can so many people keep denying that climate change is happening – Californians in particular? Yes, bottled water can be trucked in and solar panels might keep their air conditioners running, but filling a pool with bottled water will get expensive. water rationing and desalination are coming, and in the meantime, some people have painted their lawns green...

Consider the Colorado River and lake Meade, which recently set a record low – so low, in fact, that the intakes at Hoover dam will probably need to be lowered to keep the generators spinning, and lower water levels will mean decreased power production. If you visit lake Meade or lake Powell, you will see what people call "Bath tub rings" where the water has fallen and stabilized repeatedly leaving behind minerals that were dissolved in the water, "painting" the rock white. A testament to a continuously lowering water level.

El Nino and la Nina are expected to become more extreme due to climate change. El Nino is when warm water in the Pacific rises to the surface and brings more warm air to the western shores of the

United States. When the next Nino happens, it will increase the stress on the water supplies since the drought will be prolonged and more intense or the opposite could happen, it's all uncertain because many variables determine the outcome of the weather patterns. Less precipitation and higher temperatures will lead to forest fires and aquifer depletion. La Nina has the opposite effect of El Nino, bringing cooler air from the Pacific. These effects can mitigate or enhance the severity of anthropogenic climate change patterns.

The Aral Sea (a salt lake) on the border of Kazakhstan and Uzbekistan provides another example of the imbalance between anthropogenic water use and replenishing rates. Decades ago during the era of the Soviet Union, the Soviets started cultivating cotton plantations near the Aral sea by using water drawn from the rivers that fed the sea for irrigation practices. The Soviets were willing to accept that the volume of the Aral Sea would diminish considerably, they knew this would happen. As a consequence, the Aral sea has shrunk. What was once the fourth largest lake on the face of the Earth, is now only a glimmer of its former glory and splendor. It has shrunk to 10% of its original size. In order for the Aral Sea to replenish again, a dam has been built in 2008.

Eventually, the poorly constructed irrigation system and the absence of crop rotation have led to the collapse of the cotton and food cultivation in Uzbekistan. Due to spillage and evaporation much fresh water has been lost in this way. The decline of the Aral Sea is considered to be one of the biggest environmental disasters of our age. It signifies a misunderstanding and misuse of critical water resources and it shows that we do have a profound influence on the world. It's undeniable.

The world's deepest and oldest Lake provides another example of a body of water that is diminishing and becoming more polluted. Lake Baikal, the pearl of Siberia, is considered to be one of the natural wonders of the Earth. It is also considered to be the Galapagos of Russia. It is a beautiful and grand lake. It averages 744 meters in depth and is 1600 meters at its deepest point. The lake is about 700 kilometers long and 130 kilometers wide, it is an incredibly large body of water. it holds 20% of the world's fresh surface water.

Lake Baikal is home to more than 1500 species unique to the region including the Baikal Seal, also known as the Nerpa. Lake Baikal is very isolated, making it essential that we monitor the health of the lake and keep pollution at bay.

Two major anthropogenic processes have affected Lake Baikal: A large paper and pulp mill in Baikalsk and a hydroelectric power plant at Irkutsk. Due to a decline in precipitation, the lake's water level has fallen to a point at which energy generation has become impossible.

Other significant problems were being caused by the Baikalsk Paper Mill and other industrial and farming processes around the lake. And although the paper mill was closed in 2013, many of the pollutants it created are still in the lake and will take a long while to degrade. Hazardous pollution is still spilling into the lake and causes problems for the flora and fauna of the region.

From the most beautiful and impressive lake in central Asia, we move on to the Amazon. The Amazon is undergoing many troublesome developments. For example, Sao Paulo is suffering from a prolonged period of drought that occasionally leaves residents without tap water. The Amazon river, the groundwater basins, the river basins and the ground moisture levels have been drying up for a couple of years now. Also consider the effect of several dams that have a profound influence on the Amazon watershed.

In Brazil, more than 22% of the Amazon rain forest, 47% of the Cerrado and 91.5% of the Atlantic Forest have been deforested for economic gain. We have destroyed vast amounts of forest and subsequently damaged a vital circulation system that supports life in South America and the rest of the world.

This decrease in precipitation is partly caused by deforestation and the heating of the atmosphere. Normally vast amounts of water vapor rising from the rain forest, accumulate and move west to collide with the Andes Mountains, where the flow reverses, creating a circulation system that returns water to the rain forest. however, because this process is slowing down, the central and southeastern portions of the Amazonian Rain Forests are becoming dryer.

While water usage for irrigation, cattle farming, industrial and personal use are rising. with less water available for forests that create oxygen and consume carbon dioxide, climate change is enhanced, and when drought-stricken trees die and rot, the carbon they contained is released into the atmosphere. Try to imagine the sheer volume of carbon that is sequestered in the rainforests of South America.

This decline in precipitation and the increase of droughts is occurring all over the globe. Trees and forested areas are becoming dryer and more vulnerable to wildfires. Even my own country, the Netherlands, which is known for its wet climate, is experiencing more frequent and longer dry spells accompanied with higher temperatures and wind. during recent years, our few natural reserves have seen wildfires like those in Australia, the US, and the Mediterranean. Millions of trees burned to the ground, releasing enormous amounts of CO_2.

People have grown used to referring to the Amazon as the "lungs of the world". This statement is true as long as the trees are not being cut down and the availability of water does not diminish. We need to develop a comprehensive effort to save the rainforests since they are an absolutely vital part of our biosphere.

If we are to remedy our growing water troubles, we will need an educated public, more people engaged in science, advances in desalination, irrigation, energy issues and a stable population that resists consumerism. Unless we address these issues, our food production and our major source of oxygen will decline, and so will civilization and other life as well, leading quite possibly to another mass extinction – the anthropogenic extinction.

Dystopian analogies

Pick any book or movie that has portrayed a dystopian future – stories made throughout the ages by people who had horrible visions of famine and terror. Many of them, sadly enough, are quite possible or even a reality.

A country is in turmoil; Its citizens are suffering; Famine is widespread; Potable water is scarce; Energy is unreliable; Medical services are only available to government people and money isn't worth anything anymore... People take to the streets to make their discontent known to the ruling class and the government, and tolerance is low on both sides. Riot Police and the military are lined up in ranks around government buildings, a police officer yells through a megaphone that the people are to leave the square immediately and return to their homes. This is the fourth day in a week that this has happened, but today is different. There are over one-hundred-thousand people on the square.

The people are fed up. Name the reason, any reason. They have lost everything, and the eviction squads have become more active, making more people homeless. Riot Police ready their batons and shields, the people can't take it anymore, somewhere from within the masses bottles and bricks are being thrown. Sticks and planks are ripped off the vacant buildings along the square as the people and the riot police clash. It is a harsh battle, protesters, police and military have become so dispersed that is almost impossible to discern one from the other. Pepper spray and teargas are everywhere, people are tying scarves and handkerchiefs in front of their mouths.

After several long skirmishes, the people manage to get into the government building. Most of the employees have already left, including the high-ranking government officials, who, of course, were evacuated by helicopter. The people ransack the building and build barricades and prepare to occupy it. The first target is the cafeteria, hoping there is still some food left, and food they find, plenty of it! But how long will it last?

This scenario is, of course, fictional; It has sprouted from my gloomy mind. People are being repressed, consumerism is putting stress on the world's resources, and people in seats of power are making decisions that sustain the acquisition of wealth by the rich and influential. Will this be prelude to the fall of yet another civilization? Civilizations have risen and fallen. Simply look at history and imagine the rise and fall of the Persians, the Greeks, the Roman Empire, the Egyptians, the Aztecs, the Mayans, the Vikings, the Indians, etc.. Many civilizations have collapsed, but what were the causes?

One of the major and most vital resources to sustain any civilization is the availability of fresh water. Water is a requirement for all natural and anthropogenic activities. Crops, animals, trees, and humans need water. Without water there will be famine once the wells dry out, the most influential people will be able to get a hold of the little bit of water that is left if there is no replenishment of the water sources, the people who depend on it will have to migrate, suffer or die.

The problems concerning water have always been regional issues. With the increased influence of globalization and anthropogenic climate change, however, water issues of are becoming more pressing and widespread. With 7.5 billion people to sustain, we need fresh water, food, and energy for an incredible amount of people. Regions with low cultural cohesion, are subject to a repressing regime, and have diminishing water supplies will become less stable. Once water sources have been depleted and the people start to become more desperate, strife and instability are just around the corner.

We love steaks, ribs, T-bones, rib-eyes and many other pieces of meat from cows, pigs, sheep, chickens, turkeys, rabbits and many more edible animals. humans are omnivores, we eat everything from meat to vegetables and fruits, nuts and fish. We consume – and waste – vast amounts of food every day. In order to feed humanity, we've transformed large areas of land to produce food. The production of food depends on vast amounts of water.

It is estimated that food production accounts for nearly half of all the fresh water consumption in the world, but water resources are diminishing fast. This means that food production will become increasingly more difficult, and at some point, we will not be able to sustain a growing human population any more. In addition the food is not being distributed on an equal basis. High income, high wealth countries get the best and highest quantities of foods, while the developing countries still cope with food shortages and poor nutritional diversity.

As food becomes scarce, Prices will start to rise, the distribution of food will become less and famine will start to spread amongst the people, starting with the poor and destitute, rapidly climbing up the chain.

We are currently producing more food than is necessary, about 1.2 times what is needed, yet hundreds of millions of people go hungry every day. There is something incredibly wrong with the distribution of food, and it is tied to the distribution of wealth.

Dystopian analogies

The impacts of food production on the atmosphere and on fresh water resources are quite large. First of all, cattle raising is one of the most detrimental forms of food cultivation in the world. 1kg of beef requires about 15.000 liters of water, and an average beef cow of 580 kilos emits about 55 kilograms of methane annually. A double edged sword that puts tremendous stress on water supplies and adds to global warming. What is more, these cows feed on fodder or compound feed i.e. byproducts from food processing, hay, straw, silage but also antibiotics, chemical preservatives, and other ingredients.

Consider how much grain is needed to feed a cow and how many people could eat this grain instead, and how many people could eat from the meat the cow provided? Bovine cultivation is the most food and water consuming process of all food production strings.

This is wrong. Calves are fed by cows for some time. However imagine that you've just been born. When you are a few months old, you will be put into a pen where you eat the same tasteless food all day, refined food with all sorts of special growth chemicals added to it. Sunlight? All you see is the light from the fluorescent lights above you. Your life is almost meaningless, you've hardly any space to walk around; it smells like excrement and piss all day. And one day, if you've grown enough, you're body mass is satisfactory you will be taken to a different place for the second time in your life and at some point, the lights go out. You die and your body parts end up on a plate in some home or restaurant (and let's not mention halal food...).

All over the world animals are bred to provide food to humanity. Most of these beings are quite probably suffering to a high degree. How moral or ethical is it for us to look away? Do we have a grasp of the feeling of pain and grief these animals experience?

Not only is the massive industrial-scale cultivation of animals for food quite unethical, but it is also bad for the environment. We need to a change in paradigms regarding the cultivation of animals and the way we treat them. Not only to mitigate methane emissions but also to minimize the amount of suffering in the world.

I won't deny that I too love a well-prepared steak every once in a while. Humans simply need certain proteins in order to live a healthy life. But raising animals does not have to be wrong if we don't industrialize this process. I believe we can build a sustainable future with meat, with cheese and other animal products, yet different from the way we do things today. A more sensible way of providing food for billions of people is needed, a far more decentralized way of doing it. Eating more diverse and less water intensive sorts of meats like goat, sheep, chicken, rabbit, etc.

It is proven that consumerism coupled with capitalism are systems that emaciate our planet and are capricious and in the long, self-destructive. Instead of consuming more, we should become more provident and smarter about it, I am however not advocating complete austerity. To emaciate our fresh water sources is to reap the negative rewards in the form of famine and human and nature's suffering. It is also to contribute to the global warming process by adding volumes of carbon into the atmosphere that would otherwise have been sequestered in plant life.

Civilizations have collapsed due to food shortages, the Sumerians and the Mayans for instance. Our current civilization might collapse as well once we venture into a world state in which food cultivation becomes unsustainable. Hundreds of millions of people will die. Once the temperature rises uncontrollably, our water sources will deplete and our will crops fail. Crop yields are an important metric for the sustainability of human civilization. If crop yields across the world start showing a steady decline, we're in trouble.

An increasingly warmer planet will perpetuate the continued collapse of glaciers and snow packs. If all the glaciers of the world were to melt most of the shorelines of the world would expand inwards. Small island states would disappear, and we would lose a lot of land to the sea.

Would this mean that we would have to live on the seas? Probably not. However, the world's economy would collapse completely because worldwide trade would grind to a halt due to inaccessible major ports. The most heavily populated areas are concentrated along the shorelines. Cities like Chennai, Mumbai, Seoul, Lagos, Jakarta and also major cities like Shanghai, Istanbul, New York, Tokyo and Cairo will be flooded and become uninhabitable. The entire Atlantic seaboard of the United States would be flooded completely from Florida to Maine. almost all areas east from the Appalachian Mountain range would be submerged, about 30 percent of the total population of the United States would have to move, about one hundred million people. Countries like the Netherlands and Denmark would almost cease to exist. About 600 million people in China would be displaced, and the country of Bangladesh, with its 160 million people, would almost disappear completely. So it is quite right for the Climate Change movement to address rising oceans since they immediately threaten the direct livelihoods of billions of people. Yet eventually sea level rise will have a great impact on the entire world's population.

We've touched on an issue that has been around for many generations, wealth segregation, and hard ceilings. Emperors, kings, and dictators, people at the pinnacle of human segregation in terms of wealth and power. It has happened all over the world in many different forms. People have been slaves for thousands of years, castes made sure there was no climbing the ladder and there are still hard ceilings in place for women, for colored people, people from different ethnic groups or different religious persuasions. This is discrimination and racism in a fascistic way and it has been around for ages, most repression has been foisted on people by using violence, by showing power, by letting you know who's boss.

Once the wealthy people start segregating themselves completely from the lower classes, something is terribly wrong. A fence won't keep desperate people at bay, whether they are hungry, thirsty or just angry.

Once people arrive at a state of constant malaise without any relief from the people that are in power, resentment and hatred begin to grow and discontent starts festering among the people. It eventually leads to revolutions, civil wars, and the killing or imprisonment of the ruling class. Consider the Bolshevik uprising in Russia for instance, the regicide of Tsar Nicholas II and the killing of the aristocrats of Russia. La Revolution Francaise is yet another notable form of strife, civil unrest and war against the ruling class. Many of the rich and powerful were executed during and after the French Revolt, most notably of course King Louis XVI and his wife Marie-Antoinette.

Many revolutions followed the American Revolution, The Cuban Revolution, the Iranian Revolution, The American Civil War, etc. Throughout the ages, we've seen innumerable rebellions and revolutions because they were the only means by which repressed peoples could undo themselves from the manacles of the powerful. Some of these rebellions, however, were unsuccessful, having been beaten down by the ruling classes. We're still living in a dangerous and unstable world. We are near flashpoints. Strife, revolts, and wars are around the corner everywhere.

This neo-capitalistic, unbridled consumerist dystopia is already here. The incredibly rich and powerful keep satiating their thirst for wealth and power in autocratic and dictatorial ways. In their wake, people and communities get destroyed and are left to rot. Once profitability can be found somewhere else, large corporations are gone. Just look at Detroit. The car companies got an astronomical bailout and yet they forsook Detroit for the sake of profitability elsewhere, turning this once bristling city into a barren wasteland, almost like a "warzone" riddled with forsaken buildings and houses, old disabused cars in front lawns, burned homes and roads full of potholes. Instead of keeping this community alive, the big capitalist corporations left, for the sake of profit, guess that's the point of capitalism, right?

Medical care is barred from people who cannot afford it. Good medical care for the rich alone is yet another form of wealth segregation. In order to keep the profitability up, they keep the price of medicine and medical care as high as possible, at the lowest possible cost. I recently read an article where pharmacists in India recreated a drug for cancer at a fraction of the cost. In Europe, a treatment with this drug would cost somewhere in the area of 65.000 euro's while in India the same compound and the same amount of compound would be available for 150 dollars.

Eventually, the rich will become increasingly segregated from the "lower classes". Superior health care, superior food, and services would be available to the rich only. They would surround themselves with people who are willing to protect them from the "plebs". They would share some of their wealth and services with these people while the rest of humanity is left out to flounder in the backwash, destitute and desperate.

It is quite simple to make the case for all these horrendous visions of the future. Psychopathic and evil people have been in seats of power for a long time. Is it the power itself that corrupts these people? Just take a look at any of the great dictators in the history of man, where these people evil to begin with? Were they corrupted at one point in their lives? Historians are looking for the answers. It is very likely that a new sociopath or psychopath will rise to power once more. One could only imagine what kind of new horrors would be conspired to make humans feel more insecure or even terrorized.

What if future police duties are performed by emotionless robots, the ultimate dream of any self-respecting fascist psychopath, with the unquestioned use of [lethal] force against human beings, no more discussions between law enforcement and civilians. Enforcement- or terminator robots would be another technological horror which could become a reality by the steady development of robotics and artificial intelligence.

Thermo nuclear war could end humanity whether we would be fighting killer robots or each other makes no difference. The possibilities are endless, we could build giant autonomous bombers, jets, tanks, human-like robots, animal-like robots or even insect-like robots, to do the job of starting wars by killing humans in seats of powers. Just imagine a robot the size of a fly, with a hypodermic needle filled with some kind of nerve toxin, zooming through a building and injecting someone with a lethal dose? Using robots to kill humans is trivially easy, once you figure out how to build these machines, micro and macro.

This message is also being shared by Stephen Hawking, Bill Gates, and Elon Musk. The robotization and development of A.I. are a clear and present threat to humanity.

Imagine one of the world's superpowers (The US, Russia or China) developing some sort of super-warrior, a breed of terminator robots that will be unleashed unscrupulously on unsuspecting antagonists... It would set off a global war. National Security undermines Global Security. The security of humanity should be more important than the geopolitical interests of one country or a group of countries united in some sort of federation or alliance.

The ultimate and complete ending of the human race would be easy and probably self-induced, the threat of nuclear war has been an ominous reality for years. All that is necessary is for some delusional or psychopath to push the button. There have been plenty of "leaders" who were capable of doing it. Even the United States, under Truman, has done it. About 2500 nuclear bombs have been detonated by the world's superpowers.

Just think about it, the scale in which axis and allied bombers have concentrated their efforts on destroying human beings, They extensively bombed civilian area's: Tokyo, London, Rotterdam, Toyama, Hamburg, Fukui, Bochum, Dresden, and the list goes on and on, it is extensive. It is estimated that roughly two million people have been killed during these "strategic bombing missions". Imagine Nazi Germany with a nuclear bomb, would they have dropped it on London? These forces were in the process of exterminating peoples anyway, what would deter them from dropping a nuclear bomb? Or two in the case of the United States?

The only fortunate thing I could possibly think of in that context would be that many other countries do not have any nukes of their own so worldwide nuclear retaliation wouldn't be possible, yet.... Dropping the bombs on Hiroshima and Nagasaki has instilled a new fear in the hearts of humanity, and one could argue that ever since nations have been deterred from using "the bomb".

Let's look at it from another angle, whoever lost this war, would have been prosecuted as war criminals because they were bombing non-combatants. If Curtis Lemay had been captured and tried, he would have been convicted of war crimes. Firebombing practically all the towns and cities of Japan could be considered a war crime, yet it wasn't... He had won the war, dropping two nuclear bombs brought Japan to its knees, and victory over Japan was secured. The brutality in the US - Japanese war has precipitated unspeakable atrocities. If you want to know more about this subject, I suggest "The fog of war – Eleven lessons from the life of Robert S. Macnamara"

Or consider this question: who is accountable? Simply read "*the trial of Henry Kissinger*" by Christopher Hitchens and learn how power individuals evade accountability.

Human beings are flawed, however rational they might seem. People in seats of power aren't necessarily rational, they have been put in office by popular vote or other means. We can never be certain about the motivations of world leaders as there are no psychological evaluations prior to their election. A nut in office, having the keys to the nuclear arsenal is all it takes to obliterate humanity. I shudder at the idea of a rapture Christian being President of the United States...

Once the button is pushed, whether it is the US, China or Russia is irrelevant, human civilization will be reduced significantly and could even go extinct.

Let's face it, we have been looking down the gun barrel of nuclear war for many decades now, we came close during the Cuba crisis and have been living on full alert ever since. Humanity can be wiped out at the push of a button. Who is constraining who? What psychopathic and hawkish leader would actually press the button? An ominous and ever looming question.

We can get rid of the threat of nuclear war, but it will take commitment and trust – which we lack.

Other cataclysmic endings of humanity might involve some sort of uncontrolled carnivorous fungal bloom. A meat eating fungus that adapted to nourish itself of any type of meat, including human flesh. What if these fungi formed spores that are airborne? Flooding the Earth's atmosphere with meat eating spores, obliterating and consuming all land and air based animals. These are almost science fiction like speculations.

Dystopian analogies

Bacterium and viruses could overtake us. One pandemic could end humanity as we know it. We adapt poorly to certain diseases. Some we are able to destroy, others, like Ebola, are so hard to contain that if they strike, thousands can die.

The doomsday clock is dangerously close to midnight. And now also the Earth's health is being included as a factor regarding how the doomsday clock is set. Humanity has jet to grasp that we can grow to our full potential, not by ideology, dogma or creed but by applying our critical faculties and looking for new paths that maximize the worth and well-being of each individual and in which the Earth's resources and its ecosystem are elevated over economic gain and geopolitics.

This is part of my imagination, this is fiction... And yet I suspect that if you would press scientists to make predictions about certain climate scenario's they would tell you the same things, of course, some nuances here and there. There are certainly elements in these stories which are already a reality or have been, and there are certain aspects which will become a reality if we do not acknowledge the trouble we are in.

People might accuse me of fear-mongering, which is fine. I will not deny that I am scared of the future, especially the future of my two sons. I think we should be scared and acknowledge that the issues we face are scary. It is my hope that this angst will encourage humanity to do the right things and engage in becoming better.

From experience and imagination, these dystopian stories were born. We have the capacity to see good and bad outcomes. We must look first at the evidence and then try to extrapolate what the outcomes could be. We are on a highway to dystopia. The knowledge we have, combined with the failure to commit to solving the issues, lead me to believe that dystopia is becoming probable. In fact, many people are already living in a sort of dystopia. Is it fair to disregard their hardship? It is up to us to help one and other, to make the human story one of adventure, discovery, knowledge, and compassion.

It will be a great challenge for humanity to survive the twenty-first century. We can do it, but in order to do it, we must become more reasonable. We still move on along gloomy highway to dystopia.

Obliteration humanity

In times of desperation, people will believe anything, they need a crutch to lean on, someone to protect them, someone who looks after them.

As if all that has been written previously was not depressing enough we will now venture into the deep, into the abyss where the dark and evil monsters lurk, longing for the chance to feed upon our hardships, our misfortune, our grief and sorrow, the reversal of humanity and the demise of civilization. These monsters will be addressed in this chapter, the epitome of my dystopian visions, it is here where we will discuss the true evils that infest civilization.

We start by addressing mass hysteria and the belief in primitive superstition, religion.

Religion captures people and stifles critical thought. What *they* do is terribly simple and efficient. Once you start thinking critically about religion and its teachings, you will be coerced out of it. There are several doctrinal modes to achieve this, it begins with demonizing the people who are outside the cult, outside the religion, "*they are wrong and we are right and they will suffer for it.*" Secondly, it will paint a horrible picture of what awaits those who continue in their blasphemous ways, and thirdly it appeals to group authority. If you question the faith, you will hurt those near to you, they will be hurt by your decision to question the validity of their religion and the authority of god, yahweh, allah, and the prophets.

This is the reason why I have become an outspoken atheist and anti-theist, and I am opposed to all these man-made practices designed to keep people ignorant, stupid, downtrodden and subservient despite all the evidence. It is important to note that I have never been a true believer, one of the virtues of have being born in the Netherlands, one of the more advanced secular states on this planet.

The amounts of gods conjured up by humans number in the thousands. The human psyche is hardwired to find explanations for things we do not understand. Without a scientific understanding about what is happening around us, this was the best thing we humans could come up with, to appoint imaginative figures with magical powers. Over time the animal, tree, rock, sun, moon, sky, sea, fire and thunder gods merged into singular gods. People believed that these gods were responsible for everything that happened, and we began to appeal to them for help and gave them sacrifices in order to gain their favor. After thousands of years of believing and worshipping, it was only a matter of time before messiah's would appear, people claiming to be able to speak for these gods. The silence of the gods needed to be broken, and that's where these "mediums" found a needy and longing group of impressionable and superstitious people. A deep desire to hear a word from god made and kept them susceptible. Enter the first true con-artists.

Many people believe that scripture is the literal word of the divine despite the fact that these texts contain paradoxical claims, incredible stories and fairy tales of an unbelievable sort. I'm not buying it, though. Am I to believe that Abraham would have stabbed and barbequed his son if not for some "angel" coming to poor Isaac's aid, stopping Abraham just before he delivered the fatal blow? Is this supposed to be a moral lesson or should we take it as a savage age slapstick? Does anybody actually believe that Moses split the Red Sea in two? Did he really throw a staff at the feet of a pharaoh, which then turned into a snake? Did he really talk to a burning bush before receiving the "Ten Commandments"?

The story of Noah is also unbelievable. A man building a wooden boat to save every species of animal on the face of the Earth, including the Dinosaurs?! Have you ever seen the skeleton of a Brachiosaurus or a Diplodocus? Try to fit any of these creatures into a wooden vessel that must have been a really impressive ship... And then there's a flood that couldn't have happened because there isn't enough water to submerge the entire earth. What about bringing all these creatures back to their respective continents? How did the Penguins get to the Middle East? What about the Grizzly Bears from North America? How did all the carnivorous animals survive without eating their shipmates? Or try to establish that Noah took with him on this epic trip any marsupials. Or why aren't they even mentioned? It is quite obvious isn't it? None of the illiterate desert dwelling people have ever heard of, nor ever saw any of them. This is a nice bedtime story, but way too preposterous to be taken seriously, and as such all "ark-projects" should be deemed a lost and unnecessary quest to depict a fictional story. I'm not really sorry, but Ken Ham, you are wasting your time and taxpayer's money...

Also consider the horror of the rest, left out of this epic journey, god surely was very moral killing many innocent creatures who had nothing to do with all this supposed sinning going on. And how did all the plants survive being submerged for so long?

Am I to believe that Jesus walked on water? That he turned it into wine? That he, like Mithras, Melchizedek, Attis, Buddiah, Dionysus, Hercules, Krishna and Osiris, was born from a virgin mother? Isn't it obvious that this story has been told before?

Highway to Dystopia

Consider the horrendous doctrine of original sin: A human sacrifice justified by the notion of "the unbelievable story of the first two humans", Adam who was created from dust and Eve whom was created from a rib of Adam, committing the original sin by eating a piece of fruit from a forbidden tree... With this, he supposedly sealed our lot in life, an immoral form of moral capture. Did god really need to forgive humanity for the "sins" of two people who never existed? Why did Jesus need to die a horrible death? Because some non-existent person committed this "crime"? Why did we need a human sacrifice in order to be forgiven? Was Jesus sent here to die as a scapegoat? Was he really resurrected? Why are all of us supposedly born with "original sin"? These stories are ludicrous at best. It is these kinds of doctrines that appear in other religions as well. Judaism, Islam, Zoroastrianism and many other religions are simply gathered myths and legends, often copied from each other. The single most obvious fact is that these religions and stories have been made up by humans.

We have to face up to the fact that these religions are founded on savage age superstitions. These holy scriptures are nothing more than a bundle of unbelievable stories.

If I owned these books, they would sit beside the Arabian Nights and the fairy tales of the Brothers Grimm. However, to be knowledgeable about European history, it would help to be acquainted with the stories of the bible in order to understand why Galileo and Copernicus were condemned as heretics, or why the Albigensian Crusade was so bloody (God will know his own...) and how the knights and lords of the medieval ages came to be. In a historical sense, it has some value, but it also reveals that most religious leaders were filled with spite, hatred and an insatiable desire for dominion over other men.

Where is the evidence for the mythical claims made by [any] religion? Where is the evidence of the things Jesus supposedly did?

The accounts of his supposed actions were written well after his death, by people who had never met him. It is all highly circumstantial, furthermore, if Jesus really did these things, there should be many written accounts so many that the history of his life would be irrefutable. An explosion of written accounts would have been found if these incredible things truly happened and were witnessed. The stories about Jesus would be widespread, long before he died. Ancient Palestine would have become a magnet to the thirsty, needy and the sickly. We would have found evidence that many people would have migrated to this place where this wondrous figure roamed, this man that could cure you, or give you food. There is no such evidence.

We are left with the fact that imaginative people have been trying to make us believe that Abraham, Moses, Jesus and all the other supposed divine spirits did all these incredible things, but proof of these actions is yet to be found. And let's be honest about it, it is probably never going to happen. Many people have searched for years and came up with nothing. In the meantime, a circus has been created around these myths. Nobody understood what was happening back then, scientific understanding was near nil, so they conjured up all sorts of vague stories about the origins of humanity and the Earth, let alone the universe. Let us please accept them for what they are, age-old superstitions, nothing more and nothing less. The stories in the bible, for instance, have been transcribed from centuries of storytelling, and many of them disagree. How warped do you think these stories have become?

Christianity spread across the Mediterranean, and the Roman Empire Eventually became the Holy Roman Empire. The first council of Nicaea, which was held about 300 years after the death of Jesus, sought doctrinal unanimity among the clergy and the subdivisions in the faith, creating modern Christianity, a misogynistic, xenophobic, greedy and world domineering sect designed to ensnare people. The desire for influence, wealth and power has always been a motivator for Christianity. As a consequence, religious zealots tore through Europe and south America, subjugating people in the name of their god, who, of course, needed money to support his priests and acolytes and to construct this vast and world-spanning network of churches and other holy places. Christianity quickly morphed into the "thing" we know today, once the influential people at the head of the church saw the potential.

The supposed piety and goodness of Christ was part of the honey trap, the false and unsubstantiated promises and threats about your destiny after death did the rest. The notion that you could burn in hell for an eternity if you didn't follow the doctrines of Christianity provided an excellent motivator, especially among the impressionable, the superstitious and those who were afraid of nature. Imagine these horrors forced upon children, telling children that they had to abide by the rules or they would roast in hell. This is outright child abuse. The children who really believed it must have been mortified of the notion of hell and frightened of the god that could send them there. "Are you a god fearing... ?" This is one of the methods by which children and young adults are being pressured into staying true to the church. It is out of fear that they stay. Subsequently generational indoctrination by priests has spawned billions of followers, people with parentally and priestly induced convictions. The mind of the child is hardwired to trust their parents without question... It is the next generations brought up with these beliefs and convictions that have spawned the thousands of religious zealots ready to do anything for their religion, for their god. They are true believers.

Early in the seventh century, another messiah or prophet emerged, and his name was Mohammed. Mohammed plagiarized from the Jews, the Christians, the Greeks and the Persians and created a new religion called Islam. Again we are asked to believe that archangel Gabriel compelled this man to take note of the wishes of god and to compile them in the Qur'an. Even though I don't like it, I'd suggest you read the first couple of chapters where it basically alludes to how the jews and Christians were wrong. Also, be very keen to read the – often deliberately and only partially – cited 5:32 verse (which was meant for "the people of Israel"). Don't forget to read 5:33 as well. To add insult to injury, Mohammedans often claim that the Qur'an is the perfect word of god, but how could it be? Consider the origins of this book: In an illiterate part of the world, an unlettered man – Mohammed – had a "vision" while being in a cave, a cousin of his wife was someone who knew some of the stories of Christianity and Judaism, and proclaimed that the new messiah had arrived and Mohammed fashioned himself the "slave of god" and started the religion of Islam, which is heavily influenced by the stories of Abraham and Moses and Jesus. Also consider that the holy texts and verses are ambiguous and that they weren't even finalized until after the prophet had died, to whom did Gabriel speak to help them finalize the document? When Mohammed died the first real schisms emerged, who was to be the rightful successor of the prophet? Enter the Shia/Sunni divide. And why is there abrogation (2:106) in the Qur'an? Why is it necessary for newer verses to override older verses, and how can we determine which one is the newer one? The Abrogation verse is the nail in the coffin of the validity of the Qur'an, and to me makes this story completely and utterly unconvincing, if you have to add a caveat...

Probably one of the most relevant stories in Islam is the one where it is claimed that Mohammed had a nightly flight from Mecca to Jerusalem on a mythical winged horse. Why Jerusalem? Perhaps because the myths of Jesus had originated there? Or perhaps because it had become a wealthy and powerful city by then? Whatever the motives were, the implications of this story still are being felt present-day. The Al-Aqsa mosque and the Dome of the Rock are two of the most controversial buildings in the world, and some people think it is justified to commit murder over these supposedly celestial properties.

Also be reminded that the promise of eternal hellfire exists in Islam as well. It's inserted quite early in the Qur'an, perhaps the first real feat of terrorism.

Muslims are expected to live by the example of Mohammed, but was Mohammed a perfect role model? I don't believe he was, on the contrary, he would be the perfect role model if the violent spread of Islam were the objective, so living by his example cannot bring about lives of peace and love. He was infamous for his successes in war and the atrocious deeds he committed afterwards. *Infamous* is a word I chose deliberately because his "auto-biography" had been written down no earlier than one-hundred years after his death. We live in the 21st century, not in the 6th, nor in the 1st, nor six millennia ago. Sadly enough his spiteful and aggressive example shines through until today.

Now consider barbaric practices like the mutilation of young girl's and boy's genitalia (Brit Milah/Bris?), the submission and the inequality of women and ultimately the barbaric punitive practices encoded in Sharia. However, this isn't just an Islamic problem – Christianity, Judaism, and other religious denominations have enacted equally inhumane Practices. these practices are backwards and barbaric and should go out of use, extinct if you will, as fast as possible.

For thousands of years, religions have been trying to subjugate and convert people of different persuasions with torture, holy wars, crusades, jihads, inquisitions, and ethnic cleansings – all committed in the name of religion. Delusions of holy grandeur have led to the deaths of millions. There are a hundred fold more stars in the Galaxy than there are people on Earth and from this perspective the king-of-the-hill game of religion matters not.

Obliteration humanity

Even today many people are being terrorized in the name of religion. Look at the history books – the few that really tell the truth: The ethnic cleansing in Europe by the Nazi regime, whose soldiers had the creed "*Gott mit uns*" (god with us) on their belt buckles; Do a little research into the ethnic cleansings in Yugoslavia, Ruanda, Turkey, Iraq, Syria, and you will discover that they are almost always religiously inspired. Xenophobia, greed, and bloodlust are extensively interwoven into religious scripture and it isn't that surprising if we acknowledge that these modes are also embedded in the human psyche, had we not been like this, we wouldn't have survived, but now it is time to move on and away from these archaic behaviors.

Religious conflicts occur all over the world, currently particularly in Iraq and Syria, North and Central Africa and in parts of the Asian subcontinent. I call it sinister narcissistic religious zealotry. People with unquestionable faith. Individuals who fight "for the greater cause" or try to become a martyr. I call it an ultimate form of myopia, these people fail grotesquely to see the big picture because their judgment is clouded by their absolute belief in the rubbish written down in a couple of age-old books. They really believe that there's a life after death, and they are convinced that their cause is just. Consider the Islamists, Jihadists, Christian fundamentalists, and the right-wing Jews. Their behavior is terrifying, yet I am convinced that they absolutely believe the scripture and that their actions are justified. Many religions want to make people believe that life on Earth is merely a journey to the end-station, an after-life in either a place of eternal bliss or horror and agony.

Bronze Age scriptural nonsense is used to justify the loss of life, needless suffering and the destruction of heritage and knowledge. Scriptural nonsense is also being used by people to justify many forms of bigotry: hatred of homosexuality, the submission of women, and other forms of inhumane and xenophobic activities. It is despicable that people take the supposed truth of scripture seriously without any credible evidence, and then use it as justification for hurting and killing people.

This is primate behavior ("And it shows" – Christopher Hitchens). We form groups, we perceive threats to our groups and want to defend our group, often by destroying "the others". Or one could be part of an aggressive group on the prowl, to justify the actions of the groups, false pretexts are conjured up, in many cases these are scripturally embedded xenophobic excuses.

The doctrines of the second coming of Christ, the end of days, judgment day, the rapture and all sorts of prophesies predict cataclysmic endings. It almost seems that these people want this world to end. The construction of nuclear weapons, the strife in the middle east, the new caliphate, the war in the Ukraine, with some Christians almost gleefully waiting for the rapture. These selfish people expect to have an eternity of bliss and say that those who belong to the wrong religions or no religion at all will fry in hell for being different. This is the kind of coercive pressure that is being used to win people over. It happens in many different religions. It is the natural mechanism of sticking together for survival that is being played upon. Once you step out of the herd your survival is at risk, we know this instinctively.

Welcome to the club of people who claim to know all about our existence and the nature of our cosmos. Lacking evidence, they rely on "knowing" and "feeling". These people also try to push political and ideological agendas. People who threaten unbelievers with the expectation of damnation in eternal torment are sociopaths and psychopaths. Imagine them ascending to heaven, then looking down on their fellow humans suffering from eternal torment, some of whom they might even have known. What are they going to say to their sky dad? Good job Yahweh!? Good job Allah!?

Obliteration humanity

Can you imagine seeing a friend or loved one in excruciating agony and then meeting "your maker" and then not plea for the well-being of the soul of your fellow? No redemption comes, how are you supposed to continue on in eternal bliss, knowing that someone you knew is now suffering? I would be quite distraught actually, I would try to save this individual from eternal punishment, thus completely negating the prospect of eternal happiness.

Christianity's opposition to science has been fierce, long lasting, and is still ongoing. Why? Because knowledge threatened the power of the clergy, many of the scientific discoveries brought charges of heresy that could coerce scientists into submission. Thomas Aquinas wrote in his "Summa Theologica" that people who were convicted of heresy should be put to death.

These doctrines have led to the persecution of many notable scientists and theologians like Copernicus, Bruno, Galileo, Campanella, Rene Descartes, Pietro d'Abano, Cecco d'Ascoli, William of Ockham, and more. It is said that doctrinal persecution happens still, and if you look at some of the deeds of politicians all over the world, this claim can easily be justified. Unfortunately, the descendants of these know-nothing clergy can still be found in the American congress, where far too many members still deny the existence of anthropogenic climate change.

In its zeal to maintain the purity of the faith, the catholic church created the Index of Prohibited Books – a list of works not to be read by anyone. Pravda mechanics have existed long before they were used in Russia. Imagine people not being allowed to own any bible, at first, then later, a bible written in English – a rule imposed on the people by the church itself for many years.

The stagnation that religion and certain ideologies impose on freedom of thought, speech and the quest for scientific progress is dangerous. It makes people stop thinking about the fundamental questions about ourselves, our world and the Universe. Religion pressures people into conformity, throttling their thirst for different views and new ideas while keeping them in the mundane religious flow of mediocrity from the cradle to grave, in glorification of death and the afterlife.

Among the most evil things we have practiced are ritual human sacrifice and executions, vile acts inculcated by religious and ideological dogma. The glorification of the torture and death of Jesus, for instance, is sickening.

Executing people because of their nature, because of their expendability, their ideas, and their crimes has been common. Especially when religion was concerned. Whenever someone is put to death, it is barbaric. No amount of man-made scriptural nonsense can be used to justify taking somebody else's life. And yet this practice of human sacrifice goes on even today.

Consider the horrifying attacks on Atheist and Secularist bloggers in Asia, or the incarceration and flogging of secular blogger Raif Badawi, and the possible beheading and crucifixion of protestor Ali al-Nimr in Saudi Arabia. Freedom of speech and the quest for secular values and the betterment of peoples are under attack. I am baffled by the existence of the alliance between the US and the utterly barbaric Wahabi theocracy of Saudi Arabia, which is one of the worst in terms of human rights. And to add injury to insult, they head the Human Rights council of the United Nations. I'm still trying to figure out how this is possible, I don't get it, the hypocrisy is beyond me.

Human life, self-determination, human dignity and the freedom of speech should be sacrosanct. I am a relentless defender these issues and especially of free speech.

It is often claimed that morality comes from religion, but which religion? If religion gives us anything, it is a warped and crazy morality. To me, religious morality looks like "no one in their right mind would do this – except when supported by scripture." Let's face it, religions endorse atrocities like keeping the women of your slain enemies, child rape, mutilation of genitalia, genocide, filicide, xenophobia, hatred, submission and oppression.

Even the origins of "modern" religions like the Mormon Church and Scientology are highly questionable. Consider the ludicrous stories of L. Ron Hubbard, or Joseph Smith. No one in their right mind would believe these stories, and yet many do. This puzzles me. These predatory pseudo-religious groups are everywhere, encroaching on the impressionable and the desperate in order to capture their minds and especially their money.

The scars of religious and ideological zealotry are still fresh, deep lacerations torn through the fabric of human history, the rending–unfortunately–isn't over.

There is no reason to believe that the Bible is the word of any god. The Bible was written long after the death of Jesus, some of it hundreds of years later. In addition, the Bible is a translation of a translation of stories, and it often contradicts itself. Isn't it surprising that "the perfect word of god" is so incoherent? That a *messiah* has to *come* to denounce parts of it or "amend" it? Very curious indeed. There is no rational or compelling evidence for the existence of god or gods and these supposed rule- and story books should not be taken literally, nor serious.

Nevertheless, I still have hope for those who have a benign sense of faith, the people who use their critical faculties and teach their children to be critical and skeptical as well. I have faith that these people, or their offspring, will eventually conclude that religion is unsubstantiated nonsense, and religion will become a marginal activity. It has happened in my country, religion has declined steadily over the last decades, and also consider the Scandinavian countries. It is my hope that critical thinking will propagate through the internet and other gateways to reason and knowledge.

Highway to Dystopia

A lot of fatalistic people and regimes try to force some sort of Armageddon on human civilization. The prospect of nuclear or biological weapons in the hands of terrorists is quite scary, just as the possibility of regimes like Iran, North Korea getting their hands on nukes, or the antagonists India and Pakistan, China, Russia and the United States with their fingers on the trigger, with their nuclear arsenals on fifteen minute alert all the time. Or consider Saudi Arabia, yet another country full of murderous religious zealots in a terribly unstable region. Why are we still "friends" with them? Can anyone tell me this? The answer is obvious, but that's the irony of our double standards. Many people are convinced that the Wahabi Regime of Saudi Arabia is one the co-sponsors of jihadist terrorism all over the world. Perhaps even an instigator in the Iraqi and Syrian wars.

Religious and ideological people with doomsday weapons at their command is not a nice perspective and we've not yet freed ourselves from the imminent threat of thermo nuclear war. The current problems in the Ukraine, Iran, Syria, North Korea, China, Russia and the United States make the world an unstable and unsafe place. All the forces are moving around and sucking in as much oxygen as they can get. The conflict in Syria is sucking in NATO and Russian involvement. We are literally living on a knife's edge, World War III is just around the corner, a cataclysmic thermo nuclear war, Armageddon.

Note: during the finalization process of this second edition, Turkish fighter jets have gunned down a Russian aircraft, thus increasing tensions between NATO and Russia.

Make no bones of this, the Syrian conflict will be "won" by Al Assad, Iran, and Russia, "our" involvement there has to end as soon as possible. The next President of the United States that emerges from the 2016 elections should pump the brakes and reach out to all parties involved and seek a diplomatic way out of this mess. Also recognize that the complete and utter destruction of daesh is required. If we are to continue the fighting in Syria and Iraq, we must commit multilaterally. We have to involve the Syrian Government and Russia and cooperate with them in this fight against daesh. We owe this to the innocents that are suffering from this horrible war.

The point about nuclear weapons is that the amount of nuclear warheads vastly exceed the amount of warheads needed to destroy all life on Earth. Why do we have nuclear weapons in the first place? Why do we have so many nuclear weapons? Are we going to see the political will to vastly diminish the amount of nuclear weapons? To turn megatons into megawatts? Questions that come to mind when thinking about the nuclear threat that looms above our heads, like the sword of Damocles.

In 2015, 46 members of the American Republican Party signed a letter addressed to the "Leaders of the Islamic Republic of Iran" – Rouhani – telling him that any agreement reached with President Obama wouldn't survive. Undermining the President's efforts to secure peace in the Middle East seems to be a treasonous act. It is claimed that the letter has never been sent, but it is available nonetheless, signed and all... see the appendix for the link.

These politicians are endangering all of the inhabitants of the world. Are they really thirsty for war, or are they providing justification for increasing America's astronomical military in the name of "national security" and the obvious acquisition of wealth?

The same sabre-rattling can be seen in the Ukraine when a civil upheaval ousted President Viktor Yanukovych, which led to the annexation of the Crimean Peninsula by Russia, bringing us close to war. NATO has stationed extra fighter jets in Poland and the Baltic states to cope with the threat of Russian bombers, and some countries are considering arming the Ukraine, a very dangerous development.

Highway to Dystopia

The well-being of people is no longer an issue in this "game" about greed, power, and wealth. Our rights and interests do not count. I question if they ever have. Psychopaths and sociopaths in seats of power make sure that the stranglehold on humanity continues.

Religious people, conservatives, and liberals can be strange allies. Many of them try to stifle free speech under the guise of eliminating remarks that could offend the religious. I am completely opposed to this. Nothing should be above ridicule or criticism. To stifle freedom of thought and freedom of speech is reprehensible and should be challenged whenever.

Foisting falsehoods on people, the labeling of children and religious division perpetuate and deepen the chasms that divide humans. Belief without evidence smoothens the path to extremism.

We are yet to free ourselves from the fanatic modes of reprisal and reciprocity. The idea that what someone or some state did to another person or state has to be set right by equal means is putting us in a never ending spiral leading into the darkness where the evil monsters lurk that yearn for our demise.

And as if this all isn't bad enough we will progress into some other harrowing developments that are a threat to the survival of civilization. unfortunately, there are also forces out there to get us, which aren't us. I'm not talking about Aliens, we have not yet discovered them. I'm talking about outbreaks of deadly viruses, deadly Pandemics. Overuse of Antibiotics have caused many viruses to grow resistant to them.

Microbes are evolving faster than we can develop medicines to fight them. Vaccines have put an end to polio, smallpox and have almost defeated measles. Despite all this, some microbes like the influenza virus are evolving even faster, outpacing our capacity to fight them.

Obliteration humanity

Diseases like Ebola, SARS, the bird flu, swine flu and tuberculosis are wreaking havoc among the vulnerable. The 2014 outbreak of Ebola in Western Africa killed tens of thousands, and new diseases keep jumping over from animals to humans. In this evolutionary arms race between humans and microbes, we just might be losing the battle. It is a matter of time before a pandemic could wipe out a large portion of civilization.

Science has conquered Chicken Pox, Diphtheria, Pneumococcal Disease, Polio, Tetanus, Typhoid Fever, Yellow Fever and the Smallpox, but no number of prayers have done the same. However, the anti-vaccination fringe has created a dangerous hole in our battle with germs. Microbes have dominion over us, not the other way around.

We mammalian primates called humans or homo-sapiens, kill each other for wealth and power. These barbaric behaviors evolved into killing each other over superstitions, doctrines and ideologies, often providing a quick path to power and wealth. Some of us are willing to take the chance to become king of the hill at the expense of anything and everyone while others kill for the promise of martyrdom. However, we can outgrow our nature and become better than it.

We have a great deal of history books and chronicles to substantiate these claims. We have archives full of the annals of humanity, the extensive narratives, and recitals of our history that attest to the despicable, greedy, cruel, vile and murderous nature of man. And yet there are many who provide a glimmer of hope: mainly the humanists, naturalists, and secularists – individuals with the immense power of empathy and compassion. I don't want to come over as a persistent nihilist.

Science cannot prove nor disprove the existence of an omniscient, omnipotent metaphysical being that supposedly crafted the universe, the galaxies, the stars and the planets. I do however contest that any man made scripture is proof of anything, it only shows the propensity for human imagination and I regard all religious scripture as such, it contains no authority or evidence for anything at all, let alone of the existence of a god or gods.

Science doesn't care what one's beliefs are, it is only concerned with finding knowledge and truth. Science is a binding factor, a secular endeavor that brings together people from all backgrounds, religious or non-religious. Petty human differences can be set aside on the great treks devised to unfurl the unknown. Look for instance at the stupefying SETI, LHC, ITER and ISS projects. Thousands of scientists and engineers from all over the world gathered in an attempt to find answers to the fundamental questions that occupy the human mind, regardless of their personal world views.

It might be a hard conclusion but most people are probably wrong about their destiny in death. It is highly improbable that heaven or hell exist. Neither is it probable that we will reincarnate. Instead of dedicating our lives to something – for which there is no evidence – wouldn't it be more sensible to dedicate our lives to make sure we leave this world a better place than we found it? To engage in endeavors that benefit humanity? To engage in finding out what makes this world and the Universe so beautiful and magnificent?

We have become a danger to ourselves, we have become a danger to nature and to our world. We are the cause of much hardship and distress, pollution, and destruction, terror and death. I wonder if we will ever learn to become less hostile, more provident, emphatic and compassionate.

There is nothing more important than the right to think whatever you want to think, the right to say whatever you want to say, the right to ridicule whatever you want to ridicule, the right to be who you want to be, the right to love who you want to love, the right to engage in the quest for knowledge, truth and understanding.

Obliteration humanity

Nothing is more important than to fight for our own and each other's freedom.

We must realize that ideological and doctrinal capture and pressure is detrimental to our well-being and civilization. Tribalism creates unjustifiable acts. It ties people together in inhumane goals, not for the common good, but for the perpetuation of division and satiation of greed.

I feel completely comfortable stating this here: There is no god, we've conjured up god and gods because we were scientifically naive primates unable to understand what was happening around us. We've formed all sorts of god hypotheses and have grown accustomed to them. We have yet to understand that these hypotheses are completely unsubstantiated and untrue. We are still following primitive ways of thought and are incorporating them in modern day live, thus stunting any significant form of human progress.

We have to recognize our own mortality. You and I are going to die and there is nothing, no afterlife, one ceases from being, everyone around you ceases from being at death, there is no fairy tale, no heaven, hell or paradise. Every living being on the face of the Earth has a finite lifespan, and death is certain. What are you going to do? Help them? Show some empathy, compassion, and altruism? Make this world a better and more beautiful place? Holding this view of death is liberating! It makes you a better human being if you acknowledge that your life is precious, that you can make a difference in other people's lives. We are here to make our own meaning. We can try to find out how everything came to be with science and reason.

Religious authorities should be held accountable for the harm done by their unsubstantiated claims. They shouldn't be exempt from taxes. Neither should they hold any special position of authority, influence or power. I hope that religion will diminish into something unimportant. We can do better without it. We can do great and inspiring things in technology, sports, art, music, social activities, etc. And we can do all of this without religion. Non-religious people do beautiful and inspiring things all the time.

I do not care that this statement might be considered offensive, people might be saying that I am rude or hateful, that's fine. I didn't intend to do any harm by writing this chapter, I did have to address these issues because I sincerely believe that they are profoundly dangerous to humanity. If you feel hurt by my comments, that's a shame, I am not going to apologize, I want you to open up your critical faculties, I want you to be skeptical, seek and/or demand evidence, and use reason.

It might be considered rude for me to say that believers spend their lives believing a lie, giving all this time and money to a cause that isn't true or just. Try to think about religion from a different viewpoint and acknowledge that it isn't sacrosanct to critique and shouldn't ever be. Religion is not off limits.

I like religion to go extinct, not by regulating it away, I think that is impossible, I want every new generation of children to be free to join the ranks of the "non-affiliated" people, the agnostics, the atheists, the anti-theists, the non-theists, the unbelievers. How to help this process? To keep voicing criticism of religion is a start. I'll also insert this caveat here: I wouldn't mind people remaining spiritual, feeling "something", but we will have to push for the complete and utter extirpation of harmful [religious] dogma, doctrine and the forces that try to enforce it.

I really like Daniel Dennett's proposal: teach the good, the bad and the ugly of all religions to children. Make them look at religion from a historical perspective, teach them that all of them claim to be true, show them what has happened in the name of religion. Show them the controversies and the contradictions. This will quite possibly steer enough youths away from Religion to such an extent that the influence of religion will start to diminish quite rapidly.

Why do we keep engaging in primitive behavior fueled by age-old myths and legends? Religious dogma is nothing but the assumed truth, without any reason or evidence to back it up. Truth does not matter in the mind of the believer.

The extinction of religiosity will be a gradual process, it progresses as more people become more knowledgeable, reasonable, and more skeptical. There is ample reason to become more skeptical, just take a look at the headlines every day, and wonder why.

Change happens bottom up. It can start with you and me. If you are religious, please stop drinking the snake-oil and come to your senses and join us in the world of reason.

This is one of the reasons why I want to make clear that religion is not off-limits. I encourage all secularist, agnostics, non-believers, atheist, anti-theists to speak out. Why? Because I'm absolutely certain that there are more of us than we dare to dream off. And it is absolutely essential that we do so because non-religious and/or secular people are targeted for their outspokenness all over the world. We need consciousness raising campaigns. Richard Dawkins, for instance, is a champion for the "openly secular" campaign. We need more of this. Don't be afraid to come out as a secularist or humanist. Depending on your situation I would also say come out as an Atheist... *unless* it poses a grave danger to you. I don't want anyone to get hurt on my behalf!

Religious taboos are going to be broken, with the right ideas and effort religiosity will be set on a steady decline, of that I'm sure. But it is up to us to make a difference. In the meanwhile people like Senator Ted Cruz may accuse me of "*attacking Christianity*", don't worry Ted, yours is not the only one I am "attacking" (note the quotation marks – this is a quest in the realm of the mind, not the physical world, I fight with words, not with swords).

I am afraid that much blood will be spilled, especially by Islam and Judaism and Christianity, because these faiths have tied the knot of war in their quest for world-domination through the absolutist claims and doctrines written down ages ago, and the interpretation thereof... The religious right, whether they be Islamic or Christian, remain contemptuous of our secular values and mutual understanding and freedom, and they will keep pushing their abhorrent and ancient goat-herder-cults with their morals and ethics from savage ages. Not if I have a say in any of this. I will ridicule them and oppose them.

Please bear with me, we are going to delve deeper into the mess humanity has created. There is some light at the end of the tunnel, though. Nobody is going to set things right for us, the mess we have created we need to clean up ourselves, and will.

Power, greed, dishonesty and false commitments

In today's world of economics, people make money instead of earning it. The incentive to care for each other in the neo-capitalistic world, the world of capitalistic Darwinism, and the world of unimpeded consumerism, is gone. Countless people are burdened by the rising cost of education and degree-inflation, stagnating wages and increasing workloads while capitalism ships jobs to countries where people are more dispensable and labor is cheap. People are a means to increase wealth and a platform on which to exert your power. Consider the minimum wage, for instance, if they could pay you less, they would. People are sacrificed at the lower expense of generating wealth. The lower the wages, the bigger the profits, thus the whip of greed dances around.

Our current economic models and makeup of the countries do not facilitate human intellectual and cultural growth. They do not facilitate people who have an appetite for wonder, at least not for everyone. However, there are some notable exceptions, like Germany, Finland and Denmark where all forms of education are accessible to anyone and almost completely free, this in stark contrast with the college systems of the United States, where admission to a college is withheld from people who cannot afford the highly commercialized acquisition of knowledge. The government of the Netherlands is in the process of making access to college harder by raising its cost. Potentially brilliant students are being forced to weigh their chances, and they have to acknowledge that they will start their working career with a substantial debt. Many bright young people will be put off by this prospect and might be lost in the struggle to contribute to society, condemned to work on an assembly line or in an office cubicle until they are 65 or 70 years old and then die from a heart attack or from cancer, always living from paycheck to paycheck, while paying their bills, but never having the opportunity to really experience the beauty and wonder of life itself.

It is detestable that human progress flounders because of these injustices. The distribution of wealth by rich industrialists and bankers to people in seats of power or representation in order to keep their precious cash flowing is the name of the game – the pinnacle of Darwinian Capitalism and Consumerism supported by greed, dishonesty and willful ignorance. Neoliberalistic strongholds built to make way for the unimpeded growth of banks, pharmaceuticals, fossil fuel industries and great manufacturers. The subjugation of lower and middle-class employees, the diminishing of the unions. Processes which are corrosive to human dignity and oppressive to those who have no choice but to keep muddling on in order to get a penny, to remain healthy, to take care of their families and to "make their contribution to society". The yoke lies upon the shoulders of the workers, they have to pull weight of the carriage of greed along the road of growth. If someone slips, the carriage squashes him. For the sake of growth, the carriage doesn't stop. Those on the carriage wouldn't even notice, they are too busy counting their money and plotting a course to new sources of wealth. Those who see it happen only can look back in agony and horror and try to keep pulling the carriage of greed on to the next pitfall. Nobody gives a damn, especially those on the carriage. Eventually, these systems will collapse when there's no one left willing or able enough to remain pulling the increasing weight of the gluttonous rich.

Power, greed, dishonesty and false commitments

People in the current economic context are expendable and disposable, the value of the individual has been diminished significantly. Most people are trapped in numbing routines, hardly ever experiencing any challenge other than constant exploitation under the increasing stress of deadlines and job insecurity. The psychic destruction of workers is taking a toll, and there's an unprecedented high in people suffering from mental illnesses such as depression and burnout. A war of attrition is going on, as people are expected to work harder, longer and for less money than ever before.

Capitalism is not the "perfect model" for a stable civilization. The signs are obvious and ominous, and they support my claim.

How we should shape civilization, I do not really know but I contest that capitalism is the best way, because it grinds people into pulp. The ever-inflating bubble will explode at some point. A growing pinnacle that crushes its own base will eventually topple over.

Countries in the European Union, for instance, are under the yoke of an autocratic regime in Brussels. Spain and Greece were forced to cut spending in areas that impacted the lower and working classes the most. A routine of complete austerity was set in place in order to alleviate the financial stress. The pressure to pay back debts lands on the shoulders of people who didn't cause the debt in the first place. This process is going to repeat itself as capitalism depends on unsustainable growth and a non-existent, yet ever inflating corpus of money.

Climate change summits, for instance, are being planned more frequently. Every time the world's leaders come together and discuss how they are going to counter the effects of anthropogenic climate change, they commit to reducing their emissions. However, these commitments are really just symbolic and do not amount to much. We are still encouraging companies to plunder every possible fossil fuel reserve.

It is all a facade. We are talking about a world crisis, global warming and anthropogenic climate change in the context of World Economics. After our leaders have left the building, they will call up the oligarchs and industrialists and ask them how they can help them make more money.

There is a huge discrepancy between what needs to be done and what really gets done in order to fight our negative influence on the Earth. We are not doing enough to save the future of our children, that's perfectly clear.

When I watch debates in the house committee of Science, Space and Technology, I wonder how people can be so willfully ignorant or dishonest. That these senators are even allowed to talk about these matters as if they have something valuable to contribute is ridiculous. They are there to pass judgments on matters they don't even understand. It's one big Muppet show. And I'd like to reserve a special spot for Ted Cruz, who I like to call a real life Gargamel (the bad guy in the Smurfs). If he could catch all the Smurfs, he'd do it. The man is a genius, really, he cooks bacon using his assault rifle, while kids are being killed on school campuses and the Death Rate by guns in the US overshadows the casualty rates of the Vietnam or Iraq or Afghan wars. Cruz stands for the spread of religious zealotry, by industry bought influence, he is a dangerous and disingenuous man.

If you don't believe me, look at a YouTube video called America is an Oligarchy – on the Secular Talk channel – in which Donald Trump admits that he gives money to politicians: "*When you give, they do whatever the hell you want them to do*" & "*I give to everybody, when they call I give, and you know what? When I need something from them two years later, three years later, I call them, they are there for me...*"

Donald Trump said this on the Fox News GOP debate during the 2016 Presidential campaign. In "Is it good that Trump is in the GOP Primary?" he says similar things.

On this issue, Trump is honest. He tells it like it is. and what is even more telling is that the people who've received money from Donald Trump were on stage with him. He honestly tells the people of the United States on Fox News that the game is rigged in favor of those who pay the politicians.

Think about the kind of favors industrialists, bankers, pharmaceutical companies and other groups ask from these politicians. They don't spend millions to get a free pass on some insignificant permit. No, these "investments" are done to secure high yield policies and the protection of their income streams. To know more about money in politics visit *opensecrets.org*, the website of the center for responsive politics. Or visit *fec.gov*, the website of the Federal Election Commission. Money in politics is real.

These politicians are being sponsored by the elite, the industrialists, the bankers, the oligarchs and the pharmaceuticals who share some of their wealth with politicians and leaders in regulatory bodies to bolster the Monopolization of power and profit. The foxes are guarding the hen house. As they say: "*Presidents don't get elected, they get selected.*"

Highway to Dystopia

Here's an example of American political antagonism: "I'm from tribe A, every idea from tribe B is designed to attack us and get our money, so I'm going to oppose them in whatever way I can." The American political psyche is based on greed, antagonism and power – and that stands in the way of the pursuit of progress through truth, reason and scientific understanding. The quasi-ideological cards are played from the hand that pays the bills. Constituents are led to the notion that the people they vote for represent them ideologically, religiously or protect their interests. This is of course untrue, simply look at the swinging about of politicians, some of whom eventually end up opposing bills they've worked on. They're a bunch of fucking shite hypocrites (as one of my best friends used to say).

Conservatives clasp on to power through postponing agreement. In order to keep the discussion going and to keep the people unbalanced, they spread the idea that the scientists do not agree. This continuous stagnation is frustrating. Progress is being stifled all over the world. We are getting nowhere because if progress puts money into someone else's pockets, the wrong person, politicians will slam on the brakes. Consider this to be the influence of our greedy nature.

Which eventually leads us to another reason why this happens, we are xenophobic creatures. We demonize "*them*"! Communists are evil. Liberals are Marxists are communists. Labor movements are communists, the left calls the right Nazis, the right call the left communists. Atheists and secularists are leftist, elitist commu-nazi's. Stalin (a failed priest), Hitler (a Catholic), Mao Zedong and Pol Pot were atheists and thus atheism is evil, etc.. Hispanics, African Americans, Blacks, Niggers, Gooks, Chinks, Jews, Redskins, Monkeys, Irish potato eaters, Italian meatballs – the list goes on. We demonize *them*, whoever it might be. I've experienced this first hand. I've been called A leftist Nazi and a right-wing Communist. I'm a tree hugging nuclear proponent, an anti-religion fascist and what not (I'm exaggerating). The demonization of people and groups is perpetuated by powerful people in order to keep the masses unbalanced, to hold on to power, by creating the "us vs. them" feeling, and to keep the people from making a difference.

Barack Obama for instance elicits instant pavlovian responses from Republicans. Consider all the derogatory names given to the president: Barack The Magic Negro, Barack The Wealth Spreader, Barack Obabykiller, The Campaigner-in-Chief, The Chicago Charlatan, The Dog-Eating Sarong Boy, Dumbo, The Food Stamp President, Fraudbama, The Leper Messiah, The Mohammedan Mouthpiece, Obama Bin Laden, Obi-Wan Nairobi, Stuttering Clusterfuck of a Miserable Failure, and zero. There's an extensive list of derogatory names on the net dedicated just to him. Just take a look at what the Republicans have done to stifle anything he has tried to do. Anything he did to save the US from bankruptcy and to create jobs is hated by the Republicans. I neither love nor hate Barack Obama, but the balance is slightly positive. As a person he makes a reasonable and friendly and amiable impression. I especially applaud his effort to create promote healthcare for all Americans and to talk things out with Iran and Cuba. However, I dislike the actions that have benefited large corporations, while these corporations raised the pressure on their workers in the pursuit of renewed profits (For instance the effects of the bail-out and several world-spanning trade-agreements).

This antagonistic and greedy nature is being projected onto the world as well. The relationships between the US and Russia and China exemplify this. Rather than talking about *global* security and stability they look at the world affairs from a *national* security standpoint. Everything they do is to protect the homeland and to ensure their geopolitical influence, but you cannot have national security if there is no stability, cooperation and security on the world stage.

Highway to Dystopia

True progress is being held back by geopolitics. Power and greed and doctrinal interests inhibit improvement in equality, health services, access to clean water, sanitation, food safety, energy prosperity and most importantly cultural and intellectual growth.

Europe isn't a utopia either. It is an autocratic regime, with a democratic facade. Consider the European Central Bank, an ancillary of the European Union that works the same way. It is a tremendously important organization with great influence, yet it is autocratic. in fact, Europe is a trade union built to facilitate the unimpeded growth of Banks, Pharmaceuticals, Fossil Fuel Companies and big Industrials. Forget about "Glass-Steagall" like legislation.

We are living in a house of cards. Massive bailouts, costing the people billions, have been necessary to keep several banks and big industries solvent. We are borrowing money that doesn't exist and cannot pay back. Our bank accounts are overdrawn, our countries are in debt, and we cannot pay this money back because these are astronomical figures. We are once again headed for a big collapse. When are we going to put the well-being of humans in front of "making" money?

Let's look at a list of the greedy and atrocious clubs of tyranny and oppression: the overarching corporations of the banks, the banks themselves, the oil industry, the energy companies, the pharmaceuticals, the big industries, the former empires such as Russia, England, Germany and the United States and institutions such as the European Union and NATO.

Imagine what the world would have looked like if the Middle East hadn't been partitioned for the sake of the distribution of wealth, mainly wealth from oil. Imagine what the world would look like if the Soviet Union at its fall didn't get dismantled the way it did. New fault lines of ideology, culture and ethnicity ripped through areas in which autocrats were used to holding the reins and usurping the wealth. The birth of new conflicts through the division of territories and the appearance of a new greed for power with those new borders, the reshuffling of cards, today the king of hearts rules your area, tomorrow the king of spades...

The fossil fuel and energy industries have a wealth of knowledge, great engineers and scientists, and they should be aware of what is happening to our Earth, yet they keep pushing fossil fuels. Why don't they want to change? Is it out of laziness or stubbornness? The most rational answer would be that corporations are obligated to maximize profits to fill the coffers of the shareholders. If an executive fails to satiate the thirst for wealth, he or she will be supplanted with someone else.

The fact that representatives in seats of power that get paid to play the cards in favor of the industry is very disturbing. Also scientists have been paid to engage in this detestable form of fundamental dishonesty. It adds fuel to the fire of controversy, it keeps the debate going, for the sake of profit.

Another example greed is the military industrial complex. Money has to be made, even if humans are going to be killed in the process or because of it. The United States, Russia, China, England, France and Germany are the biggest weapons manufacturers and exporters in our world. Countries like India, Pakistan and Saudi Arabia are net importers of these weapons. Why? here's why.

The weapons trade, a multibillion dollar industry, is responsible for repression, fear and tens of thousands of deaths each year. The manufacturers are driven by greed, so much is clear. They produce everything required for war: Pistols, Rifles, Grenades, Mines, bombs, Rockets, Armored Vehicles, Tanks, Jets, Attack Helicopters and Ships. This continued production of weapons could lead to a cataclysmic ending of our civilization. Open war and terrorism would not be possible without a constant influx of weapons.

Why are these countries stockpiling weapons? To put fear into the hearts of their own citizens or their neighbors and enemies?

Take a look at India and Pakistan for instance, these countries have been partitioned out of religious motives. Despite partitioning these people into two nations, tensions remain, mostly over contested land. Did you know that India and Pakistan have an arsenal of nuclear weapons? That they have massive armies and India, at the very least, could be considered an emerging military superpower. Why is it necessary for these countries to stockpile weapons? These countries, India and Pakistan, are antagonists and this arms race between them could be seen as a small cold war in the Asian subcontinent.

Because more than half of all countries are net-weapons importers, it is no surprise that militant groups can get their hands on weapons. Some of these arms importing countries might even be handing out these weapons to militants in order to fuel their proxy wars. Look at the wars in Yemen, Iraq and Syria. What is more, many weapons simply were left in these countries. A massive cache of weapons was left by the United States when they withdrew from Iraq in order to rebuild an army that could keep the country from collapsing, but this ploy clearly failed, as Iraq was left void of any all-inclusive government that would be able to provide unity and stability.

The US is my favorite vacation destination, I am absolutely in love with their countryside and some of the cultural aspects of their nation. Boston, for instance, is one of the most beautiful cities I've ever visited. But that doesn't exonerate this nation from criticism. The US has made every error in the book. Just look at the revenue made by the military and the weapons industry, the amount of poverty, the student-debt crisis, or ask this question: How many allies of the United States have turned into bitter enemies of the

Power, greed, dishonesty and false commitments

United States? Russia, China, The Afghan resistance, Pakistan, Iran, Iraq, Saddam Hussein, Ho Chi Minh, Bin Laden and Stalin.

Why? Because of ideological and geopolitical pursuits in order to gain influence and power. The only wars in which the US participated that were justified were the First- and Second World War. Although the committing of war crimes, the targeting of civilians with strategic bombers, from the allied part is often being swept under the rug. Maybe Desert Storm was also justified, Saddam Hussein was an absolutist, a terrible and malicious and sadistic dictator – who did use WMD's against the Kurds. But back then they should have stuck with it, and should have made the region more stable and safe instead of leaving it in turmoil. Although I think it was justified to get rid of Saddam, I am not sure about the motives of the US. Afterwards during the Bush Junior administration they did the same thing again. But after the second campaign in Iraq, they left it completely void of any reasonable or all-inclusive structure, leading to the wars and atrocities we witness today, total instability, a festering quagmire of war and atrocities. Iraq needed a generational rebuilding commitment, and I will submit to you that the military occupation has been ended at least a decade too early, and now it is too late...

Don't mistake me for a leftist regressive, I don't think the US is responsible for all the hardship in the world. Many other factors are involved as well.

Strangely partitioned countries and regions are common, they are a legacy of continued power struggles and divisions. The Kurds for instance is a people of millions living together in large parts of Turkey, Syria, Iraq and Iran. Why haven't they gotten their own country? Their ethnicity and geographical concentration would have been a justification to do it. But also consider yet another "Pakistan-India" scenario with conflicts over contested regions, the areas where the religious and ethnic fault lines are.

Iraq is a highly illogical partitioned country. The existence of Saudi Arabia and Jordan and many other countries is questionable. These countries were not created with any regard for the well-being of the people. they were divided with the distribution of wealth and power between empires, large corporations and rich and influential families in mind. Religious fault lines run straight through these countries and fuel constant sectarian instability and violence.

History teaches us that the "oil" wars have done a lot of harm. The war between Iraq and Iran, the invasion of Kuwait, Desert Storm, the invasion of Afghanistan, the war in Sudan and the recent problems in the Ukraine have led to an increased influx of weapons in these regions. These wars are being fought over strange partitioning practices resulting in an intense selfish desire to grab hold of swathes of land, either for their commodities or for religious and dogmatic reasons.

The current Ukraine crisis is putting tremendous stress on the relationships between Russia and NATO. The annexation of the Crimean peninsula by Russia in February 2014, has led to economic sanctions against Russia. The rebellion crisis in the East of the Ukraine is being fueled by the Russians in the East and NATO in the West. It looks as if this is a war about sectarian differences, between people who speak Russian and people who speak Ukrainian. However, we cannot ignore the fact that the Ukraine has vast amounts of gas and oil deposits. What is this war truly about? The suspicious mind sees NATO encroaching on Russia, or a war over the commodities of the Ukraine. It looks like a facade, raised to conceal a proxy war between NATO and Russia. Which people suffer and die from this? The Ukrainians...

Who benefits? The prime benefactors of these wars are the military industrial complex and the oligarchs hungry for new oil and shale gas deposits. They are on either of the NATO - Russian divide. Ideology in this case is just a facade, or at least it looks like it especially when you ask yourself the question who will benefit from this war. Let's be honest, how many ideological differences are left on either side? Make no mistake, even though someone could benefit from it, the war in the Ukraine is dangerous. It could have dire consequences globally, nuclear powers are showing teeth and are growling at each other in this proxy war. The Ukraine has long been a reasonably stable country, it is no coincidence that all of a sudden a "civil war" has erupted in the Ukraine: it's geopolitics and greed.

Consider the blithering members of the US Senate who want to bomb Iran (they say it on National Television), rather than trying to work things out with them. Isn't that just plain crazy? These people are far too blood-thirsty for comfort. Again, the question: who can possibly benefit from this? Simply look at Syria for instance, is it a surprise that the US goes to war without even declaring it? They [and we] are at war in Syria, yet no war has been declared. Who benefits from this? Thousands of pounds of ordinance get dropped every day...

Why does the US spend more than 50% of its money on military matters? Who benefits? "*The welfare of the US is warfare*", a phrase coined by Kyle Kulinski from the Secular Talk YouTube channel. While decent education is unaffordable for people from the lower classes, the United States spends hundreds of billions of dollars on the military. The US still has a questionable track record in terms of affordable health care, they do not take care for their downtrodden people, their homeless, and yet they spend astronomical amounts of money on the military. For every homeless person in the United States there are five vacant homes, but military expenditures remain astronomically high.

Many "wars" have been constructed to keep this high-tech weaponry and military rolling: The cold war, the war on drugs, The instability in the middle east flowing into the war on terror... We have conjured up all sorts of pseudo-noble and quasi-moral reasons to keep intervention forces, to keep massive military and heavily armed police and federal forces. Again, who benefits?

Take heart, I don't want to pick on the United States. The European Union recently had its share of problems too: The Greek collapse, the Spanish collapse, The Irish collapse. The ending of the DSB (Dirk Scheringa Bank) and IceSave, the massive bailouts of countries and banks by the ECB. The current interest rates are near zero, encouraging countries and banks to borrow more money, adding to the deficits. One might be inclined to ask: which people are responsible for these debts? Who is going to pay the debts? How are these debts build up? This enormous bubble of meaningless money is growing. At one point the bubble will burst, leading to increasing instability, decline of food and water availability, massive unrests and possibly civil war. By 2015 Europe was emerging from a recession, and there were signs that the economy of the EU was growing again, but how far will the bubble grow until it bursts?

Isn't it strange that not a lot of people benefit from growing economies that are a boon for speculating stockholders and big banks. The average Joes, the people who have to work the line and drop dead at 70 for having lived an unhealthy live, don't get a raise. They need to work even harder or else. The amount of people that have lost their jobs to efficiency and lower wages is staggering.

Policies in Europe are being made by the banks, the pension funds, and the true leaders of the European Union, the ones that operate in non-electable seats and in the bureaucratic backrooms. In the meanwhile the banks, the industries, pharmaceuticals and the big insurance companies have been sheltered, their money-making machines still a-turning.

I sincerely hope that these paradigms will change, for this to happen a broad base of people need to unite and form a movement against it. This can only be done on a national or even international scale.

The unsung heroes in this story are the people in Iceland who didn't buckle under the pressure from Europe after their bankers drove their small country into bankruptcy. Something unimaginable happened. They jailed their bankers and flipped the bird at Europe! I applaud the Icelanders for their bravery. Their well-being is far more important than to flounder in the backwash of the oppression by economical might. The "Boom-Bust" cycle (Another one coined by Kyle Kulinski) is crushing people.

The signs are everywhere: the failing of states like the Ukraine, Iraq, Syria, Pakistan and Afghanistan, North Korea, Yemen, Libya, Mali, Nigeria, Somalia and Zimbabwe, the capriciousness of the markets and the prices of commodities, the increasing amount of mental illness and the growing discontent of the masses.

In the 2010's, we've seen collapses in countries like Syria, Iraq, Libya, the Ukraine and Afghanistan. Other states might follow due to political or economic instability or because of geopolitical interests or religious conflicts.

Patriotism, a seemingly beautiful thing, connects people in a struggle for survival. I really love Henry Wadsworth Longfellow's poem about Paul Revere, which tells an excellent story about the patriot Revere doing what he must for his countrymen at the very beginning of the war for independence in then colonialized America (No taxation without representation). Patriotism in a sense of loving your country can be beautiful, it brings about a lot of symbolism and cultural beauty, but it can be utterly meaningless. Do people really think it is worth fighting over trivial, territorial idiosyncrasies? Patriotism is one of the mechanisms that fuels the sense of needing to stand up, it is the sense of pride and a spur to action. But it can also be the refuge of scoundrels. Let's consider this from a slightly different but parallel viewpoint.

Highway to Dystopia

Do we see the same things happen in nature? Yes, we do. Chimpanzees are only half a chromosome away from human beings. There are many similarities between Chimp and human behavior. Patriotism is the enforcing of the "us" feeling. It contributes to the sense of community, it builds pride, trust and bonds (which are chemically driven processes). However, these trust relationships have been built on the idea that the group an individual belongs to is special and needs to be protected against potential enemies. To me, it seems that patriotism is the bedfellow of faith. It can be a means to justify violence against other groups, just as religion and scripture is a means to justify violence against fellow human beings.

Don't mistake me for a pacifist. If there's an evil, genocidal or torturous regime out there which needs to be fought, we have to fight it. But we have to be sensible about it, it is morally completely reprehensible to kill people out of greed for wealth or power. If we ride out, multi-laterally, guns a blazing, it may only be for the aid of fellow human beings in distress.

I like patriots in a historical sense, and I enjoy patriotism if it is in a cultural or symbolic fashion. Yet, it has a "murky" and "evil" nature below the surface.

I don't regard myself as a patriot. Suppose we meet, I would be enthralled to know where you're from, from a cultural viewpoint, I want to know you, what thoughts you would like to share, how you regard life on Earth. I regard myself as a citizen of the Earth. I adhere to the idea that we are all of African descent. Our ancestors walked around in Africa and gradually, over thousands of years, dispersed around the world. I care for my fellow human beings, I care deeply for the health of the Earth and all its inhabitants.

I have a dim view on politics and many politicians. This doesn't mean that I am a complete nihilist however, I am confident that there are a great number of politicians who really want to make the

Power, greed, dishonesty and false commitments

World a better place. I salute these people, and I salute anyone who wants to make a positive difference in people's lives, who wants to be committed to helping people. We absolutely need you and I express the sincere hope that more people with proper morals and ethics engage in politics. Not out of greed or the lust for power, but out of altruistic motives, to make the world a better place.

Also take note of people who truly vie to reform their respective world's, people like Maajid Nawaz and Sam Harris who, despite their considerable differences, sit down and have a rational discussion and try to look at ways on how to reform Islam for instance. Also consider people like Bill Maher, Dave Rubin, Maryam Namazie, Sarah Haider, Faisal Saeed Al-Mutar, and Ayaan Hirsi Ali. These are people that are out there and are trying to make a difference by annunciating criticism of religious doctrines and dogmas. My personal stance on this ? Something that isn't true doesn't deserve to determine what people do. I rather have people become unbelievers, and for this to happen we will have to diligently spread skepticism and knowledge as this will gradually erode the base of religions.

Suppose you would ask me what a good and stable future would look like to me:

We would build a society that strives for personal improvement, to obtain new knowledge, to build new skills, to take care of one and other, to have a culture full of sports, art and music. A society that develops new (peaceful) technologies and reaches for the stars.

It would be a democratic semi-meritocracy with policy-making based on evidence and reason. A state in which your qualifications and past experience merit a candidacy for a position in the government, mostly committees. People then get to choose which person they want in office. There will be checks and balances. A position is only maintainable if enough public votes in favor are cast on a regular basis. It would be a complete secular state where everybody is considered equal and gets equal treatment under all circumstances, regardless of color, creed or sexual orientation. A state in which religion does not get a special position, nor any tax exempts or deductions. There will be no teaching of "pseudoscientific controversies". True scientific subjects like Math, Physics, Chemistry and Biology would not be watered down. I would also be an advocate of completely open, transparent and institutionalized medical care, pharmaceuticals, research, education, public transportation, water and electricity services.

Safety concerns would be viewed in context of city, state, country or the world, no repression or subjugation of people would be permitted, nor would people be spied upon.

"Those who would give up essential Liberty, to purchase a little temporary Safety, deserve neither Liberty nor Safety." – Benjamin Franklin

I would favor global cooperation and outreach projects to help each other develop access to amenities such as clean water and sanitation, good food, electricity, medical services and perfect and free schooling. The emancipation of the women in the developing countries would be one of my main objectives. The goal: to build a sustainable civilization in harmony with nature, a fair society in which freedom, personal growth, prosperity and happiness would be maximized.

What would its name be and how would we get there? Let's call this my personal utopia. Something to fight the darkening dystopia in my depressed head. If I would have to give it a name, it would be the "Star Trek future" in which money is no longer the arbiter of what we do, we live to better ourselves, to be beneficial to other people's lives, to explore the Universe and to find out new things!

How do we rid ourselves of dogmatic practices, doctrinal forces, ideological divisiveness and the specter of greed? It is high time that humanity starts seeking ways to educate all people, the more knowledgeable the people are, the more they will apply their critical faculties, the faster we will win the battle against the destructive forces of greed. We have yet to acknowledge that greed and the insatiable thirst for power is destroying the Earth.

Many of us are already living in a Dystopia while many wealthy people are living in blissful ignorance, with their machines of greed pushing down on us while they enjoy a life of luxury. We have no need for gods, demigods, great and dear leaders, the elite, superimposing regimes, doctrines and dogmas. Human beings are perfectly suited to co-exist peacefully and to engage in wondrous and awe-inspiring endeavors.

Let's keep holding on to hope, there are still good people in the world, especially in seats of power and influence. We can make a difference if we want to, and should. Change starts at the bottom, it starts with you and me.

Homo Stupiditous

People in office have contested or tried to disprove the fact of anthropogenic climate change for a long time, by claiming that global warming/anthropogenic climate change was not happening. These politicians and hired scientist are conveying these false and misleading messages to the general public. The claim of the deniers-side is that climate scientists are in fact liars out to make money out of scare-mongering or even worse, that they are all involved in one big conspiracy. This is absurd. Scientists get paid to do scientific research, to make observations, find out what is true and false (to a reasonable degree of certainty) based on evidence, and to build and share knowledge for the benefit of humanity. Also consider the sheer amount of non-profit organizations and institutes of intellectual mentation and the thousands of students and scientists that are engaged in the quest for understanding anthropogenic climate change, this makes the "*denier stance*" even more crooked and untrue.

Those who contest the reality of ACC should watch the videos on this YouTube channel: UQx Denial101x Making Sense of Climate Science Denial, which is provided by the University of Queensland. These free programs can help you deal with ACC deniers. Another great resource is the Skeptical Science website, or view any of the videos made by Bill Nye on the subject.

Governments are compelled to provide basic services to their people in order to build prosperity. They are a part of the world's economy. And in order to remain stable, their people have to have access to clean water and electricity. Especially electricity is one of the big motors behind economies. Without it, you aren't in business. That's why emerging economies are trying to get their hands on as much energy production as they can get, of course at the lowest possible cost. Enter the rich fossil fuel industry with their power to manipulate governments. Also consider the relative low technological threshold to participate in the carbon economy and you're set to participate in the financial circus of the world.

The prime drivers behind the denial of science are economic power and ideology. Some politicians conjure up reasons to evade the truths of science, while others have even been paid to lie about science by corporations that want to keep selling fossil fuels, regardless of how it affects the environment. Industrial lobbies have mounted expensive campaigns to convince the public that ACC is a hoax, just as the tobacco companies fought efforts to prove that tobacco is carcinogenic, and eventually lost.

Society is played by the notion of antagonism, us versus them, the affluent versus the poor, have's versus have not's, liberals versus conservatives. All of this happens at the cost of the credibility of the scientists, the science and the search for knowledge. Many feigned skeptics simply adopt the stance against the science of anthropogenic climate change by faith. Furthermore they question every scientific endeavor up front and are unwilling to accept the evidence presented, since it is perceived as a threat to their beliefs or their way of life.

It is harrowing to see the members of the United States house committee of Science, Space and Technology display scientific ignorance and worse, scientific illiteracy. These people are expected to pass judgment on science issues and propose policies based on testimony from experts. How on Earth is it possible to become a member of this committee without having the aptitude to understand what scientists are saying? Worse yet, some of these religious zealots deny science because of some silly piece of religious scripture. I've seen enough snowballs and false graphs already, it is time for scientifically literate representatives to take place in these committees.

Science within the dance of economics is shoved aside at a mere whim, considered a nuisance, discredited as lies from have-nots. For years, economic growth has taken precedence over doing what is right. The expanding pinnacle of capitalism has gained a strangle hold on governments and people. Massive incentives for mining, drilling and pumping fossil fuels have become routine, and the most ridiculous tax rebates and subsidies are devised to keep the industry going. This simply is corporate welfare.

Fossil Fuels are highly subsidized because they provide thousands of jobs and enormous tax revenues. First you pay tax on the gas you put into your car. Then you pay for the use of the road and the pollution emitted by your vehicle. If you add up these costs, you will discover a giant stream of money that is linked to the fossil fuel industry, a giant cash-cow.

Governments are highly dependent on these streams of income, and in some cases they get about 50 to 75% of all the money that is trading hands during a fill-up transaction.

Even though many of us already know that emitting carbon monoxide, carbon dioxide, nitrous oxide and sulfur dioxide is harmful to life on Earth, we keep consuming fossil fuels and continue to push on in the quest of finding more deposits.

It is also well known that burning any fossil fuel creates harmful chemicals and particulates that can cause different types of cancer and pulmonary diseases that lead to untimely deaths. According to the World Health Organization, about 7 million people die annually from ailments caused by air pollution. Even worse, people do not understand the damage these pollutants do to our atmosphere. If the effects on their health doesn't scare these people, it's not likely that they'd care about pollution's latent effects on our biosphere?

The fossil fuel companies routinely thwart progress by persuading people that the science of Anthropogenic Climate Change is unproven or is debatable. It is like squeezing a lemon, every last ounce which could be squeezed should be squeezed, they want their material gain, it is almost like talking about addicts. There's no limit to the greed of the oligarchs and industrialists, and they will do everything to satiate their thirst for money and power.

Enter the world of broken politics, broken regulations, political capture, and regulatory capture. Distributed wealth to capture seats of influence and power in order to support the eroding base of the pinnacles of greed, unimpeded consumerism, and Darwinist capitalism. It happens on either side, lines are drawn, trenches are dug and flags are raised. No one gives a damn, no one gives an inch. An antagonistic non-consensus culture that postpones any significant progress required to set things right and to progress.

Not only big companies and governments engage in this dangerous game of postponing consensus by denying the truth of science, it is also being done by a lot of environmentalists. This might sound quite paradoxical, since these factions are in a sense fighting each other, but both sides cherry pick science in order to support their own stance.

One of the most poignant stances the environmentalists take for instance is on nuclear energy. Disproportionately addressing accidents transpired in archaic designs and totally disregarding the safety record of the entire industry and the possibilities and the research that has been done in order to improve nuclear designs immensely.

At the same time they present Renewable Energy as the holy grail of green energy, the emission-free energy sources that can create many jobs and *completely* power the world with wind and that beautiful nuclear reactor in the sky, the sun. However, every means of creating energy has a downside that must be assessed. Unfortunately, wind and solar are intermittent, which lowers their efficiency. Without subsidies, neither would survive.

The danger of this *environmentalist course* is that we do not get enough bang for the buck. Thanks to the low energy densities we will be required to do vast amounts of mining, purification, chemical processing, manufacturing, transportation, installation, maintenance, decommissioning and recycling. And to cap it all off, I am absolutely certain that these technologies will never provide more than a quarter of the energy required by civilization, at least not in terms of billions of people.

Later in this book I will show you a comparison in the materials-cost per KWh of generation capacity, and how this is affected by something we call "capacity factor". This should be the nail in the coffin of the push for *renewables*, if we really care about mitigating the denuding that is going on.

I arrived at these conclusions through free inquiry, and by doing the math and by checking the physics involved, which is what the environmentalists should do as well!

What these people are doing is providing negative evidence and nothing else. These people not only feign skepticism, they don't provide evidence to support their claims. They are being skeptical about something because it conflicts with their political view, world view or ideology (cognitive bias). Instead of following the evidence they follow their convictions. This selective ignorance, this selective denial costs too much time and effort.

A special spot should be reserved for so-called "woofuckery", pseudo-science, black magic, superstition and all sorts of untrue malarkey. We are talking about the charlatans and quacks who prey and parasitize on the impressionable, often with dire outcomes. We know them as snake oil sellers, faith healers, psychics, shamanists and witch doctors. They perform all sorts of cons in order to swindle people. Subject them to double blind tests, to controlled circumstances and their supernatural powers falter. Simply take a look at any of the videos of James Randi, a magician, skeptic and freethinker who subjected people claiming to have extraordinary powers to controlled tests and debunked their claims.

Some people suffer from cancer, and instead of going to a real doctor to get the proper medical attention, put their well-being in the hands of faith healers and psychics.

New age pseudo scientists make good livings off ignorant impressionable people – by telling them to "metabolize" time differently, to do quantum-dodaa's and whatnots. They make a great living by selling books on these disingenuous and untrue non-issues. I do not trust that these people actually mean what they say, I think it's all a big ruse.

And then there's the anti-vaccination movements and people who claim to know everything about the effects of certain foods. Many movements with beliefs based on unsubstantiated claims, with blithering charlatans in their midst, engaging in activities that endanger either their own health or the health of the general public. These people should be educated first, and if they persist in refusing immunizations, they should be charged for endangering public health and safety.

Let's have a look at the spread of mass-delusion by the church, the proclamation of *"miraculous healings"* and the declaration of sainthood. No compelling evidence has ever been presented to prove that it was divine intervention that has helped these people recover from their [terminal] ailments. Nevertheless, claims like these keep people attached to their faith because they long for a supernatural protector, someone who cares for them in times of need or peril.

In a sense the entire denial based community of feigned skeptics oppose solid evidence by faith. They follow their dogmatic influencers and demagogic leaders and are not susceptible to any evidence. Deniers often try to engage in discussions presenting cherry picked facts and once these facts are put into context, they play the blame card or act as if they are being offended. Once the Ad Hominem card is cast, it is time to claim victory, that's the moment when your opponent has run out of arguments. Also consider the use of "moving of goalposts" and "circular logic" by the religious and the "skeptics".

Irrationality causes people to lie and commit daily fallacies, idiocies and atrocities just to destroy their opponents' arguments, well-being or even lives. Their actions often justified in scripture or some kind of idiotic ideology, in the name of some god or great leader. Conjecture and hear say are almost forbidden to use in a court of law, they are the least credible statements one could make, yet you can swear on the bible that you are going to tell the truth. Do you see the irony?

Dare I say it, many people do not grasp the seriousness of science illiteracy and/or scientific ignorance, be it willful or not. It shows how far we are removed from running a civilization based on rationality, truth and evidence. Scientists must speak truth to institutions of power and encourage people to use empirical evidence in deciding what we do as a civilization.

"Democracy cannot succeed unless those who express their choice are prepared to choose wisely. The real safeguard of democracy, therefore, is education." – Franklin D. Roosevelt

Homo Stupiditous

Instead of teaching foolish controversies, children and young adults need to be taught proper science and the use of critical thinking in order to determine what is really true instead of just taking things at face value. To assist them we need a free Internet and a completely independent press.

There's such a great discrepancy between what is being done, what we are committed to do and what needs to be done that I question if humanity will be able avert catastrophes at all, especially in regard to Anthropogenic Climate Change. If we want things to change, we must be diligent when choosing our representatives. Time is running out. We need to cut carbon emissions aggressively, not by 2050 but in the 2020s at the latest. We need humanity to gradually move away from irrationality, speeding up this process however is essential. Because our survival and the survival of the biosphere depends on it. Even if we cut back emissions soon, there is already enough excess CO_2 in the atmosphere to bring severe problems to us and our planet for many years.

If we allow people to keep sprouting nonsense all over the place, to influence people by dumbing them down with falsehoods and pseudo science, we are certainly going to end up worse than we can imagine. There are idiots in office, in seats of power and influence who have the audacity to form policy and make decisions based on ideology rather than on empirical evidence and real data. This is extremely dangerous. If for instance the monitoring of the Earth by specially designed satellites gets shut down, because some ideological wingnut on Earth doesn't believe in anthropogenic global warming, we will be going blind. We will not be able to gather any data anymore, and then what? We won't be able to show the public what is happening on Earth. Are we supposed to go on, do business as usual and sleepwalk into oblivion?

Sometimes the stupidity of Homo Sapiens is unfathomable. I think we have evolved, we've reached the next step: Homo Stupiditous.

And it only took us about two hundred thousand years to get here. It must be a new record on the evolutionary scale of the hominids.

Women of the world

There is an unbalance in the world that needs to be addressed and that is why this chapter is specifically written to advocate women's rights and to signify their importance.

I want to stress that I'm not a proponent of the "new feminist movement", "the regressive left" nor of the "MRA movement". Why? Because these people want to stifle societal cohesion, they've been engaged in a polarizing debate, I'm completely egalitarian and liberal in terms of gender and sex issues. Sure enough there are some gender issues that need to be ironed out, there always will be, but don't try to fit everything into conformity, accept that there's a broad spectrum. I am a proponent of normal male-female relations, friendships and interactions, in terms of chances and wages I'm completely egalitarian. I don't really give a damn about the feminism - masculinity divide in terms of sexuality. Why would I tire myself with these trivial and divisive factors that breed hatred? I am confident that you will figure it out. I am all for using common sense in matters of masculinity and womanhood. Sure there will be women looking hot, and men looking like he-mans in films, magazines, games and websites or porn. So what? Individuals claiming to be offended by caricatures or by "hot", augmented or photo-shopped individuals are out of luck. I honestly think that the subject-object dichotomy is a piece of garbage. Just as there are beautiful women in games and magazines and in movies and on TV, so are there portrayals of beautiful men. It's part of human nature. Many years ago I actually nearly fell in love with princess Leia lying there in a metal bikini in front of the giant disgusting space slug called Jabba the Hutt, I wanted to save her for myself. Guess that's a natural thing for a teenage boy. I don't care enough to write anything more about it, I will not be a hypocrite, I like seeing beautiful women, just let it be. It is human nature to be fascinated by other people, by intelligence, eloquence, beauty and yes... sex.

Having said that, I would like to move on and present my arguments of why I think that raising the bar on women's rights everywhere and not just in the West, is something that is going to help civilization progress.

There are mothers in the world who are less fortunate than your own: There are hundreds of millions of women who do not have free choice, aren't able to be engaged in fulfilling their dreams, and have no control over their own reproductive cycle number. In contrast, we have a couple of hundred million privileged women living in the "West" who do lead happy, fulfilling lives while being in control of their own destinies (not all of them are fortunate, but the overwhelming majority is). There's a huge gap between the women of the developed World and the women of the Developing World, but one thing unites them: they all have the same hope for their children, regardless of their background. They all want their children to live better lives than they do. Most importantly, they want them to be happy!

There's a distinction that needs to be made. Women in the developed world have [nearly] equal status to men and have all the means to pursue any of their dreams and they are self determined. The inequality I am about to address mainly concerns the women of the developing world. In the developing world a difference needs to be made within the next decades if we are to curb population growth and build a better society as a whole.

Women of the world

Human population is growing at a rate of more than 200.000 individuals a day and it is estimated that by the year 2050 there will be nine billion of us. We have to start wondering about what will happen once civilization becomes that big. We already have more problems than we can handle, including Climate Change, which is becoming more severe year after year.

The empowerment of women is key to the development of a healthy society. But in many countries, having many children is the means to secure one's future. Wondering "who will take care of me when I am old?" is prevalent where there's no sense of security. This sense of security will increase with the rise of living standards and the emergence of social security and free and widespread healthcare.

Procreation is advocated by several religions as a means of growth, to leverage their own position on the global scale, and to increase their power. Consider for instance the dogma of the church regarding condoms. Their crusade against contraceptives is especially harmful in Africa where females are having trouble being in control of their own reproductive cycle, the teachings of the church in this regard only increase the problems.

The church causes much harm by imposing false claims on these women, by advocating "*abstinence*" as a means to remain safe from diseases like aids. By doing this, the church is foisting fear on them and capturing them in a morally warped sense. It is a dark path that can lead to abuse, mutilation and "*honor*" killings.

As a contrasting feature in the west there's a strong correlation between the religiosity of a certain demographic, a specific cultural region and the amount of teen pregnancies, abortions, the lack of contraceptives, advocating of abstinence only, this is no coincidence. Consider the Bible-Belt in the US for instance.

The same claim can be made of Islam, consider the statements of some of the [past] leaders from the Islamic world:

"We have 50 million Muslims in Europe. There are signs that Allah will grant Islam victory in Europe — without swords, without guns, without conquest — will turn it into a Muslim continent within a few decades." – Muammar Gaddafi (source: wikiquotes)

The implication of which seems obvious: conquest through the womb.

Or consider the mutterings of Erdogan, the "supreme leader" of Turkey.

"Our religion (Islam) has defined a position for women: motherhood." – Recep Tayyip Erdogan (source: vocativ)

In this respect, all religions are equally vile to me. It is no coincidence that the fertility rates in Africa, the Middle-East and the Asian sub-continent are so high that the populations in these regions are growing exponentially. Even with the ensuing refugee crises from many of these countries, the population keeps growing, a telling sign that something is terribly wrong.

These practices of religion are completely and utterly backward. In the quest for domination women have been forced into a pattern of endless pregnancy. It is in religion where men with barbaric tendencies find their justification for breeding without end. There's no morality nor truth in religion, and its doctrines regarding women are particularly harmful and as such should be relegated to the domain where it belongs: far, very far away from the families and the women of this world...

About 800 women in the world die during child birth every day, roughly 30.000 a year. Most of these women live in the developing countries, some of them live in the developed world. Some deaths are simply unavoidable. What are common causes of women dying during child birth?

Women in the developing countries do not have the status and are not often not allowed to decide whether they could seek treatment. Delaying the search for care is a contributing factor of death during child birth. Many don't know that some pregnancies can bring about serious complications, often life threatening, in which case medical help is required in order to survive. If they live in a hut a couple of hours away from the nearest hospital they could be too late in the case of an emergency. Many of these people do not own cars, and getting to the hospital is either expensive or a long trek by foot.

It would be smart to head to a clinic in advance, in order to be to be able to receive proper care if required. However many people favor traditional childbirth practices, like home deliveries over deliveries in health clinics. And let's be honest, it is hard to actually plan child delivery, if the clinic is far away, one could be away from home for days or even weeks, which in some circumstances isn't preferable.

And then there is the problem with the health clinics themselves. Health clinics in the developing countries face all sorts of problems during operation. They might have a problem keeping rooms and equipment sterile, there can be a shortage of skilled people and after care might not be available for budget reasons.

It might seem strange and contra intuitive but child survival could eventually be a means of curbing population growth. Fortunately children surviving birth and childhood is a good thing, one would almost be inclined to think the worst of me, starting of a subject in this manner. I love children, I am always amazed by their capacity for inquiry and wonder! Children bring the best out of people.

Statistical research shows a positive correlation between surviving child birth and the fertility rate (The average amount of children per woman). If the child mortality rate goes down, so does the fertility rate.

Several institutes, like UNICEF and the World Health Organization are examining these correlations. Information regarding these ongoing researches can be found on their respective websites.

Relying on better health care, improved hygiene, access to potable water and medical services always produces a decrease in the mortality rate of mothers and children.

We can save a lot of these women and children and make a significant difference in their lives. Will we be able to save them all? Probably not. Death tied to child birth cannot be eradicated, but it can be diminished significantly, of that I am quite sure.

What can we do?

The magic word is, as always, education, I will repeat this creed Ad Nauseam. The more knowledgeable people in the developing world will become, the smarter they will be about pregnancy. A reasonable first step would be to train and send educators to communities to teach young women and men about basic healthcare, sexuality and the possible complications of pregnancy before during and after childbirth.

Getting these women to health facilities before labor is essential. This means providing these people with efficient and fast means of transportation, or building some sort of medical transportation network.

Health clinics need to be sufficiently and adequately staffed, many of them need to be renovated and equipped proficiently. And we could easily provide hundreds of thousands of people with new and meaningful jobs, training them to be community health workers, people that not only provide maternal care, but could also perform routine check-ups on other people as well, improving the general health of all the people. There's enough people to do it... What we lack is willpower.

Inequality in face of the law also needs to be ironed out. Even in some parts of "the west" women are still not on par with men in face of the law and vice versa (for instance in divorce matters). In the "developing world" women are mostly inferior in the face of the law. Gender inequality is always worse where countries are more religious. Cultural and religious differences drive deeper the wedges of inequality.

If we take a look at several maps in which gender inequality are addressed, we see similar patterns in terms of religiosity. Gender inequality becomes worse as the countries are less developed, or more religious.

Religious doctrines like Sharia are pitted heavily against women in general. The rigid role and the limited rights of the woman are encoded in Islamic doctrines. In countries like Saudi Arabia it is forbidden for women to drive because they are under the "care" of the men (which by itself is incredibly patronizing). Women are also not allowed to engage in sports. In countries like Afghanistan and Pakistan, women are afraid to go to school if there is one. Men do not want women to go to school, because it is enshrined in doctrine. These women are being pushed into traditional gender roles. They must become mothers, prepare food, do the dishes and wash the clothes.

There are doctrines and cultural uses in which child marriage is encouraged. Where the woman i.e. the girl is considered to be property that can changes hands for material gain or the pro-curement of land and power. The woman doesn't have any choice in the matter. All over the world women have to face bodily punishment just for being a woman. They can be stoned to death, if they fall in love with someone who isn't their fathers' choice. For women, infidelity is punishable by death, as is leaving the faith, the latter also applies to men. Fear of death keeps the women (and the free thinkers) subservient and quiet.

Girls in these cultures have no say in their own well-being; their fathers can force them to have their genitalia mutilated. What kind of religiously driven barbarism is that? Girls die during these "procedures" which makes you think "What is the medical necessity of it?" In short, there is none... Millions of women all across the world are just fine with the vaginas they had when they were born.

Fortunately there are some organizations that fight for the rights of women all over the globe. I remain confident about my claims that in the end education will liberate all of these women. The more knowledgeable and optimistic all people become about the future, the better the world of the women will be. I look forward to a time when all men and women learn to appreciate each other, when our relationships will be normalized and we do not need to speak antagonistically about matters of masculinity or feminism anymore. Be and let be.

We must talk about amending all sex discriminatory nationality & citizenship laws, give all girls proper non-religiously imposed, *secular*, education and create Job equality especially in terms of pay. We also have to create equal opportunities, but not try to force equality everywhere. It is nonsense to force girls into science if they don't want to, just as I don't think it is a healthy practice to create quota for X amount of women in a company and vice versa. What it all comes down to is this, we are still talking about giving the women something, which is wrong. We shouldn't be giving women anything, they should already have it... Women all over the world deserve a better outlook on the world. we should help them contact people who can make a difference. In essence, the women of the third world need a little nudge, we can help by trying to win the intellectual battle in terms of theocratic principles, but just as the women of the west have risen up, so should the women of the developing countries.

However, let's avoid the divisive methods employed by the ultra–feminist movement: the attacks on free speech the push to limit the experience of men and women in terms of sexuality and sexual expression. Don't be hostile to free speech (even in matters of sexuality) and leave the authorities out of it.

Women deserve self-determination and must have equal say in a relationship. They must be able to control over their reproductive cycles, go to school and engage in work where they are assessed on their qualities, rather than their gender.

Education will remain the keyword in practically all of my arguments. Education is the propagation of knowledge and research is the acquisition of new knowledge. Women are equally capable of doing this, imagine all the brainpower we would unlock if we would empower the women of the developing countries, imagine the brainpower we would unlock if we would bring *non-religious, secular,* and proper education to the women and children of the developing world. Teaching them languages, arts, and giving them the opportunity to learn true and unadulterated sciences like biology, physics, and chemistry. It would propel them into an optimistic and beautiful future. We need everybody on board in order to solve the issues of humanity, in this quest we need all able people to jump in. Good and individualized education should be freely available to anyone, everywhere.

There are some great organizations working tirelessly to promote a better future for the women of our world: Women for Women, Oxfam Novib, Weforest, the AHA foundation and the American Humanist Association.

Weforest for instance gives women the opportunity to engage in tree planting. A double edged sword addressing two problems at the same time, firstly it addresses the need for good jobs for women in the developing countries. To give them a meaningful job, is to empower them. And secondly it addresses the need to plant more trees in the world, making it a tremendous force for good. The nice thing about Weforest is that they give women jobs planting trees, in the meanwhile empowering them and making it possible for their children to go to school.

Women for Women helps the most marginalized women transform their lives. They teach these women how to earn and save money by using basic business skills and help them starting small businesses of their own. They teach them how to manage their reproductive cycles and how to become more knowledgeable about hygiene and health. With these assets, they will become more influential, more self-determined and more successful.

Ayaan Hirsi Ali, who shares my nationality, is my hero! I'm deeply saddened that she had to leave our country, but she has found a new life of love and meaning in the United States. Ayaan is the founder of the AHA Foundation. The AHA Foundation focuses on Female Genital Mutilation, Honor Violence and Forced Marriage. The AHA Foundation offers help to women who are facing any of aforementioned issues.

In league with all of these organization is Oxfam Novib. Oxfam Novib provides humanitarian aid wherever it is needed, they help people get out of poverty by helping women and young people to shape their futures. They also work actively to help women overcome bodily abuse, and gain control over their own reproductive cycles. They work hard to achieve this by trying to change attitudes and beliefs regarding the role of women in society.

Women of the world

Empower the women, and you'll see entire communities lift up socially, economically, and culturally. This is a maxim often and passionately annunciated by the late Christopher Hitchens.

Many of the issues that need to be addressed to set things right lie deeply rooted within religion, and to diminish its influence we need to fight the religious capture of children. Children are born without any notion of god or gods. Give a bunch of unrelated children a playground and you'll see amazing and funny things happen, no faith required... The idea that religious dogma's and doctrines count for children as well is ridiculous. Children should be busy discovering things, being inquisitive, playing and making new friends.

"The greatest invention in the world is the mind of a child." – Thomas Edison

Which brings us to another thing we need to get off the table: Faith schools. These schools have a clear segregating function, they are driving a wedge between children of different cultural backgrounds. Faith schools serve to indoctrinate children, not only by propagating the teachings of religion as fact, but by questioning other religions and even established science – like the Theory of Evolution and The Big Bang Theory. Our children should be playing together, not being kept apart by doctrinal differences. We do not need to separate our children from each other, with this separation, we create antagonism. faith is the most divisive factor on our planet. However, there is a place for separation – and it's between religion and state.

Exposing children to religious dogma is tantamount to child abuse.

Faith and religious zealotry brings me back to the exception to the rule: The United States of America and its Protestant Taliban extremists. In 2015 the Republican party fronted a fraudulent "snuff" movie to discredit Planned Parenthood under the guise of being pro-life. False material like this hinders planned parenthood's clients' ability to avoid unplanned- or teen pregnancies, to get contraceptives or to learn about STDs and STIs. This "video" has already led to the defunding of valuable services provided by Planned Parenthood on a state level.

Wingnuts like Louisiana Governor Bobby Jindall are trying to defund planned parenthood where their services are needed the most. If you would draw two layers with the degree of religiosity and unplanned and teen pregnancies on the map of the United States, you'd see the two layers overlapping almost perfectly. These maps can be found on the websites of Gallup and other public polling and research institutes. The Christian Taliban obviously is so blinded by dogma that they fail to recognize that they are actually hurting American society, mostly those living in the bible belt.

This is going to get me into trouble, but I also have to inject prostitution. I'm not so naïve or simplistic to think that it will go away if you crack down hard on them and by them I mean the pimps and the women who sell sex. But what I do advocate is this: Legalize every bit of it, tax it, regulate it, and enforce those regulations. Yank this industry out of obscurity. Don't forget the lessons of the prohibition period and the subsequent rise of the Mafia. Once booze became legal again the mobsters had to go and look for other income sources.

It's the same for prostitution, puritanical people or "social justice warriors" might not like what I've got to say about this, but there's a demand, and the demand is now being satisfied in obscurity and in lots of cases against the will of the women. It involves heinous crimes like abduction and human trafficking and slavery. Get it out of the domain of obscurity and give the women a choice to become masters of their own fates and provide them with a framework in which they are protected.

I feel the same way about [soft] drugs. Isn't it ridiculous that you can be sent to jail for having smoked a plant, a victimless crime! But I digress.

The rat race of consumerism and capitalism has dehumanized our world. Our destinies are largely determined by fortune of birth. Will you be famous or rich? Will you be poor and starving? Are you born into the *"one and only true religion"*? Why do we ask these questions? Aren't we supposed to be of equal value? Shouldn't we all have an equal chance to succeed?

Humanity is still far, very far from achieving its true potential because we withhold opportunities from people who are have-nots. In a picture of hungry kids, so often seen when addressing for instance the immense hunger in Africa, might be the next Neil deGrasse Tyson, Mahatma Gandhi or sir Isaac Newton, but we will never know. They are the have-nots. These children lack clean water and food, the safety of a warm home and a family or community, access to sanitation, electricity, proper education and a fair chance to contribute in our world.

750 million people have to travel or require help to get potable water – and a slightly larger number are illiterate. How can we change these embarrassing facts?

Why not promote secularism, the separation between religion and state, but also the separation of religion and healthcare, work, and education? The conscious and deliberate dismantlement of theocracies and theocratic principles. We should emphasize the good of helping people progress in life without being hijacked by religion. Religion has its own, separate agenda and it's not necessarily for the betterment of humanity. It denigrates women by urging excessive procreation. Religion also works to evict real sciences from education, which is one of its more harmful practices, keeping the flock ignorant and uneducated, making sure that they believe without question.

We need to curb population growth, not by using unethical means but through smart strategies. Through the empowerment of women, through education, through the push for a more meaningful existence, by eradicating poverty, disease and inequality – especially in the developing countries. Curbing the growth of the population will only be possible if we can raise the living standards of the people of the developing countries. The *developed* countries have already reached their natural growth ceilings – with fertility rates decreasing. The only growth happening in the developed countries is through migration.

If we could raise the standards in the developing countries as well, the migration of peoples would stabilize itself. These people are roaming around in search of safety and stability and prosperity, and to be quite frank I don't blame them, It is a natural thing to do.

To raise the bar on all accounts we have to learn how to emancipate and empower the women of the world. They hold the key to stabilizing population growth. They will have a profound influence on their children's development. Just think about the sheer volume of intellectual and scientific potential that could be unlocked, just by empowering and properly educating the women of this world. Free and widespread [deliberately non-religious] education for girls and boys and men and women will be the tip of the spear in our quest to curb population growth.

A more egalitarian society will be reached when we provide proper education to everyone, empower women, advocate secular values, end theocratic principles and encourage skepticism.

The golden rules like "Be and let be", "do unto others" are secular values, formed through necessity, to survive as a communal species. These should become our guides, and everybody should have the right of full self-determination.

Forests and more

Reforestation and conservation efforts across the world are dwarfed by the sheer magnitude of deforestation. In so doing we are consuming our own life support system. Forests play a vital part in the world's atmospheric cycles because they turn carbon dioxide into biomass – and release oxygen in the process – A thing often overlooked: trees also play an important part in the hydrological cycle through evapotranspiration.

The world's carbon cycle has been in relative equilibrium for millennia, the carbon cycle showed a finite amplitude and a definite pattern. We are going out of bounds in the measure of these patterns. One of the more serious issues that has aggravated this problem is mass deforestation. Deforestation damages the eco-system's propensity of recapturing carbon dioxide. Deforestation and our increased carbon emissions from industries and fossil fuel burning has made the carbon cycle go out of bounds significantly.

Orangutans, Tigers and many other species living in the woods and forests are in danger of losing their living space. Whenever forests are cut for wood or creating cropland, many animals and insects lose their habitat – their homes. For some, it will mean death. And for some species – extinction.

It sounds strange but I'm going to classify deforestation superficially, a lesser wrong still is a wrong, though, so don't mistake me for being in favor of lesser evils. Some forms of deforestation are worse than others. Cutting down the trees without purpose and just for the wood is the worst we can do, but cattle ranching is obviously also bad as it will increase methane emissions. Using the ground for cultivation is the least harmful because it is still being used to capture carbon, yet the density of these sugar cane, soy bean, palm oil or cotton plantations is significantly less, only providing a fraction of the former carbon capture capacity. The most serious problem is the release of carbon from peat, the impoverishment of the soil, and the drying of the soil.

South East Asia is a ticking time-bomb, there are great peat lands. Peat consists decaying vegetation in the soil. The forests in South East Asia are being burned down, if you burn the forest which sits on peat land, you'll burn the peat as well. There is a stupefying amount of peat in Indonesia, disturbing these forests and releasing the carbon content of the peat is a really dangerous activity and we need to stop it immediately!

A recent TV program about gold and mineral mining in the forests of south America showed huge machines converting acres of forest into big mud holes, and I wondered how common this was. The same happens with other valuable minerals and ores. Bauxite, for instance, the world's main source of Aluminum, is being strip mined at the cost of forested areas in countries like Brazil, Suriname, and Guyana. And in Canada, many acres of forest have been destroyed to get at the tar sands that lie below. Any commodity will be torn out of the ground at the cost of what was above it.

We also cut trees for energy, the so-called "Biomass" burning power plants often burn wood pellets, pellets that come from trees, cut down elsewhere on Earth. Biomass, in fact, is partially responsible for destroying our Ecosystem.

Forests and more

NASA is keeping a keen eye on deforested area's in the Amazon and have concluded that the top soil in the Amazon is actually becoming so dry that small patches of barren land are appearing. Whenever a large enough area of forest is destroyed, the land that remains no longer contributes moisture to the air, and it can become more barren in a process that leads to desertification. The fresh water basins and the aquifers have been put under tremendous stress and some major cities in Brazil have experienced prolonged periods of drought and decreased water availability.

Once the soil and the underlying aquifer starts drying up, trees and plants lose their capacity to capture carbon, since Photosynthesis is dependent on both water and carbon dioxide. This is the basic reaction for photosynthesis:

$6H_2O + 6CO_2$ (+ energy from light) $> C_6H_{12}O_6 + 6O_2$

No photosynthesis can take place without at least six water molecules ($6H_2O$), this means that if the soil is becoming more dry and the aquifer that feeds it is depleting due to a decrease in precipitation, it will lead to trees having more trouble creating new biomass and oxygen at the cost of carbon dioxide, water and energy from the sun. To be honest, photosynthesis is infinitely more intricate than the simple formula I've shown above, but the basic premise is clear. In the absence of water, photosynthesis basically grinds to a halt.

Also I've omitted the necessity of other nutrients like nitrogen, phosphorus, and potassium but they play no big role in my arguments.

Consider that the drying process also takes place in several other vital places in the world, namely the South American rainforests, the African rainforests, the forests in China, the rainforests in South East Asia, the great plains of the US and many other places. We can conclude that something bad is going to happen if we do not take care of this growing problem.

In the American and Canadian West, evergreen trees are struggling to stay healthy as they cope with higher summer temperatures, shortage of rain and warmer winters that increase the survival of insect larvae that destroy the trees in the coming summer. And with every tree that dies, we lose its ability to capture carbon dioxide and liberate oxygen. These larvae turn into beetles that roam in the forests of Canada, The United States, Europe, Russia, and Asia. How to counter this problem? We do not know but it is paramount that we find a way because the carbon sequestered in these trees will be released once they die.

The destruction of the rainforests, the diminishing of their vital water supplies, the diminishing of the photosynthetic life forms in the sea and the oceans are going to add up to terrifying effect. It will make carbon dioxide levels rise way beyond the current – unprecedented – levels. We're already in a state of serious carbon debt and this debt will increase even more if we fail to put a halt to these issues. That's why talking about forests is so tremendously important and why I do so vehemently.

Deforestation rates are the highest in Brazil, Indonesia, Russia, Mexico, Papua New Guinea, Peru, The US, Bolivia, Sudan, Zambia and Nigeria.

Fortunately foresters from all over the world are committed to saving the forests. Foresters from all over the world are working on possible solutions to save the forests. In Brazil for instance, the government works actively to keep people from cutting down trees. How do they do that?

The Brazilians for instance have wrought an intricate and wide-spread process. They monitor the amount of deforestation, where and when it happens via satellites. The logs which were illegally are confiscated, and the offenders will be arrested. The confiscated wood is processed and sold, with the profits being used for re-forestation and conservation efforts.

Furthermore the areas that have been deforested cannot be used for agriculture or raising cattle because people will not receive any funds from the banks or the government to do so. In this way deforestation becomes unprofitable. Thanks to efforts like this, Brazil has reduced its deforestation rate from a staggering 25.000 square kilometers a year to roughly 5.000 square kilometers a year. Still a high and undesirable number, but it is a vast improvement and it actually helps me become more optimistic about our chances of saving the forests and for them to bounce back.

According to Tasso Azevedo, an avid leader in the fight to save the rainforests, Brazil has prevented about three billion tons of carbon emissions. Nevertheless, we've cut roughly 40 percent of the historical tree cover of the world, and we show little signs of stopping. Tasso Azevedo has given some very interesting talks on this topic, one at TED.

I would like to propose a four tiered plan to save the forests of the Earth:

The first tier would be to mimic the Brazilians: criminalize illegal cutting. Keep a keen eye on the world's forests and crack down on the people that are logging illegally and make sure that produce from illegally logged areas cannot be sold.

The second tier would encompass communal reforestation pro-grams that involve schools and local authorities. We could create school programs, teaching children about the importance of the woods, how trees propagate, how to select nuts, germinate and plant them. We could work together with local authorities reclaim denuded fields where children and their parents could plant trees. We could then, try to enlarge these areas, steadily giving back more land in order to let forests grow freely again. As a bonus children [and parents] would become more knowledgeable about nature in this way.

Third, encourage organizational reforestation. Work with local authorities to secure pieces of land, auction them off to local organizations and let them plant trees, as a gesture to the local communities. These organizations could then also be asked to sponsor family or children's tree planting projects.

We could also use roofs to grow bamboo or fruit. manufacturing facilities have huge roofs, these roofs could easily be repurposed to be gardens or orchards or even woods. Instead of using vast amounts of land, we would actually find a double or even triple purpose for it. France for instance has passed legislation requiring that each new roof should be "green" or have solar panels – an excellent idea that should be adopted throughout the world.

Shubhendu Sharma of Afforest has developed a method of planting dense forests nearly everywhere, increasing biodiversity tremendously. I suggest that you visit his site if you are interested in small scale reforestation efforts.

The last tier is essential in reforestation and conservation efforts. We pay our taxes, and we may expect something in return: energy, electricity, running and potable water, medical services or transportation. I think providing a habitable environment with clean air and healthy flora and fauna is on par with aforementioned governmental services. Governments could do more to keep the forests healthy, they could easily increase their spending on extending, keeping and protecting national reserves and parks. They should also actively seek out people who cut down trees illegally and not punish them, but help them find a different and better way of making money. There are plenty of ways to make a decent living without having to cut down trees that aren't supposed to be cut down. Governments should help people who have cut trees illegally by leading them to a better way of making a living, perhaps by re-educating them, helping them to become foresters instead.

Let's support tree planting professionals and non-profit organizations like Weforest, the World Wild Fund, Trees for the future, Afforest and many other conservancy groups. We need more tree planting and conservation efforts going on. We've destroyed enough. We can turn this around, we can and should.

However, no matter what they accomplish, it is absolutely essential that we stop mowing down our forests and replace our dirty, carbon burning, carbon dioxide creating power plants with a mix of modern rooftop solar cells and clean, safe, efficient nuclear power plants that make no $CO2$.

I am not a believer, I am as a matter of fact an anti-theist and an atheist. I do however *"worship"* trees, these amazingly distant and obviously different cousins of ours, these wonders of evolution, making life as we know it possible. There is no higher purpose in trees, they came to be through evolution and play an tremendously important role in our ecosystem. Without them, many will die, for they give us food and air. I love trees, majestic trees like the great sequoia's, sturdy and ancient oaks, lush and opulent wisterias, haphazard maple trees, and beautifully red and pink hued cherry trees. All trees are amazing and enthralling to me.

The Energy Challenges of Humanity

Population growth is going to drive energy, water and food demand upwards. Approximately 4 billion people consume less than average amounts of energy and water. 3.2 billion of these still live in circumstances of energy poverty. These people will be pushing for more prosperity, they are going to want more electricity, water and food. The fertility rate of these 3.2 billion people is high, meaning that their needs will grow exponentially. It is expected that the 3.2 billion people of the developing countries will double before the end of this century. The only way to curb this explosive population growth is by education and increased prosperity.

Access to energy is essential for the betterment of humanity: having light at night, access to running water and a washing machine (look up Hans Rosling), being able to call a distant family member and to have access to the internet. Energy can propel people from the developing world into new forms of civilization and modernity, where population growth will stagnate and the standard of living will shoot through the roof.

The Energy Information Administration (EIA) estimated, in 2012, that our energy consumption of 550 quadrillion BTu will increase to 850 quadrillion BTu by the 2040s, which could be a low estimate. If we convert these numbers into Terawatt hours we get the following: current energy consumption is roughly 160,000 TWh and future energy consumption will be 240,000 TWh or more. These figures are all inclusive, and electricity only constitutes about 10 percent of the total.

The fundamental questions we are going to explore are: How much energy do we need? What are the requirements to create this energy? What do we use it for and how do we use it?

Defeating fossil fuels will be the prime focus in the coming chapters, but we are also facing different challenges like the electrification of transportation, manufacturing and production processes, capturing and sequestering Carbon Dioxide, and solving the problems concerning the anthropogenic processes that use [fresh] water.

As explained in the chapter "diminishing water supplies", our fresh water supplies are under tremendous stress. The increase in water demand and the decrease in precipitation are major causes of the depletion of water supplies. Also the warming aspect is having a negative effect on glacial water supplies, putting the usage of water for irrigation and other vital uses at a direct risk. In some countries and states, quotas for irrigation and other agricultural purposes have already been set at zero.

To solve anything, we first have to acknowledge that it will take energy to get there. So it is also with finding the solutions to the fundamental problems about the water supplies. Water and energy are directly tied to each other, we can have none without the other. Not only is it a matter of learning how to use water more efficiently but also look at possibilities to draw water from other sources, possibly from the air or the sea, both of which will require massive amounts of energy.

Food production, manufacturing, energy production and transportation will be impossible without either energy or water. Energy comes in several forms: Solar radiation, heat, combustion and electricity. Producing food to satiate the hunger of humanity is quite a challenge, most of it requires irrigation, machinery and transportation.

Transportation is a big factor in our energy usage. We travel around the world using cars, trains, ships and airplanes. All this energy required to move around has to come from somewhere. Most of this propulsion comes from the combustion of gas, diesel and other propellants, also the amount of electrical vehicles is starting to rise.

With the steady decline in water and food security we are mortgaging the future of our children and grandchildren. It is time we start thinking about the way we utilize *stuff*, the way we transport things, the way we generate electricity and distribute it and how we produce things and grow food.

I am not advocating austerity. I like to travel. I like to see new cars and airplanes being developed. I like to go to bars and watch games. I love to go to the restaurant with my wife and eat a well prepared meal. All these things would be impossible if we go all-in on austerity. Instead, we need to become more intelligent and provident and, not to forget, we also need to distribute our collective prosperity, there's enough for everyone.

We need to start thinking about carbon remediation. All things we do or use require some form of energy, whether it be electricity or heat. When you use your cell phone not only are you using the energy stored in your battery, but without the energy needed to sustain the network and the services you use, your cell phone would be useless. And the water running from your tap would cease without the electricity that constantly powers the pumps.

If you buy a toy from a store, you might not realize, but it has a large carbon debt attached to it. What is this carbon debt?

The Carbon debt, or carbon chain can be quite extensive. Computers, for example, are made from aluminum, copper, plastic, silicon, lead, gold, magnesium, neodymium, gallium, lutetium, tantalum and rutherfordium – and probably more – I just named thirteen different elements... It is an incredible and intricate machine with many different components like motherboards, chips, capacitors, hard disks, video chips, heat sinks, and cooling-fans. All these materials need to be mined, many of these materials come from different mines and go through different purification and manufacturing processes before they reach the components factories where the materials get turned into components. Many types of components get built in the same factories, subsequently, these components get transported to the lines where these computers get assembled. Once the computers are built, they will be distributed all over the world, first to distribution centers, then to main hubs for shops, and then to the shops themselves or directly to the customers. Once you look at a computer from this angle, you come to realize how extensive the carbon chain of a product can be. The production and transportation of all these goods takes energy that is largely created by burning carbon.

One could easily extend the carbon chain even further, let's say that the machines required to mine all the required elements need diesel fuel, we could attach an entire chain of diesel fuel production and transportation to the existing computer production carbon chain. We could go at this ad infinitem but the message is clear. This is true for all the products we use: computers, TV's, laptops, phones, refrigerators, microwave ovens, alarm clocks, game consoles, speakers, cars, bicycles, you name it.

Every form of energy generation has a carbon debt. Solar, Wind, Hydro, Geothermal, Nuclear, Gas and Coal incur a carbon debt during their construction, and without being in operation. The debt is hidden in materials & feedstock i.e. mining, purification, transportation, manufacturing, and construction. When talking about energy generation, we need to consider the full picture, not just the operational part, which is far too simplistic and naive.

Highway to Dystopia

It is popular to believe that renewable energy sources will be adequate enough to satisfy the demand for energy, however, these currently amount to less than a percent of the total energy production on the Earth. Belief doesn't create electricity and it is very doubtful that renewable energy sources will ever be able to supply even 50 % of our needs. Many environmentalists drive home the message that the renewable energy revolution is ongoing, this is a misleading and dangerous statement. Not only does it fool many people, but it also deludes policy makers. And that's where I draw the line. Renewable energy sources will never be able to supplant current energy sources on a one for one basis. Not even if we would cut fifty percent of our current energy consumption and double the efficiencies of all the renewable technologies. The limitations against renewable energy are set in stone.

To significantly reduce the amount of carbon created during the generation of electricity we should use the most efficient method available – and that method by all standards is nuclear power. I'm not being paid by the Nuclear Industry for saying this, some of them even loathe me... More on this later on.

The water footprint of food is another significant issue we must address. It takes lots of water to make a cow or a chicken grow or to raise crops. Each of these "food sources" requires different amounts of water. A cow is arguably one of the most water consuming land animals we eat. It takes about 15.000 liters to produce 1 kilogram of cow meat. It takes 2.200 liters to produce 1 kilogram of chicken meat, 5.527 liters for goat, 11.309 liters for lamb and 5.418 liters for pork meat.

We could also consider it from a pollution viewpoint, by looking at methane emissions per kilogram of meat produced, it is no surprise that they roughly coincide with the water consumption per animal.

I don't want to dictate what kinds of meat we should and shouldn't eat, I love them all. But we need to start looking at ways to alleviate the stress on water supplies, we could take a look at balancing out the production of meat. Where more yield per unit of water is favorable. The same applies to crops. Growing food accounts for roughly 50 to 70% of all fresh water consumption. If we want to survive, if humanity is to be around for the next centuries, we have to acknowledge that we need to become smarter about our consumption, the ways we produce food and the ways we use our fresh water supplies.

It takes many years for water to accumulate in reservoirs like glaciers, snow packs or aquifers. We have to keep a keen eye on the depletion rates of these reservoirs because short periods of average or above precipitation doesn't replenish these vital sources of water. This basically means that once a certain level is reached, the reservoir needs to be cut off from the water network and left alone.

Anthropogenic water usage has been depleting these sources for decades. In California, a state plagued by droughts and water scarcity, people are already wondering how long their water reserves will last, and it is quite possible California's reservoirs will run dry in just a few years. In the meantime, fracking for methane continues, and fracking requires huge amounts of water which it pollutes and pumps back into the aquifer.

Reality is going to dictate economics. Quite soon we will be forced to start throwing money at solving problems that would have otherwise been overlooked. Consider the drought-stricken state of California for instance, wouldn't it seem logical to start investing heavily in a network of desalination installations and a complete overhaul of the complete water infrastructure?

Domestic water usage in terms of using water for drinking, washing, filling bath tubs and swimming pools doesn't amount to much. However, these activities will become unsustainable unless you have deep pockets and are willing to pay for it, water will become so precious that at its prize will start to rise.

These issues are widespread and are going to add weight to the already existing energy challenges. We won't only be talking about getting rid of thermal engines and the use of fossil fuels. But we will also be forced to re-examine our mining, production and manufacturing processes, and incorporate carbon capture and sequestration and water desalination practices on a world scale.

The harm of the extraction economy

It is undeniable, industrialization and the use of fossil fuels has propelled human civilization into new heights of prosperity and possibilities. Without it we would never have had automobiles, airplanes or space exploration. The boon of the industrial age is tremendous, it has given people more convenience and time. It has made our civilization grow like never before. It has taken decades to find out, but we are about to reach a point where it becomes common knowledge that burning fossil fuels is bad, now we have to translate this knowledge into actions.

While I write this, halfway 2015, 491 billion barrels of oil have been extracted and consumed since the year 2000, this equals 79 quintillion liters (that's 18 zero's). Oil production alone accounts for 75 to 90 million barrels a day. We have also extracted and burned roughly 119 billion tons of coal and 48 trillion cubic meters of gas, and common sense tells us that this cannot go on forever.

Consider these mind boggling numbers, the sheer volume of fossil fuels consumed by human civilization. If we keep consuming fossil fuels at these rates, we will run out of fuel within a matter of decades, if we are lucky and find some new places to *suck it up*, we could stretch it a couple of decades more...

Ever wondered why fossil fuels are called "fossil"? It is because they are millions years old remains of things that have once lived on Earth like trees and plants. When plants and trees in the swamps and bogs and wetlands die and become submerged they are replaced by other plants that also die in an endless cycle of "birth" and death. At some point the peat (the submerged and decomposed remains of the plants that died) become buried under soil and rock, and as more sediments accumulate, the pressures and temperatures within the peat begin to rise as if it were in a pressure cooker eventually the peat got "squeezed" and "cooked" so hard that it turned into what we know today as coal.

Petroleum is a fossil fuel that formed from diatoms, which are tiny photosynthetic sea animals much like today's phytoplankton, which died and sank to the bottom of the sea over millions of years. There, once covered by sufficient layers of sediments, they were transformed by compression and high temperature into hydro-carbons – long carbon chains with hydrogen atoms attached. Natural oil has no general formula, it is a mixture of compounds, that's why we need to refine the oil using a distillation column, compounds with different boiling points come out at different stages of the distillation column.

Natural gas or methane (CH_4), however, can form from animal or plant life in a much shallower circumstances, even in lakes and ponds. Tiny microorganisms called methanogens decompose the material, producing methane gas in a process that is called methanogenesis. Capturing methane from sewage and landfills is considered by some to be a renewable source of energy.

These are just some of the theories that explain how fossil fuels are formed. One thing about these fuels is true though, their reserves are finite. It took millions of years and special circumstances to form these compounds. These reserves are being pumped up and will not replenish. What will humanity do once we run out?

The electrification of our future began when we began to burn coal to create the steam that powered primitive steam engines roughly 250 years ago in England. Coal and lignite (brown coal) soon became the dominant sources for energy. There are thousands of coal-fired energy plants all over the world, and, unfortunately, even more are being built.

There are thousands of coal plants strewn around the globe, burning coal in order to generate electricity. It also produces huge volumes of a waste product called coal ash, which consists of the elements that did not get burned – elements like lead, mercury, arsenic, beryllium, boron, cadmium, chromium, cobalt, manganese, molybdenum, selenium, strontium, thallium, and vanadium. Some of these are carcinogens, while others are radioactive.

Some of this coal ash is released into the atmosphere in the form of fly ash, and the heavier waste products is dumped somewhere aboveground on a coal ash hill, or a coal ash pond, every coal-fired power plant has at least one.

In 2008, Kingston Ash Slide released 1.1 billion gallons of coal ash slurry into a river and the nearby town of Kingston, crushing several homes and enveloping the town in hazardous materials. The authorities tried to calm the residents by telling them that the coal ash was not dangerous, but who in their right mind would believe such a thing. The 2008 Kingston Ash Slide is one of the biggest environmental disasters to have happened in the US.

Another example of the horrible miscalculations of the energy companies is the toxic ash in Little blue Run lake. Hazardous and poisonous substances are seeping into the groundwater and destroying its usefulness. I would not recommend anyone to drink water from a well that is contaminated with chemicals from a coal ash pond.

Just to remind you, there are thousands of these coal plants, coal ash heaps and coal ash ponds around the world and each year hundreds of millions of tons of coal ash are added to these waste dumps.

Oil is essential to the propulsion and plastics and synthetics industries. Without oil we wouldn't have had plastics, we wouldn't have been driving around with cars and trucks and busses and we wouldn't have been able to fly around the world, we would still be burning wood and coal. We've chosen to follow the "path of oil" in order to propel ourselves into the future and this was not inconsequential.

We cannot be trusted with oil, we're much too nonchalant while handling it. Even though Oligarchs have become tremendously wealthy because of the exploitation oil, and gas and coal, We don't seem to be mature enough to handle it. If you Google "oil spills" or "oil disasters" you will find long lists of disasters. Just the first Wikipedia page (which, by the way, is an excellent starting point for any non-scientific person engaged in a quest for understanding) lists of 183 oil spills, with an unknown amount of oil being spilled.

In the first three months of 2015 alone, four oil transport trains derailed in the US and Canada, spilling thousands of liters of oil that caught fire. Pipeline failures are so frequent that they draw little attention, although they contaminate everything with traces of carcinogens like benzene: The Keystone spill, the Mid-Valley Pipeline spill, the Black Sea spill, The trans-Israel pipeline spill and the Yellowstone river spill, yes that Yellowstone – and more.

Mining Canada's tar sands is another environmental disaster caused during our quest for fossil fuels. First, we cut down all the trees that stand above the deposits, then we scoop it up in large quantities, and then we have to heat the tar in order for it to become viscous enough to flow. In the meanwhile a third of the oil content gets burned, before we actually get to use any of it. It's as dumb as it gets, but it gives Canada untold wealth with the tradeoff of a completely denuded and destroyed countryside and a significant reduction in biodiversity, carbon capture and oxygen creation capacity.

The harm of the extraction economy

Hundreds of supertankers carry oil around the globe. One such tanker was the Exxon Valdez, which struck a reef in Prince William Sound in 1989, releasing enough oil to contaminate 2100 kilometers of shoreline, kill hundreds of thousands of seabirds, and hundreds of otters and a lot of fish. This disaster also had great implications in a political sense, this however did not prevent future oil spills from happening.

One of the biggest oil spills ever to have happened was during the Gulf War in 1991. Its cause was a deliberate act of sabotage by Iraqi soldiers, under orders of the sociopathic dictator Saddam Hussein. In addition to several thousands of tons of spilled oil hundreds of oil wells were also set on fire in Kuwait. The Gulf War Oil Spill was an unrivaled catastrophe in terms of oil spillage and air pollution. It is estimated that there are about one million cubic meters of oil sediment along the Persian Gulf, which is by now, more than 20 years later, nearly impossible to clean up.

On this Highway to Dystopia we pass disaster after disaster effortlessly. Consider the Deepwater Horizon oil spill of 2010. This oil spill had and has such a negative impact that it has many names: The BP oil disaster, the BP oil spills, the Mexican gulf oil spill, and the Macondo blowout. Experts say that this is the largest *accidental* marine oil spill in the history of mankind.

The Deepwater Horizon oil rig sank after it was severely damaged in a methane explosion on April 21st, 2010. The subsea oil well itself broke loose and oil jetted from the sea-floor for 87 days until it was finally capped. Even today, in 2015, oil from this spill keeps reaching the surface of the gulf and the coastal areas of Mexico and the US. It is estimated that British Petroleum's negligence caused a staggering 795 million liters of oil to pour into the Mexican Gulf. Over 8.000 animals died, and the end is not in sight as the coastal areas of the US and Mexico remain contaminated with oil.

The list of oil spills seems endless. It has already become a multibillion dollar problem, not that I care about the money by the way, money is superfluous, since it is being made anyway. The real problem of these spills are the detrimental effects on nature, these spills kill wildlife and contaminate water sources with hazardous chemicals dangerous to all life.

Although natural gas is the least harmful of all the fossil fuels, it is not off the hook. The Deepwater Horizon disaster, for instance, started off with a methane gas explosion. If you are interested in a list of natural gas accidents, simply Google "natural gas explosions" or "natural gas accidents" and you'll get a long list of accidents caused by the natural gas industry.

Shale deposits of natural gas and oil are being tapped by a process called fracking, which is the hydraulic fracturing of underground rock formations that contain deposits of oil and gas. In order to fracture these rocks they force water that contains toxic chemicals through a pipe into the ground in order to destroy the rock, and push the fossil fuel out of the ground.

Fracking is thought to be the new energy revolution, at least some statesmen and oil barons say so. If you want to see the impact of fracking on the countryside, simply go look for the immense patchwork of wells in Alberta Canada or Texas in the USA. Like any other means of getting fossil fuels out of the ground, fracking is just another means to perpetuate the usage of fossil fuels. And in so doing we risk contaminating our groundwater reserves with fracking fluids that eventually could spread through aquifers.

Wherever fossil fuels are being mined, transported, refined or sold, contamination of seawater, the soil and groundwater becomes an issue because we build imperfect transportation networks in which spills are unavoidable.

The harm of the extraction economy

I don't trust the big oil companies to drill for oil and gas in the Arctic. These companies, however, are pulling the strings, they have the means and they have the power. Because of all the risks we must not allow the oil companies to drill for oil and gas in the Arctic. The track record of these companies is worse than questionable. The destruction that has occurred due to their sloppiness is unfixable.

Besides the carbon dioxide produced by our fossil fueled economy, we pollute the atmosphere with a wide array of harmful emissions: carbon monoxide, sulfur oxides, nitrogen oxides, volatile organic compounds, free radicals, nano particles, soot, toxic metals, ammonia, chlorofluorocarbons and many more elements.

When concentrated in large urban areas with certain weather patterns, these pollutants can create smog, a vile soup of harmful elements that kills or handicaps many people every year with afflictions like COPD, strokes, lung cancer, heart disease, etc.

It isn't that hard to understand, right? When the air is saturated with harmful elements, it is not *nice stuff* to breathe! Burning stuff in great quantities has been a boon for humanity, however we've pushed the limits on for too far. Air pollution has been proven to shortens life spans significantly.

Consider Volkswagen's emissions-scandal. Rationalizing this down to the basics: this company has traded lives for profit, they cheated the system to enhance their profits. Exhaust-pipe emissions kill people. And it's not just Volkswagen that has to take a hit here, there have been other companies that cheated as well.

Smog and air pollution are big problems. Look at Beijing or Paris, Los Angeles and London. Many cities have seen smog caused by stagnant weather patterns and the voluminous burning of fossil fuels. Air pollution is causing millions of deaths each year. This is preventable if we were to throw off the shackles of the fossil fuel industry, by investing in clean, carbon dioxide-free methods of producing energy.

What we do to the air, we also do to the oceans with the plastics that we mindlessly throw away, and the amount that gets into our sewers, rivers and oceans is increasing every day.

All across the oceans plastic is floating around. Many plastic wrappers and containers are thrown away mindlessly. How do these plastics end up in the oceans? The problem with all these single use plastic containers, is that they are everywhere, they get flushed through toilets, they get tossed out of the windows of driving cars and people on ships toss them overboard as well. The amount of plastics that get into sewers, rivers and oceans is vast and increasing every day.

The oceans are big, really big. 75% of the Earth's surface is water. But although the ocean is large, it is polluted with 270.000 metric tons of plastic, and, unfortunately, that amount is expected to double within the next decade.

These plastics frequently get eaten by fish and other sea creatures, many of which also get entangled in the debris, especially fishing nets and bags.

Almost all of the shops we visit sell their products encapsulated in some sort of plastic container, and most of these plastic wrappings will be discarded. Imagine the sheer amount of plastic containers and wrappings in shops. Plastic is everywhere! We call these wrappings "single use plastic containers" because once the product is used, the plastic gets thrown away. The production and transportation of products has become easier do due to plastic containers. We move all of these wrapped products around on a staggering scale.

The harm of the extraction economy

How can we make sure that less plastic ends up the oceans and how could we clean the oceans?

We have to start by changing our behavior. We have to become more knowledgeable about the consequences of producing throw away stuff, which is directly tied to capitalism. Several paradigms have to change in order for the volumes of throw away stuff to get smaller instead of bigger, we produce too much of the stuff that can be thrown away to easily.

Which brings us directly to the first step: start using less plastic. It isn't rocket science... We have to become more thoughtful about the way we package products. Some entrepreneurs have started "bring your own container" shops, where all the products are sorted in large containers, and you bring your own, reusable container to transport the products you buy, which is an excellent idea that has to become more widespread over time.

Another great idea would be to use standardized glass and paper containers for food and drink. All the manufacturers would be required to use this, and we would be able to set up a re-useable glass and cellulose container economy. An economy in which you return the container, after the products have been taken out, the containers get washed and returned to manufacturers for re-use.

The use of plastic bags, and plastic wrappers must be reduced. Why would you wrap your sandwiches in a plastic wrapper? Why not use a lunch box? Some of these things are so incredibly simple. We have to become far more intelligent about the way we carry our goods around.

Recycling everything we can should be our standard. Fortunately, in most of the developed countries it already is. Here in the Netherlands we separate electronics, plastic, paper, cardboard, glass, metals, wood and chemicals and bring them to special recycling centers for free!

It should be like this everywhere, and don't forget that we already are good at recycling, simply consider all the things we recycle already: Steel, Copper, Asphalt, PET Bottles, Paper, and Water.

A cradle-to-cradle principle for all materials has to be set up. Most of the material used in our products can be used again. Even though recycling itself is a water and energy intensive process, it is a more sensible and even more economical than to just toss everything away.

We could for instance easily adopt a reusable container system for a lot of products, especially electronics for instance. You buy a product, get the container, open it, get the product out and return the container to the vendor, which in term returns it to the factory, which uses it again to encase another product, keeping the container in a closed loop.

We could also use biodegradable containers instead of plastics. As long as we keep using them in a loop, in a cradle-to-cradle context with some form of reprocessing in the end.

And why do we package meat in plastic instead of paper, which can even be made from rapidly growing bamboo. Bamboo could also be grown for a more sustainable form of wood, instead of using age old (wild) trees.

Cleaning the oceans, once we've addressed the single-use plastic pollution, is such a huge problem that many people doubt it can be done. However, we have no choice.

The problem with trying to fish plastic out of the ocean is that you will have to introduce large systems, like gyres, that separate the plastic from micro organisms like plankton. This is something that is terribly difficult. Imagine other aquatic creatures becoming entangled in some way. And also consider how many of these contraptions are required to clean up the ocean?

The harm of the extraction economy

Instead of treating a symptom, we need address the cause: let's stop being so damned wasteful.

Fortunately, some of the plastic will eventually wash up on the beaches where it is more easily gathered. We have to stop dumping plastic in the oceans in the first place, and secondly have to be patient and let the plastic wash up on the shores of the oceans, and clean those shores up. We could make a job program out of it. Give people something meaningful to do? Working on the beach would be a great alternative to working in a noisy or smelly factory.

We live on a finite world in a finite universe. Just as the sun has a finite amount of hydrogen, so has the Earth a finite amount of resources. Even the cosmos has a finite amount of gas, required to create new stars, at some point no new stars will be formed anymore, and the old ones will burn out. Fortunately, many people are starting to realize that fossil fuels are also finite sources of energy, we will run out of them eventually.

However, oil production keeps rising. At the end of 2014 the price of oil had dropped to an all time low due to increased production and slightly lower demand. The United States Congress approved the construction of the Keystone XL pipeline which would encourage further exploitation of Canada's tar sands. Fortunately President Obama vetoed the bill, but he then agreed to open up the East Coast of the United States to oil exploration for the first time since decades.

All these actions contradict with the idea that we are dealing with "stuff" that has to remain sequestered and is finite.

Also consider this unpopular question: What would you rather have? A relatively safe pipeline (no guarantees there) or frequent train-derailments? This is not a false dichotomy, simply ac-knowledge that as long as fossil fuels are being transported around, we need to implement the most safe technology available, and that isn't trains...

What about the fossil fuel companies? Do they realize that they will eventually run out of product to sell. Their CEOs can be expected to put profit first and planet last, as they have done for years. Short term gain keeps these companies short sighted and indifferent to the future of humanity.

Sometimes they conjure up products they advertise as a green and sustainable, but do they really endorse it? It looks like a silly facade to give us the impression that they care.

Fossil fuels aren't the only finite sources on Earth. Everything on this Earth is finite, resources, energy, food, lives, everything.

What about raw materials like iron ore, bauxite and copper? The fact that copper is harder to get has made its price soar. The creation of steel is directly tied to the use of iron ore and coal. A brief look on the industrial commodities page of "intelligence unite" of "the economist" for instance shows that Natural Gas, Copper, Lead, Natural Rubber, Steel and Gold production and consumption forecasts are all expected to rise by 2 to 5% from 2015 to 2016. The only production forecast that is expected to decline is the production of gold, while its demand will rise, as will its price. I wonder how long we will be able to keep producing these commodities, what are the limits and when will we reach them?

Most ores however are quite common in the Earth's crust and pose no direct risk of shortage. The amount of fossil fuel consumption however, dwarfs the yearly production of different kinds of metals. It is prudent to acknowledge that we have been mining the deposits which are easy and cheap to get. Once we run out of these *goldilocks* deposits, we will have to find new deposits that will probably be less valuable and will require more intricate methods of refining, which will mean an increase in the price of the final product. It also means that we will be denuding new and untouched natural territories.

What lies beneath the glaciers of Greenland? It is a pristine land and hasn't yet been mined on an industrial scale, meaning that it is probable that there will be lots of valuable materials and substances in the ground. Many companies are keen to go prospecting Greenland, they believe that Greenland is especially rich in ores and fossil fuels.

The same crows are also circling Antarctica in the hope that one of the glaciers will collapse and to gain access to the soils below, soils that could contain all sorts of materials, including fossil fuels. The rich and greedy could easily mount expeditions to go and look for these materials once these glaciers and ice sheets have collapsed, and they will.

The Arctic and the Antarctic should be left alone. They are vital parts of our ecosystem, and though there isn't much life there, the buffering functions of these regions are indispensable. If we find oil in these areas, it would be disastrous.

Our questionable track record of handling these substances and keeping a keen eye on the consistency of these area's is poor. If we start drilling for oil, we're just one disaster away from ruining these areas for good.

The potential for finding oil or gas in the Arctic and Antarctic is immense. We already know that the Arctic holds vast amounts of methane, and that could also indicate the presence of oil. Fossil fuel companies are keen on drilling in these areas. That's one of the reasons why we need to reduce our thirst for oil. We need to start using less oil, and if this fails, their incentive for extracting it from the earth for profit remains intact.

Highway to Dystopia

We must create treaties to protect these areas. Access to the Arctic, Antarctic and Greenland should be restricted. These treaties should be enforced by specially trained enforcement agencies. The protection of these areas is far more important than the scavenging of its natural resources at the cost of irreparable damages.

In order to stop the average temperature from rising above two degrees Celsius, we need to drastically reduce our fossil consumption aggressively, otherwise, we will be unable to keep our planet and especially the ecosystem healthy. This requires paradigm shifts in energy economics. I'm quite confident that we have the technical prowess to do it, but we must start by admitting that we are pushing the limits of the Earth's ability to tolerate our excessive use of fossil fuels. The finite and polluting nature of fossil fuels will force our hands, and make us go look for alternatives, we have to start now.

Oil, gas, copper, zinc, tin, silver, lead, and gold are resources that are running out. We could easily reach the end of these resources in the 21st century, so the time to recycle is now. The time to look elsewhere has also come.

If we have not found new deposits elsewhere in our solar system, we will be forced to start recycling these materials. Which should be doing anyway. We should end the dependence on oil and gas in order to stave off the crash that would occur once we run out.

There is a huge waste pile and it has been built up through the massive consumption of single use products or products with a limited lifecycle. Most of these products contain plastics, but there are also precious materials in there like gold, silver, indium, copper, aluminum. These materials are there, in landfills and waste piles and are being carted around the planet, either to be covered with dirt and be sequestered indefinitely or to be transported to India and China, where little children use their little hands to rummage through this waste in order to get these precious materials out.

How can we fix these issues? Let's stop transporting this waste around the globe and keep it where it is. Why would we invest the energy in carting it around? We have to start recycling these products on site, there are a multitude of options to separate a lot of these materials and get them out of the waste.

Secondly, and this is far more important, we need to stop being so wasteful. Why do we need to produce all these short lived products? These are mainly containers for moving produce and products around. Most electronics have a limited lifecycle, they normally last for a couple of years. We should "cradle-to-cradle" these processes better, and we have to make them more durable.

What is more, we have to rid ourselves of the thirst for "earth commodities". We could easily begin with shrinking our dependence on oil and gas, this is a trivial matter from a technical viewpoint. We could also significantly reduce the use of coal, but as long as we need it to produce steel and silicon, we cannot get rid of it entirely.

We should venture out into space in search of new commodities. Iron and copper for instance are quite common in the universe.

The moon for instance holds deposits of gold, cobalt, iron, palladium, platinum, tungsten and helium-3. Mars is believed to hold deposits of magnesium, aluminum, titanium, iron, chromium, lithium, cobalt, nickel, copper, zinc, niobium, molybdenum, lanthanum, europium, tungsten, and gold. How do we know this? We have found trace amounts of these elements in rocks on the moon and mars, and from Martian meteorites.

The missing piece however are spaceships that could effortlessly land and take off again from giant gravity wells, planets like mars.

We could start by using ferry-missions between space stations. So it would be natural to start by prospecting the moon, or big asteroids. People are already suggesting that lunar and asteroid mining operations could be cheaper than terrestrial mining operations.

Can we go to the moon to mine thorium? Can we go to mars to look for gold, silver or other expensive and rare metals like titanium? It all comes down to costs and the willingness to do it. Rather than seeking for these commodities on Earth at the expense of our own biosphere and ecosystem I think that it is far more interesting and valuable to be an engineer or a scientist that works on finding practical solutions to make extra terrestrial mining and purification operations possible. The value of our biosphere vastly exceeds the costs of looking for these so-called rare materials and resources that might be ubiquitous on other bodies in space.

Pulling the plug on fossil fuels is easy, getting there requires a concrete plan: to electrify the combustion economy, to find extra-terrestrial material deposits, to waste less, to recycle more and to help people transition into a new way of life and help them get better and more meaningful jobs.

Speculating about transportation and energy changes

We talk about disruptive technologies when we can utilize *stuff* that does things differently from what we are used to, and which has the propensity to push business as usual aside.

Paradigms can be changed by introducing disruptive technologies, and a good example is provided by the development of Battery Electric Vehicles (BEVs). The first BEV was conceived right after the dawn of the first gasoline-powered car, ever since verged of breaking through for three times. In the eighties and nineties GM developed the EV1 but then took it off the market again. Finally, nearly twenty years later, a billionaire named Elon Musk resurrected the BEV in spectacular fashion with an EV sports car based on a Lotus Elise, the Tesla Roadster.

There's absolutely no question about it, the adoption of BEV's and other electric forms of transportation can cause a big shift from carbohydrate fuel consumption, mainly gasoline and diesel, to electricity consumption. It is this possible paradigm shift that makes the BEV a disruptive technology.

Cars, motorcycles and airplanes take us places, they help us discover more of this planet than would be possible without them.

Highway to Dystopia

On December 17, 1903, the Wright brothers realized an age old dream and opened up the world when they took off from Kitty Hawk in their powered, heavier than air Flyer. Thanks to their contribution we can now venture virtually everywhere. It took humanity only sixty years from flying a couple of feet to setting foot on the moon. The jet engine was developed forty years after the first flight, allowing us to reach speeds in excess of the speed of sound and achieve great heights, we can now circumnavigate the entire globe in a single flight.

Since the beginning of the industrial age and thanks to the invention of powered flight, thousands of airplanes, thousands of boats and millions of trucks, cars and bikes have been produced in order for us to travel around the world and to transport our goods.

We have grown accustomed to having a car and being able to fly to distant destinations. We have also grown accustomed to having electricity at the flick of a switch and the convenience of stores having all sorts of products and produce.

None of this convenience would be possible without transportation on a mind boggling scale. Nearly all of the products we use have been transported for thousands of miles before reaching the shop. Therefore, not a single product comes without some form of carbon debt, so we need to start thinking critically about our transportation systems. How are we going to shift the paradigms in transportation? Will we need new forms of technologies? Many companies are already looking into avenues possibly leading to solutions.

Transportation equals carbon emissions. A paradigm that is about to change, but it will take some time and a lot of development. The millions of vehicles that roam the earth predominantly use two forms of combustion to propel themselves: The internal combustion engine, with pistons and a crank shaft to build momentum or the Jet engine. These engines use the energy content of gasoline, diesel, petroleum, methane or jet fuel to build momentum. This momentum in term gets used for setting the vehicle into motion.

Most engines are inefficient, the energy content of the fuel being lost producing heat and in getting all those mechanical parts to move. We are burning a lot of fuel in this way, which increases the problem of emissions because there are a billion cars on the world, ten thousand cargo ships, millions of trucks and tens of thousands of airplanes.

One thing is certain, we need to develop far more efficient means of transportation, but is there a sustainable future in transportation without emissions? Can we maintain this scale of transportation when we do so?

Let's begin by considering airplanes, which will probably be most difficult sector to significantly upgrade. Over the last 30 years, many innovations have led to a decrease in fuel usage. Specialized wing tips, innovations in engines, wing designs, hull designs and all sorts of things have made airplanes more efficient. Yet there is still a lot to be gained.

As this book is being written, a team from Switzerland, called Solar Impulse, is traveling around the world using an airplane that runs on the energy captured from the sun by solar cells. Also consider the E-FAN made by Airbus, a fully electric, small training aircraft that made its debut 2015 by flying across the English Channel. Innovations like these will inspire engineers to develop new means of propelling vehicles. Although it will be difficult, I'm optimistic about our chances of building a more sustainable way to fly around our planet.

The trucking industry (although incredibly important to sustain our way of life) is primarily powered by diesel fuel, is probably the most polluting method of transportation – emitting tremendous amounts of CO_2 and other harmful compounds.

Mass road transportation however is absolutely necessary if we want to retain this prosperous and plentiful way of life. It also provides a lot of people with a meaningful and enjoyable job. What can we do to make this form of transportation smarter and cleaner.

We could use vacuum tubes to drive frictionless trains at high speeds or we could use Maglev Trains. Maglev stands for Magnetic Levitation, which uses vast amounts of electric coils and magnets. There are a ton of possibilities, we have to pursue them all. Innovation and research are needed to perfect the way we use mass transportation, by road and by rail and otherwise. It starts with vision, and there are a lot of very smart and visionary people!

The massive cargo capacity of enormous ships like the Maersk Triple E's make them the ideal means to effectively transport large quantities of goods over the oceans. These giants of the seas are a staple in the world economy. They are a vital part in transporting goods around the globe. I like them very much, however I don't like the way they propel themselves. These ships have gargantuan internal combustion engines, running on tons of crude diesel fuel. Looking at military submarines and aircraft carriers one could only wonder how clean these cargo ships could be if we would retrofit these ships with small reactors like the ones that run submarines or newly developed MSR's. It would be a giant leap forward in terms of mitigating emissions. However there would be a lot of stringent safety issues that need to be addressed first. If we would unlock the secret of scalable and sustainable nuclear fusion, we could have solved the issue entirely, circumnavigating the globe would become a trivial matter in terms of fuel.

If we were to build this more modern and contemporary means of transport, we should make the transition from sea, to road or rail as seamless as possible.

Speculating about transportation and energy changes

Let's take it one step further, how about sustained treks into space? Imagine a future in which *Millennium Falcons* become a reality, where a vehicle sits on the ground, takes off and flies into space, comes back again and lands. I think it is possible and will become a reality in this century. New technological breakthroughs will help us to expand the boundaries of our possibilities. There are engineers working on airplanes that can go into space and re-enter without any sophisticated launch or carrying platform. One of these is called SABRE and it is being developed by a company called Reaction Engines.

This spacecraft will be fueled by hydrogen and oxygen. It uses engines that can operate atmospherically and in space. It is these kinds of innovations that are going to propel humanity into the next phase of technology and optimism. I suggest you look up "reaction engines", they have an informative website, exactly explaining their technology and how it works.

And then there is also Virgin Galactic, a company that could be taking you into orbit. A promising endeavor headed by Richard Branson. They might even be able to provide cheap means of bringing satellites into orbit. Who knows what will happen once they will get their operation ongoing, they might even evolve to become more far seeing, perhaps even becoming interested in going to the moon for instance. One could only speculate at this point.

Air/Space vehicles will be propelled by new and yet unimagined or unrealized hybrid engines. Engines that run on some sort of nuclear propulsion, using argon, xenon, or neptunium, uranium or thorium. It might be small footprint fusion reactors, plasma beams or MSR's. We don't know. NASA is investigating some possible forms of propulsion and energy generation in space. There are also some new contenders in the field of space exploration.

SpaceX, another cool endeavor headed by Elon Musk, is one of the contenders in future space travel. It's most promising aspect is that they have developed rocket technology at a tenth of the budget normally allotted to these kinds of projects by NASA for instance. This kind of technological push while at the same time being extremely efficient is awesome.

It is only a matter of time before we fly to the moon again and trips to Mars and other celestial bodies become trivial endeavors. The only thing it takes is a couple of dedicated humans, that set out to do it. Just look at the staggering march of airplane technology since Wilbur and Orville Wright's first sustained flights. Right now it seems far away, but once we've done it, it will happen again. We've had a long lull since the last landings on the moon. I am quite optimistic about us flying to the moon again and pushing on towards Mars and the other planets beyond. NASA, Mars One and SpaceX are all working towards these goals.

Hydrogen is the proposed fuel of the future, but there are some drawbacks. Using hydrogen to propel cars is not a good idea. Creating the hydrogen economy will be a very laborious process which requires a new and massive infrastructure, similar to the fossil fuel industry. Many people think we produce hydrogen by electrolysis, but high volume hydrogen is produced differently. Hydrogen is predominantly created by steam reforming natural gas (CH_4) into Carbon Dioxide and Hydrogen, more than 80% of all hydrogen currently being produced is made by steam reformation of natural gas, making it in a sense a fossil fuel.

Using hydrogen as an energy carrier is a process beset with high energy loss: 1st, the electricity must be generated, 2nd, the electricity must be transported via the electric grid in which there is usually a 5 to 10% energy loss, 3rd, the electricity has to be converted from alternating current to direct current, 4th, the electricity is consumed to create hydrogen, 5th, the hydrogen needs to be compressed or liquefied and stored, 6th, the hydrogen must be pumped into the vehicle, 7th the vehicle's fuel cell must capture the electrons so that they can be used by an electromotor. Alternatively, the hydrogen could power an internal combustion engine, which is even more inefficient.

The longer the chain is, the less efficient your vehicle will be. In the Fuel Cell Vehicle chain we count at least seven points where there is energy loss involved. There is some efficiency to be gained, however the chain is still long. At any point you will lose at least 5 to 40% of your energy content, which stacks up to eventual 20~40% energy efficiency at the end of the chain. Which means that you will lose approximately 60~80% of all the energy generated at the beginning. The problem remains, even if you significantly improve one of the steps, you'll still have five others to improve. Let's be honest about it, we already have better means of creating, transporting and using energy, so why bother with hydrogen?

When the hydrogen is not generated locally, but is being pumped, or worse, being distributed with trucks, we create another problem because transporting hydrogen requires energy, which adds another inefficiency to the chain of energy loss.

Once you realize that all these steps involve some loss, you will see that it is a terrible system. We can already propel our vehicles far more elegantly than that. Using pure electricity, without useless conversion steps is a step forward. It allows for a far less sophisticated or intricate system to feed it, it is more efficient and it uses far less components in order to work. It fits straight into the already existing infrastructure. The BEV only has a "three step" chain whereas the FCV's chain has six, so why bother with hydrogen?

Biofuels are another supposed renewable. The label renewable is sacrosanct in some communities. However, High water usage and re-emission of carbon are my main concerns regarding biofuels. Biofuels (Methane once more) from refuse or sewage is a different story. I don't think biofuels are going to be a lasting solution in order for ICE (Internal Combustion Engine) vehicles to remain on the road. Why would we perpetuate this chain of inefficiency? And also consider the amount of agricultural area required to grow these crops, it's immense.

Which brings us to the most favorite powered commuter vehicle in the world, the car.

We've had cars for about 150 years. The first cars were adapted from carriages or stage coaches, and were powered by small steam engines. In the 1880's the first internal combustion engines were introduced by Delamare-Deboutteville. In the US, Armstrong Electric made the first electrically driven vehicle a year later.

In 1908, Five years after the legendary flight of the Wright Brothers, the Ford Model T became the first car to go into mass production on an assembly line, and with the subsequent improvement and extension of the (fossil fuel) infrastructure the demise of the electric vehicles was set in motion. Because of its limited range the electric car quickly fell out of fashion.

The popular internal combustion engine (ICE) created a massive increase of fossil fuel demand and brought a comparable increase in the production of carbon dioxide.

We currently produce a staggering 50 to 60 million cars each year. It is estimated that there about one billion cars in the world, and the average car emits between 120 and 180 grams of CO2 per kilometer. If every car on the world were to drive just one kilometer a day, we would emit roughly 43 million metric tons of CO2.

Speculating about transportation and energy changes

It is estimated that if we continue producing and consuming oil at the rate we are currently doing, we will run out of oil in approximately four decades, and even if we would find new deposits, it will be highly unlikely that this time span will rise significantly. Let's face it, well before this century is over we'll be in an oil-crisis of epic proportions if we don't drastically reduce our dependence on oil.

Toyota paved the road for the revival of electric vehicles. After the tragic ending of GM's popular EV1 hybrid vehicles were the champions of fuel efficiency. The Toyota Prius was an absolute success. It was way ahead of all the other vehicles of its time. It was a mass produced, widely accepted vehicle that ran on a combustion engine coupled to an electric motor. The emissions of the first Prius at some point was below the 105 grams/km mark and now have even dropped below the 82 grams/km. Even though these hybrids emit less grams per kilometer, it is still a huge amount of carbon dioxide that is being emitted considering the total sum of all hybrids on the world. If all the cars of tomorrow would by Hybrids, we would still be emitting a large amount of carbon, but far less than if we all would be driving Pick-up trucks with V8 engines.

The developments in hybrid technology have advanced since the first appearance of the Prius. Other manufacturers have accepted the technology and have started producing hybrids as well. The next step is bridging gap between BEV's and Hybrids, the "plug in hybrid". These plug in hybrid vehicles can be charged using a conventional wall socket, getting an electric range of circa 50 to 60 kilometers, after which they switch to hybrid mode.

GM's EV1 was almost successful at reviving the BEV. People who drove EV1's absolutely loved them. And yet GM wasn't happy with them [at all]. Despite many attempts by EV1 drivers to keep them, GM recalled them all and destroyed them. GM literally and callously liquidated the BEV revival, by killing off its own product.

Highway to Dystopia

The Tesla Roadster is an incredible car, the archetype of cool BEV's. With the Tesla Model S, Tesla has upped the ante for BEV's significantly. This is the first mass produced luxury 5 seat sedan with a good range and reasonable charging speed. The Model S is not a "quirky" EV, it has a nice non-EV design, it is a stretched car with beautiful shoulders, long lines, and a sleek nose. It has set the standards, it has paved the road, it has become the most groundbreaking car of our age.

As a consequence a couple of car manufacturers have become interested in BEV's as well. The success of Tesla has made them realize that the BEV might have a future. I'm pretty sure that BEV's will revolutionize the way we propel our vehicles in the future. BMW has followed suit with the stocky I3. Nissan has built the successful Leaf, Renault has the Zoë, There's a BEV Smart, The E-UP and several other BEV's have [successfully] entered the car market.

Unfortunately, BEV's are more costly than contemporary ICE vehicles because of their expensive battery packs. In addition, their limited range and their low charge speeds need to be improved. However, I am confident that manufacturers keep improving and innovating BEV technology and that they will overtake ICE vehicles within the coming decade, the march of the BEV's is unstoppable.

For some cool BEV reviews, please see Robert Llewellyn's "Fully Charged" channel on YouTube.

Another exciting thing about BEV's is that they have entered the realm of racing. Formula E, for instance, is the electrified version of Formula 1, these race cars achieve high speeds and have tremendous acceleration. It is becoming increasingly more popular. Formula E will become what Formula 1 has been for many decades, a breeding pit of new technologies and innovation in the world of BEV's. Formula E will accelerate BEV popularity significantly.

A lot of "hobbyists" are creating "home-made" drag racers with batteries and electric motors, and they absolutely smoke the old guard of drag racing. The electric engine has a great potential, and is vastly superior over internal combustion engines. It is a matter of time until they will push the ICE of its throne indefinitely.

One of the things BEV manufacturers could do to increase the popularity is to follow in Tesla's wake, make them look amazing, make them look exciting, it's easy! If a BEV looks sexy and exiting, people will buy it.

High distance and fast charging will be the key to unlock the BEV's true potential. Making people able to travel vast distances will speed up the acceptance of BEV's even more.

I'm confident that BEV and Battery manufacturers will reach a point at which the battery cost will be so low, and the capacity will be so high that a paradigm shift in propulsion will happen. The ICE vehicle will then be overtaken by BEV vehicles because most people drive cars out of practicality, so a cheaper car will be the winner. People also buy cars because of their looks, so the sexy looking BEV that is cheaper to run and more convenient than the sexy looking ICE vehicle, will win. It is going to happen, it is not a question of whether but of when.

I hope that the increase in BEVs will also bring a more durable kind of car. The number of cars produced needs to go down, in order for them to go down, vehicles have to become more durable. Ending the era of the internal combustion engine however is going to have tremendous effects on the carbon emissions from vehicles. Only, of course, if we are going to shift to more carbon neutral forms of energy production.

The future of transportation looks bright. We are on the verge of breaking away from internal combustion engines. In the meantime, other types of engines are being perfected in order for us to attain speeds never before seen except in sophisticated or classified endeavors.

The big challenge lies within air and sea travel. We might be able to build some sort of liquid hydrogen/oxygen or methane engines for airplanes to replace or enhance the contemporary jet engines.

Ships however are a different story, they need strong high torque engines and I'm not sure how we are going to replace the modern day diesel giants that propel these ships. Maybe we will be able to create small thorium or fusion reactors to run the large cargo ships. Perhaps the first to adopt these kinds of technologies will be the navies of the world. There is still a lot of research, innovation and development that needs to be done, without dedicated scientists and ardent engineers these technological advancements will not happen. Humans will travel farther, faster and higher than ever before! The future in technological terms is optimistic, I'm quite sure of that, as long as we keep pushing.

Questioning renewable technologies

There is not a single source of power without any negative tradeoffs, things that seem good often have hidden negative trade-offs or may cause some serious problems.

Instead of just asking if we can we do it, we also need to determine how much material is required, how much mining, what are the environmental consequences, what is the carbon footprint of the entire process, and what will the lifespan of the facility be – just 20 years, as with windmills, or 60 or more as with modern nuclear reactors. Perhaps even 100 years.

Why a hundred? Because that's the time we need to set our affairs in order, to make Earth a habitable and safe place for all, to go look for other habitable places in space, and to go look for and perhaps find new extra terrestrial resources. We might be able to do it earlier, maybe in a couple of decades, given the possibility of a technological breakthrough yet given our nature I'm skeptical that we will. Let's face it, we've altered the chemical composition of the atmosphere and the oceans, and we must begin to pay the piper. We have already increased atmospheric carbon dioxide levels to 400 PPM, and even if we act quickly and wisely, for a while, things are going to get worse before they get better.

So why am I going to question renewable technologies? I've been advocating renewable energy for quite a while, but at some point I realized that we need to do more with less, because we are denuding the planet at a terrifying rate. We must examine every power source, and that includes the vaunted renewables. We need to become even smarter about energy, we have to become more provident, we have to become less wasteful. So this has led me on a path to question the ways we consume energy, water and other "stuff", and after comparing all the technologies I concluded: something has got to give.

We have some time left to balance things out though, it is not too late. we still have time to create new forms of energy production that can sustain civilization without creating massive carbon emissions.

There's is a strong global push for the development of Renewable Energy (RE) sources. Shiny solar panels and wind farms are popping up everywhere, this push is born from the angst of global warming, and pollution. Unfortunately, their popularity is the result of the public being shown just one side of the energy coin by those who will profit.

In order to understand what energy sources to favor, I have investigated all the energy sources. I started from a popular standpoint, advocating solar energy, hydro, geothermal and wind power in order to mitigate carbon emissions. I initially thought that slamming solar heating and PV panels on all homes would solve our issues. I looked at it from a home to home and business to business perspective. However delving deeper into the energy issues of humanity has forced me to re-examine my reasoning. I now think more critically and also evaluate the amount of energy, materials and water consumed. If all these issues are considered, we will be less likely to adopt an idea that might look good, but isn't. The implications of our energy matters are of immense importance.

Reality must be our guide, and reality requires that we compare the energy densities, type and amount of materials used, the lifespan of the facility and the efficiency of each way of generating power. In the beginning I always do some short and basic math in order to get a grasp of the scope of things and read articles regarding energy production and consumption. Then we start breaking it down, normalize it.

We start by considering these numbers shared by the United States Energy Information Administration: Civilization consumes 550 Quadrillion BTu of energy every year, this translates into 160.000 TWh, electricity generation is roughly 21.000 TWh each year. It is estimated that energy consumption will rise to 850 Quadrillion BTu in the 2040's, this equals 250.000 TWh. The issues we have to solve tie back to these numbers. Any technology we adopt must be able to satisfy a large portion of the 250.000 TWh figure. This is the only thing that matters, even money in this regard is irrelevant. No one is going to turn off the lights. What is relevant however is how we will get to this point, and what it will take to get there?

In order to produce "carbon neutral" energy, we have to examine the monetary and environmental costs of extracting the raw materials needed to build a sufficient number of each type of facility. For example, windmills and solar panels, will require neodymium, copper, silver, tellurium, indium, zinc, iron ore, bauxite, silica, oil and coal.

"Do you, Mathijs Beckers, mean to say that oil and coal are needed to create windmills?" Yes. Steel, plastics and polymers are required to create wind turbines and solar panels and most of this begins with mining or drilling for oil. Most mining processes are incredibly destructive. We often have to remove the topsoil, which, to use the example of the Alberta tar sands, destroys thousands of acres of the boreal forest. In the search for the minerals needed to support are often wasteful society we destroy many Eco systems, comfort and riches trump the planet, climate change has taught us that the planet bats last.

Highway to Dystopia

We are engaged in the willful destruction of the world's ecosystem for short term gain, for tar sands, for lignite, for bauxite, copper, rare earths, you name it. If we can make some money out of it, we are bound to get it. Destroy the natural cover, dig in and dig in deep with big yellow diesel drinking machines that are designed to get the valuable "stuff" out of the ground. What is more valuable? The materials in the Earth, or the ecosystem on it?

Once we have extracted, these materials chances are slim that these materials are pure enough to be useable. Most of these materials need to be purified first. Purifying materials is an energy intensive process. It consists of crushing the ores, sieving them, washing, heating, de-oxidation, and chemically treatment. The silicon for creating solar panels, for instance, has to be more than 99% pure or it will be useless for solar panels, and this costs a lot of energy.

The creation, transportation, and installment of Solar Panels and Windmills are processes not free from emissions, chemical waste and fossil fuels. To create steel and aluminum we need diesel, coal and gas. Diesel to mine the ores, gas to heat the ores and melt them and in the case of steel, coal to coax it. So these first steps amount hugely to the carbon emissions of these products.

Secondly, the creation of the composite wings for the windmills require chemical processing, which of course has its own waste stream.

Finally, the creation of solar panel wafers is a chemical process with hazardous waste streams. In China, this waste is simply dumped into ponds and rivers, whereas in Europe the waste disposal regulations are stricter. We can, however, ship the waste anywhere we want. Which by the way is what we will do with the elements from the solar panels that cannot be recycled. This new pile of electrical waste that is build up from hard to separate composites will end up in China or in India, where small children and dirty and cheap laborers will be rummaging through them in order to get the most valuable parts out and earn a penny at the loss of their good health.

During the fabrication of solar panels, we use an array of chemicals and materials such as sodium hydroxide, hydrofluoric acid, gallium arsenide, phosphorous, titanium dioxide, cadmium, silver, tellurium, and indium. And this is just a couple of the known elements and chemicals used to create photo voltaic cells. The processes involved are purification, producing crystalline silicon, making silicon wafers, doping the wafers, Making the circuits and encapsulating the solar cells. Fabricating solar panels is a very intricate process that requires a lot of energy, water and also produces a lot of waste that has to be treated.

We need to become more provident and create less waste, yet it seems that the green revolution is doing exactly that. In their quest for "clean" energy they totally ignore the material requirements and the possible waste streams. These are the things that are often disregarded in life-cycle analysis. The water usage and the amount of energy required to get it, and the disposal of the waste, contaminated water, and sludge, which either need to be treated on-site or have to be transported to a special waste treatment facility, often times thousands of kilometers away.

Once you look more closely to the intricacies of solar power, you'll arrive at a stage at which you are going to question whether it is possible to effectively fight climate change. Does it actually do harm to the environment? I've come to believe that it does, and I also think that it is a terribly inelegant solution to our problems.

Given the fact that there are so many precious materials in these photo voltaic panels it is superfluous to say that recycling has to be a prime consideration. Titanium, silver, indium and tellurium, for instance, aren't ubiquitous. We have to acknowledge that the current fleet of PV panels needs to be recycled in an intelligent way, without discarding too much of the precious materials used.

Furthermore, the electrical waste pile is already looming on the horizon, we need to make sure that it doesn't grow out of proportion.

Transporting all these solar panels and windmills to their respective destinations is another contributing factor to carbon emissions. The vast amount of windmills and solar panels produced to make this supposed carbon-free future possible means that the scale of transportation will be equally great, each of these will have to be transported. We are talking about millions of miles of boat, train and truck transportation. Unless we have completely decarbonized the nature of these means of transportation, we will be emitting a lot of carbon for the sake of low-energy-density energy capture with a limited life-cycle and with murky production, waste and lifecycle concerns attached to it.

There are some life-cycle emissions in wind turbines as well, mainly hidden in the amount of energy required to construct the large steel towers that support the turbines and the generators. These steel towers will be transported from the factory to the place where they will be installed, and there they will be hoisted into place by grand cranes. In addition, wind turbines require intensive maintenance routines because they have to cope with vibrations and material stresses.

Other than from an economic, pollution, materials and manufacturing viewpoint there is no reason why every roof shouldn't be made out of solar panels or roads should be made out of interactive solar panels. If we had the materials and the means to do it, it would absolutely disrupt business as usual, it would revolutionize the way we would build roads and roofs. However, the sheer volume of materials, manufacturing and maintenance required would negate the boons of these PV "wonders". We would get into the realm of trying to get billions of tons of glass, copper, silica and other materials. Resources that are under tremendous stress already. Especially copper is hard to get and becomes more expensive every year. The volume of things make these solutions impossible. More recently there have been two companies that were trying to sell solar roadways and solar bike lanes. The idea of solar roadways has already been debunked by Phil Mason on his YouTube channel, called "Thunderf00t". I suggest you look it up, if you've ever been enthralled by the idea of "Solar frikking Roadways". His video shows just how stupid some of the ideas are. Some people are living in some kind of weird utopia in which materials are seemingly endless and already unearthed and available. These people aren't in touch with reality.

What about decommissioning all these renewable sources? The lifespans of solar and windmills are between 20 to 25 years, and at the end of their functional lives, they will need to be taken down and recycled. The more widespread these technologies will become, the more decommissioning we will need to do at the end of the functional life of these technologies. Technical parts in windmills are subject to wear, and in order to keep these machines going parts have to be replaced, also metal fatigue is a factor. The sheer size of a windmill complicates things as well, It's a heavy generator that sits way up there, the turbine blades are attached at a relatively high and hard to reach place. At the end of the functional life we will have to deconstruct these windmills and try to repurpose the materials.

The same principles apply to PV's, their limited life spans will make sure that we need to take them down again, after their economic and functional life have passed. It will be quite labor intensive and much energy will be wasted taking down and rebuilding these solar arrays and windmills.

If we are to continue the "green revolution", to try supplant oil, gas and coal by renewable energy sources only we have to recognize that we will be setting out in a wasteful and futile process once again. More about this in the coming chapters.

Due to the limited life spans of these energy sources we have to engage in recycling many of the materials that have gone into these energy capture contraptions. Some parts of a PV cell for instance can't be recycled, at least not yet. And if we would be able to recycle these parts, it would most probably be in some chemical process, which by itself will probably be harmful as well. As long as we do not find any ways to recycle this electrical waste, we will have to sequester this waste somewhere. Try to imagine the sheer volume of this waste if we would go all in, and it would double every 20 to 25 years unless we would be able to recycle all of it by then.

To engage in gathering energy through "*farming principles*" isn't the smartest way to go ahead. We will be using vast amounts of land and materials to capture the energy that would normally be absorbed of reflected by the earth. It is to engage in building hundreds of square kilometers of solar installations, and hundreds of thousands of windmills, a terribly wasteful endeavor. And wind turbines are deadly to thousands of [rare] birds and bats. many people do not recognize this. We do not need it, we can do energy generation far more intelligently and efficiently.

The challenges for renewable technologies lie for instance in the search for optimal circumstances, the sweet spots, in order to achieve higher the highest possible yields. This in turn will lead to renewed problems, since this electricity needs to be transported over vast distances, requiring long transmission lines, which in term account for transmission losses. We have not yet figured out how to transport energy without any loss, so centralized optimum renewable energy generation is rather risky. The risk increases as we put too much generation in one spot, a massive failure of any kind would have immediate and widespread effects on human activities and could even precipitate disasters. Imagine the lights going out during open heart surgery or the traffic lights failing at high speed intersections. Just two simple hypothetical scenarios that might go terribly wrong when the power fails.

There is also the intermittency problem with renewable energy sources. Solar energy depends on clear skies and clean panels to operate at the highest possible efficiency, and wind energy depends on wind, if there's no wind, there is no energy. Hydro power depends on steady replenishment of water reserves in order to remain operational. If a prolonged period of drought like in California or in the Baikal region depletes water sources, hydro power is going to grind to a halt, hardly a dependable source of power, given the fact that you are never 100% sure that your source of potential energy gets replenished.

What are we going to do during these "dry spells" in renewable energy? What kind of technology will we use for backup power? Energy storage? Energy storage will be addressed later on. Let's accept that we will be dependent on fossil fuels to bail us out of these "dry spells". Fossil fuel will remain the backup as long as it's cheap and the only practical alternative.

The use of renewable energy brings stability and load problems. Although we can forecast periods of maximum output, we have to play a balancing game between renewables and fossil fuel energy sources. When renewable sources are producing energy near their limits, the 24/7 power plants need to throttle back or shut down later to be ramped up or started again, which is inefficient.

Imagine travelling on the highway in your car at a constant speed, your fuel economy is optimal, but if you exit the highway and have to vary your speed in city traffic, your fuel economy goes down. This is exactly the same with fossil fuel fired energy plants. They are comparable to giant engines that run at their highest possible fuel economy if able to maintain a constant speed and load. And because starting and stopping generators uses more energy than letting them run at low speeds, keeping them running is a common choice, but it also creates more carbon dioxide.

Growing crops for energy like sugar cane, soy beans, and palm oil for energy destabilizes the carbon cycle because it uses large and essential areas of land for the wrong type of cultivation. We should either leave the areas alone, give them back to nature, or use them to cultivate sustainable foods or versatile materials like bamboo. Turning crops into liquid fuels and then burning them again is one of the most stupid ideas I've ever seen, it does absolutely nothing positive for our atmosphere and energy consumption. Instead it is a serious misuse of precious land plus it is a means to perpetuate the use of the internal combustion engine.

Also forget the idea of Biogas or Biofuels from algae, the volumes required make these technologies either incredibly water intensive and/or high in area requirements.

Suppose we can convert carbon dioxide and water to fuel? It is possible to turn carbon dioxide and water into diesel for instance in a process that requires electrolysis and high pressure reformation. However this is a wasteful process in which a lot of energy gets lost due to inefficient conversions. I saw an example of a plant that produced 160 liters of diesel every day. I looked at the annual diesel consumption of Americans for instance and a little arithmetic told me that the US would need 2,6 million of these plants in order to quench the American annual thirst for diesel. The main thing they forgot to tell us was how much electricity was required to produce these 160 liters of "e-diesel" a day. Once we get this missing piece, we can extrapolate how much energy it would cost us, and comment on the merit of this technology.

The point I'm trying to make here is that you always need to be skeptical about this kind of news and these kinds of claims.

Questioning renewable technologies

Without the full picture you can't really comment on the issue so always demand more evidence!

Even though hydrogen is the most common element in the universe, it cannot be easily harnessed. If we could capture hydrogen from the air, we would could use it to create electricity. However, we do not have such technology, at least not on a scale that could be used for transportation.

Most hydrogen is produced by steam-reforming natural gas, which turns methane and water into hydrogen and carbon dioxide. One could justifiably regard this hydrogen as a fossil fuel because it was created by using natural gas.

One could also use methane captured from garbage or synthesized by methanogens in an industrialized process. Then one could consider it a renewable source of energy, with carbon dioxide emissions nonetheless.

Hydrogen can also be created by using electrolysis, the least efficient process of all. It is a process strewn with losses and inefficiency. Imagine a contemporary gas station being retrofitted to serve hydrogen cars. It would first of all require a big power supply of some sort, then you would see an electrolysis machine that creates hydrogen, the hydrogen then becomes pressurized in order to compact it and then it gets stored in enormous tanks in order to be ready for the huge flow of cars hungry for their shot of hydrogen. The hydrogen economy, especially with regard to vehicular propulsion is tantamount to building another chain of inefficiency, and if we opt for centralized hydrogen generation, that would require an involved and expensive distribution system.

The hydrogen car is in effect the reverse operation, a big gas tank stores a limited capacity of hydrogen, an intricate fuel cell made out of expensive materials reforms the hydrogen with oxygen in order to create water, and during this process electrons have to pass through a membrane, which capture these electrons that can be used to make an electromotor work.

That said, hydrogen is not an elegant means of carrying energy around. As a matter of fact none of the renewable energies are. There's simply too much inefficiency going on. We need a tremendous amount of materials in order to get this process started. A huge array of solar panels or windmills, all intermediate sources of energy; Probably some storage is required down the way in the form of batteries or gas conversion, which is process that consumes energy; Transformation into electricity once more, another energy consuming process; then turning it into hydrogen, more loss; and subsequently turning it back into electricity once again losing some of its potency.

Scientists are now engaged in cracking the code of hydrogen production, there are other ways to produce it, through biological processes for instance. I'm thrilled that they are doing this, since we are going to need alternate fuels in the future. However, I'm put down by the inelegance of the whole Hydrogen Economy idea, especially for cars. Using electricity itself is far more elegant and efficient. I would advise the people working on this enigma to couple their strengths with people who are working on long range and big scale transport, long range busses and trains and airplanes. Hydrogen will certainly have a role to play, but it's not on the road, at least not in cars, that would be far too wasteful.

The more steps required to get the energy from the place where it is generated, to the place where it is used, the more energy will be lost down the way. We have to be conscious about this. There is nothing wrong with this if you want to look at it from the viewpoint of unimpeded consumerism, if for instance a large infrastructure is required it drives prices up, decreases transparency and increases profitability. Environmentalists would seek reasons to advocate this infrastructure, since it does not emit GHG nor harmful substances, and eventually one could argue that it will create jobs. It is one of the most heard arguments in the solar industry for instance, it creates many jobs. It also increases complexity, maintenance and waste production, and most importantly, it is an incredibly impotent technology that is not going to put a dent in our energy problems while causing a lot more deprivation of precious lands.

The final stroke against renewable energy (solar and wind in particular) comes from basic math. I postulated that the necessity to electrify all of our energy consumption would require 250.000 Terawatt hours, and I encourage you to do this simple math that follows for each technology:

Energy (XWh) = ((Capacity x 8766)/100) x Capacity Factor

If you start off with a capacity in Megawatt Hours, you divide by a million to get the Terawatt Hours figure. And after this divide the 250.000 figure by the number you got out of the calculation, that's the amount of "generators" you need per technology to fulfill the future demand of 250.000 Terawatt hours.

Let's do this for a 1000 MW nuclear reactor:

((1000 MW x 8766)/100) x 90 = 7.900.000 MWh or 7.9 TWh. 250.000/7.9 = 32.000 units. This is the amount of 1000 MW nuclear reactors required to generate enough energy to sustain civilization, we currently have about 600.

I am an absolute advocate of occupying people in a meaningful way. However if you start looking at it from a viewpoint of providence and efficiency, you start to realize that we desperately need to go for more effective alternatives. Do we really need all these diesel/gasoline guzzling trucks loaded with PV panels driving around, with people risking their lives climbing on to roofs to install them? It might sound shrill and strident, but I think it is justified, we can do better! Until we find a way to find the necessary materials elsewhere in the universe, we have to acknowledge that the emaciation rate of our Earth and its materials needs to be slowed down significantly.

Inconspicuous growth is what many capitalist corporations and nations want. To acquire more money than ever before. The ever growing thirst for wealth and power is almost insatiable, and the idea that an economy constantly needs 3% growth is absurd. I wonder if it is possible to keep growing, and to keep investing money we do not have into economic models that are un-sustainable. Providence should be the new guideline, don't mistake providence for complete austerity or conservation. I don't advocate a reversal, to go and live in mud huts without any sanitation or electricity. We need to acknowledge that we live on a world of finite resources with limits set in stone.

Renewables do have a small role to play, but we need an energy source with high energy density if we are to significantly reduce emissions, have a strong base for desalination and create a stable and prosperous future. I oppose renewables because they do not and cannot provide base load energy, require some kind of storage to counter their intermittency, have low energy density, require vast amounts of materials amounts of materials, and are nowhere near as green as we are led to believe. If humanity is also going to need extra energy for increased desalination, and aquifer replenishment and carbon sequestration, Renewables will fall utterly short.

Energy poverty is not an option and growing economies will grab any opportunity at cheap energy they can get. This means that they will be pushing for coal and gas, for its technological threshold is very low, and one can easily build and maintain a low-tech coal-fired power plant.

It is no surprise that even today new coal and gas powered energy plants are being build. Renewable energy is still a niche product in the world of energy generation, even though there is a strong but futile push to increase its practical influence. Trying to throw millions of solar panels on the hundreds of millions of roofs on the world, is a terribly inefficient and wasteful process that is not sustainable. I doubt it can be done, bordering on believing that it is impossible. Suppose we can do it, how often would we be able to repeat this process? If we want to generate enough energy for humanity, we have to go for smart nuclear advancements. Energy demand is going to grow exponentially, And renewables are not going to keep up with this growing demand.

I think that pursuing the course of solar and wind is a show of human inaptitude. It's also a show of dishonesty, I think many politicians and big corporations know we cannot run the world on renewable energy alone, yet we keep pushing, almost dogmatically, for the implementation of huge amounts of renewables, to what end? It's good PR, because it gives the impression that they care.

We've created this vast amount of hazardous energy generation in the form of lignite, coal, gas, and petroleum based fuels. Isn't it sad that we cannot come up with adequate strategies to combat the mess we've created ourselves? How stupid is it that we are now forced to create thousands of windmills and millions of solar panels to replace _one_ lignite power plant. Why doesn't anyone see how flawed this is? In the meanwhile new coal and lignite powered energy plants are being built! Economics dictate that a lignite power plant will be built in favor to other energy sources if it is the cheapest option, and it almost always is...

There are some incredibly smart individuals amongst our species. Enough of them roam around and if we want to solve our problems we would only have to pool their collective intelligence together and give them the means to create the sustainable solutions to our problems. We can solve the problems we've created quickly and efficiently if only we commit to it. Let's just hope it doesn't include and astronomically wasteful "green" economy that is destined to crash, just as the fossil fuel industry will eventually crash.

The nuclear stigma

Dingggg. At the sound of the bell, the dogs start drooling. Why? Because they have been conditioned to expect food when the bell rings. This exemplifies what happens when you drop the word "nuclear" into a discussion with environmentalists who can't believe that, although I support nuclear power, I am also an environmentalist, but simply one of a different, more critical and more nuanced breed. I'm an avid environmentalist who loves nature, understands its value, has a thorough understanding of the pros and cons of nuclear energy and tries to help people educate people on the safety of clean nuclear power. However, informing them is often difficult, if not impossible, because so many cling to the misconceptions and lies about nuclear safety that have been broadcast by the anti-nuclear crowd.

The true horror of the nuclear promise showed itself with the dawn of the nuclear bomb. On July 16, 1945, at Trinity Site in New Mexico, a new era in warfare began with the conception and detonation of the first of the world's most powerful weapons. Weapons that have been used to hold the Earth and its inhabitants hostage ever since. A terrible force used twice against humans at the end of the Second World War. It exemplified the power of the nucleus and instilled fear into the heart of humanity. In the blink of an eye, thousands of lives ended in a deadly shockwave that shook the Earth when "Little Boy" and "Fat Man" caused some 250,000 deaths. Although the bomb used on Hiroshima was rated at 15

Kilotons of TNT, that was "peanuts" compared to the potency bombs we store today.

The detonation of the two nuclear bombs at Hiroshima and Nagasaki catalyzed the nuclear arms race. It took the Soviet Union another four years to detonate their first atomic bomb code named "First Lightning". In the following decades, the United Kingdom, France, China, India, Pakistan and North Korea followed into the wake of the nuclear arms race, the cold war had gotten more intense and more ominous. As if all of this isn't scary enough I almost forgot to mention that Saudi Arabia is trying to buy nuclear weapons from Pakistan... The heat is still on.

Ever since the detonation of the first "*gadget*" a large number of nuclear weapons has been detonated in tests, just shy of 2.500 of them... A total yield of roughly 540.000 kilotons equivalent to TNT. Little boy, dropped on Hiroshima, yielded 15 Kilotons which is 0,0028% of all the yield ever to be detonated on Earth.

With apocalyptic weaponry in the hands of antagonistic regimes with significant ideological and geopolitical differences, nuclear warfare seems more likely every year, and a nuclear war threatens the existence of all life, including humans.

Just think about it, during JFK's presidency we've literally looked down the gun barrel of a nuclear war. Fidel Castro had recommended to Khrushchev to use the nuclear weapons stationed on Cuba against the United States – I'm paraphrasing from "*The Fog of War: Eleven Lessons from the Life of Robert S. McNamara*".

But, take heart! There is also good news to report, the world's "active" reserve of nuclear warheads has been diminishing as a result of SALT (Strategic Arms Limitation Talks/Treaty) and SORT (Strategic Offensive Reduction Treaty). From a staggering 68.000 active warheads, their numbers have declined to roughly

4000 active and 12.000 inactive. Fortunately there are means to get rid of these weapons and materials completely, which will be covered in the next chapter. Humanity has the knowledge and the means to turn nearly all of the fissile material in these bombs into energy that could and should be used for peaceful means, megatons to megawatts.

The Manhattan Project, thousands of scientists and engineers gathered together to successfully unlock the powers of the nuclear force. Not only did they unlock the secrets required to build terrible weapons, they also discovered that one could use nuclear fission to create energy.

But today, when the word "nuclear" is inserted into a discussion, words like Chernobyl and Fukushima often follow. My friend and fellow humanist George Erickson wrote a very good and well versed article in Nuclear Power: Climate Change Warrior for the 21st Century – see: http://tinyurl.com/EnergyReality – here's why

"During an equipment test in 1986, operators ignored computer warnings, disabled the safety systems and inadvertently exposed the core of the reactor, which had design hazards not present in Western reactors. This negligence led to a hydrogen explosion that released radioactive gases into the atmosphere because the reactor had no containment structure. In contrast, every water-cooled U.S. reactor has a robust, re-enforced concrete containment structure, and the Nuclear Regulatory Commission strictly supervises every plant. Chernobyl, which was built by the old USSR, was long judged by American scientists to be dangerous."

"Chernobyl was a failure not of nuclear power, but of bad design, poor training and a political system that forbade operators from sharing information about reactor problems. Chernobyl is the only commercial reactor accident where radiation directly killed anyone. Fifty four "firefighters" died from intense radiation. According to a study by 100 scientists from eight UN agencies,

'Chernobyl produced an additional 50 deaths over the following 20 years,' a tiny fraction of the deaths caused by the use of coal and petroleum..."

Suppose these numbers are worse, say a million, they still are being dwarfed by self-inflicted annual death tolls from smoking, drinking and suicide (omitting the harm of the combustion economy). I don't want to be regarded as callous, each death from anyone source is terrible, especially for those left behind, but for the sake of argument we have to put these numbers in perspective.

"Tepco's Fukushima reactors began operation in 1971, and ran without issue for 40 years, generating huge amounts of power while adding ZERO CO2 to our atmosphere."

"Following the 2011 earthquake that severed Fukushima's connections to the power grid, the plant's emergency generators, which were located in the basements, provided power to run the plant until the 18-foot seawall (that Tepco had been told was grossly inadequate – but refused to raise) was swamped by a tsunami. And, without power to run the coolant pumps, meltdown was assured. (The government could have forced Tepco to raise the seawall, but did not.) "

"Old, deeply weathered Sendai "stones" in the area had been warning for centuries, "Do not build below the 150 foot elevation." Instead, in 1967, Tepco cut 25 meters off of the site's 35 meter natural seawall to make it easier to unload equipment at the building site, which placed the reactors five meters below the crest of the 2011 tsunami."

The tsunami took 20,000 lives that day, but the Fukushima failure took the lives of just two firefighters who drowned.

"Nuclear power has been tarred by the Fukushima disaster, but the failure was NOT the fault of nuclear power. It was the caused by

corporate lying, record falsifying and penny-pinching, by the lack of government enforcement of seawall height, by building too close to the ocean, and by installing backup generators in easily flooded basements. Blaming nuclear power for Fukushima is like blaming the train that derails when the engineer takes a turn at 70 mph that is posted for 30."

Imagine building a reactor in a region known for tsunamis without including a proper seawall, and then installing the emergency generators in the basements.

It is rather painful to see that right at the moment when humanity starts to realize that we need a clean, high energy density alternative to coal-fired energy, this kind of disaster happens. Yet I see it as an opportunity. Rather than shutting down nuclear all together, we should jump in full gear, look at what has transpired, make sense of it, learn from it and improve significantly upon our nuclear practices. This should have been a moment in which we learned and gained knowledge and progressed. Yet fear took hold of us, and stifled any kind of significant progress because it unjustifiably turned the public against nuclear power..

Another stigmatic issue is the cost of building and operating and decommissioning nuclear reactors. Although some people claim that the cost of building, operating and decommissioning nuclear reactors is excessive, experts say that we can produce electricity with nuclear energy at a lower cost per megawatt than by using coal or lignite, which are the cheapest sources today. "*Thorium: Energy Cheaper Than Coal*" by Robert Hargraves, supports that view.

I'll insert this caveat here: I absolutely hold no degrees in economics, and I have to be fair that I'm not one to hold a capitalistic (nor communistic) worldview, I am a pragmatist, we should do what is right, regardless of the cost... So I won't bother too much about the economics of nuclear power. However there are some people that can substantiate that nuclear energy is cheaper than the most predominantly and cheapest forms of energy generation in use today. Looking at nuclear energy from an emission standpoint, especially in terms of human health and the overall state of our biosphere, it is cheap, it doesn't destroy our cardiovascular system, our respiratory system nor does is require denuding as much land as other energy sources do, nor does it destroy our atmosphere.

In addition, generating electricity with nuclear power creates no carbon dioxide or emissions like those that are produced by carbon burning power plants that compromise and kill millions of people every year. In fact, the "death print" of nuclear power – and this includes Chernobyl – is the least of all forms of power generation, including solar, wind, geothermal and hydro.

What about nuclear waste? It really isn't waste. Most of the material that is left after nuclear energy has been generated can now be used as fuel in modern reactors or for other purposes. However, unlike the new reactors, the reactors we have been using since the 50s and 60s are only able to utilize about 5% of the uranium in their fuel rods as fuel because the fuel in the rods becomes contaminated with fission byproducts that makes them useless in a reactor. These depleted rods are what we call "waste". Yucca Mountain repository is a proposed site to store this "radioactive waste". What would you say if I told you that this waste actually has a lot of energy potential left in it? What would you say if we could turn parts of this waste into useful elements for all sorts of applications? And what would you say if we could actually tap into that energy potential?

It is estimated by Transatomic Energy that there's enough energy in our stored nuclear waste to fuel the energy needs of civilization for seven decades. However this is not of the shelve technology we could put into action tomorrow, it still requires a proof of concept reactor to be build first. The hypothesis leading to these designs looks pretty solid and the antecedent technology required has been built in the sixties and did run for four years straight. So it is possible to do. Also consider that Bill Gates is personally involved in another nuclear reactor, designed for the same purpose..

In fifty years of nuclear power production, about 240.000 tons of nuclear waste have been produced worldwide, sounds like a big number but it is completely dwarfed if you compare this to the 110 million tons of toxic coal ash produced annually in the US alone. (Frequent Questions about the Coal Ash Disposal Rule - EPA website). That's roughly 5.000 tons world-wide versus 110.000.000 tons in the US alone, each year...

Proliferation is another concern, it is a stigma that will always stick to nuclear power generation. Certain isotopes of Uranium, Plutonium and Neptunium can be used to create a nuclear bomb , but spent fuel cannot unless it is properly refined. Fortunately, attempts to create a nuclear bomb are accompanied by radiation that is easy to detect and the processes involved are only available to highly trained professionals with the right facilities.

A nuclear reactor cannot explode like a nuclear bomb, it simply is physically impossible. In order to cause a nuclear explosion, one has to smash together pieces of weapons grade radioactive isotopes, in order for a mass chain reaction to occur. The nuclear fuel in reactors simply is not of the kind needed to create this kind of explosion, and it doesn't get slammed together like the materials of a nuclear bomb do.

If a nuclear reactor goes *wrong* it could result in a meltdown, a steam or a hydrogen explosion. The Chernobyl and Fukushima accidents were precipitated due to heat, pressure, steam and hydrogen building up leading to a critical point at which they exploded causing volatile radioactive elements such as iodine and cesium to be dispersed into the air and the water. In the case of a disaster (i.e. Chernobyl, Fukushima Daiichi) these volatile (mostly short lived) radioactive isotopes get into the atmosphere, and less volatile isotopes get dispersed in a limited area around the reactor. These remain radioactive depending on their half lives/decay. Some seep into ground water, other particles remain on the building, in the dirt or somehow get into plants. But this is quite manageable as Chernobyl for instance has shown.

We have to acknowledge that the track record of the nuclear industry is exemplary and probably the best of all the energy sources in use by human beings. The amount of deaths and accidents precipitated in the nuclear energy industry is the lowest of all the energy industries. The amount of radioactive material dispersed in the two major nuclear accidents are completely dwarfed by the amount of radioactive particles dispersed by the 2.500 nuclear bombs that have been detonated in the past. Also consider that we live on a naturally radioactive planet.

Radiation is everywhere: it surrounds us, our granite counter tops are radioactive. We breathe radon gas, and uranium particles from fly ash. We are constantly bombarded with cosmic radiation, and we eat radioactive foods like bananas which contains minute traces of radioactive potassium. In addition, many people live in areas where there is more natural radioactivity in the soil or from the air than at Pripyat, the city closest to the now useless Chernobyl power plant. Fear of radioactivity has to be put in perspective. We need to keep a rational perspective.

Radiation, which is called Ionizing Radiation in the case of Nuclear Radiation, includes X-rays and Gamma rays, and Alpha and Beta particles. Radiation can create problems if people are exposed to high levels of radiation.

The average background radiation level around the world runs from 3 to 15 Millisieverts (mSv) of radiation per year, although in some areas of India and other countries background radiation levels can exceed 300 mSv without causing any ill effects.

A Dental X-ray releases about 0.01 mSv; A full body CT Scan is 10 mSv; A Nuclear Industry Worker has a 20 mSv limit of exposure a year, and 100 mSv is the lowest level of exposure linked to a slightly increased risk of cancer. 500 mSv is the limit for short-term exposure for emergency workers engaged in life-saving actions. Near certain death from fatal forms of cancer start at 1.000 mSv and above 3.000 mSv your survival rate will be 50%, 10.000 mSv will be fatal within a couple of weeks. This information, which comes from the International Atomic Energy Agency and the World Nuclear Association, shows that you needn't be afraid of radiation.

Let's look at France for instance, a country of 66 million inhabitants, that relies on nuclear reactors to provide base load energy. About 80% of the electricity in France is being generated by nuclear reactors. They have an exemplary track record, and there is no evidence of negative health effects from depending upon the large amount of emission-free nuclear power they have enjoyed for 40 years.

Also consider pilots and air-crews that get an additional 2 ~ 2.5 per year of cosmic radiation.

Radiation by itself in small quantities is quite harmless, we are being exposed to radiation every day. Nuclear Power plants are required to contain every speck of radiation, but coal-fired power plants, which are largely unregulated, release significant amounts of radioactive particles.

We also have to acknowledge that radioactive isotopes are a boon for humanity. Not only in an energy context, but in a medical context as well. Healthcare benefits hugely from the existence of radioactive isotopes which can be used for diagnosis and the treatment of diseases. And what about smoke-detectors? They would be useless without the radioactive element Americium.

The amount of radioactive particles in the oceans vastly exceed the amount of radioactive particles dispersed into the atmosphere and oceans in the Fukushima accident. Citation would be required in a true scientific piece of work, there's a couple of links in the appendix leading to some other studies concerning this issue. Don't take my opinion on this at face value, yet try to attain a healthy and rational perspective on this issue and go seek for articles regarding these issues, there are a lot out there.

We live on a nuclear planet, plate tectonics and the heat in the earth are being fueled by nuclear decay of Uranium and Thorium and Potassium in the Earth's mantle and core. If we didn't have any nuclear decay in the core of our Earth, it would be dead, it would be stone cold, and we wouldn't have any plate tectonics, nor volcanic activity. These tectonic and volcanic activities also release these radioactive particles into the seas and the oceans, and that's how these elements got in there in the first place.

Our atmosphere and oceans get heated by radiation from nuclear fusion in the sun. Thus we may conclude that all life on Earth depends on nuclear energy to exist in the first place. Without it we would probably not be here.

The way fear seeps into the minds of the common people is through media coverage. Unfortunately, the media coverage of environ-mental disasters is governed by the dictum "If it bleeds, it leads." And if nuclear energy is involved, the scrutiny is always intense, prolonged, often exaggerated and shallow. The most frightened are sought out for interviews, and giving airtime to irrational fears can turn them into truths. In contrast every day pollution doesn't get any attention. The detrimental and hazardous effects of lignite and coal fired power plants and renewable energy generation vastly outstrip the issues of nuclear energy, yet they are more calmly addressed. Breaking the confirmation bias against nuclear energy, the stigma, will pose a big challenge.

The good of nuclear energy deserves to be addressed as well, it is not all energy, death and damnation. Nuclear energy has also brought humanity many boons, great discoveries and renewed health. NASA has an excellent article on this called "*Coal and gas are far more harmful than nuclear power*". (note the "far more" addition)

However ominous nuclear energy might seem, it actually makes use of one of the four elemental forces of nature. The four elemental forces are gravity, the strong force, the weak force and the electromagnetic force. The strong force basically keeps atoms together, the nuclear force is part of the strong force as it makes sure that protons and neutrons are held together in the nucleus of the atom. It is also the reason why so much energy gets freed once an atom gets split or fused. Nuclear energy is the energy of the sun and the cores of terrestrial planets. The sun exists because of thermonuclear fusion of hydrogen and helium isotopes. The Earth's core is hot due to nuclear decay, pressure and friction.

Producing nuclear energy by fissioning atoms is making use of one the most basic and fundamental forces in universe.

Basically what we do in a nuclear fission process is hit a fissile atom [Uranium 233 for instance] with a neutron, after which the Uranium 233 breaks apart into fission products, some radiation, a "couple of neutrons" and in the process also releases energy in the form of heat. Subsequently this heat is used to generate electricity. The energy gets released because we are disrupting the forces that keep the nucleus of an atom together, it breaks the "bonds" between the protons and the neutrons of the nucleus, the energy required to maintain these bonds is then released. It is important to get at least two extra neutrons out of the reaction, because this keeps the fission process going.

Fusion is done by making two atoms collide and fuse, you have for instance the Deuterium - Tritium path in which one Deuterium and one Tritium atom fuse into a helium atom and a neutron is left, these neutrons pose a couple of material problems, which is one of the reasons why fusion has not yet proven itself. During this fusion process about nine times as much energy is released compared to the nuclear fission process with a comparable amount of fuel. People are also looking to make A-neutronic fusion possible, a process in which there is no neutron flux. Containment is important, it is keeping the plasma-flow (plasma is superheated hydrogen gas, that can react to electromagnetic forces) contained in a beam through big magnets. Up until now we've not passed the 8 minute mark for containment.

It might seem naive or simplistic but nuclear energy is nothing more than a different means of getting heat out of elements, transfer this heat through some heat exchanger into an turbine which in term turns a dynamo that creates electricity. There are a lot of different designs, working fluids and turbine designs yet the elemental principle remains the same: get heat, use it to create momentum to run a generator. It's the same for Coal, Gas, Petroleum based, geothermal, etc.

The people working on nuclear fusion have yet to prove that we can do it in such a way that it can provide energy for people here on Earth. ITER is meant to provide a proof of concept. It is still going to take some time before nuclear fusion on Earth will happen in a scale that will benefits humanity in a sense of massive energy production, if ever. The age old adage is: Nuclear Fusion is a decade away.

I'm confident that we will make it happen. Why? would you ask. All over the world the push for sustainable nuclear fusion is ongoing, a multitude of nations and companies are working hard to make it happen. When the push is strong enough we're bound to find out how to do it. It is a confidence in human ingenuity and technical fortitude.

The biggest benefits of nuclear energy can be summed up quite easily: it has a high energy density and requires a relatively small footprint and small quantities of feedstock in order to provide large amounts of energy without any carbon emissions. New reactor designs, called Generation IV reactors, are a vast improvement over the current fleet of Generation II and Generation III reactors. Improvements include an increase in passive safety features, zero meltdown risk, high fuel efficiency, higher generation efficiencies and the possibility to become standardized in terms of manufacturing and maintenance processes. The overall footprints of these Generation IV reactors are an improvement over the old reactors. And yet a lot of designs currently in use are already incredibly dependable, reactors like the CANDU, the AP1000 and many others.

Nuclear has the smallest overall footprint of all energy sources. It has a capacity factor of over 90%, and 10% allotted downtime due to maintenance. Nuclear provides base load energy and then some. There are no harmful emissions during operation.

A conventional nuclear reactor runs on a solid fuel cycle, uranium pellets that are housed in titanium tubes. The problem with solid fuel is that it is expensive to manufacture and is terribly inefficient and leaves you with big quantities of unused fuel.

There is a billion ways we can do nuclear and most of them are safe and incredibly efficient. And let's be honest, the track record of nuclear energy as a whole has been exemplary. There are two designs in development that are particularly interesting to me. They are called the LFTR and the WAMSR, these are acronyms for Liquid Fluoride Thorium Reactor and Waste Annihilation Molten Salt Reactor.

Highway to Dystopia

It is necessary to delve into the history of the MSR in order to put things into context. By the 1950s, the U.S. Navy had commissioned the first nuclear submarine in the world, the Nautilus. The United States Army had their own reactors and the Air Force had none. So they cooked up the idea of a nuclear aircraft that could circle the globe almost indefinitely. Alvin Weinberg proposed that a Molten Salt Reactor, which would use a liquid fuel, could be built to serve this purpose. Weinberg conceived the idea that you could have a working fluid that would simultaneously be a cooling fluid as well. The Molten Salt Reactor initially was designed to create a nuclear powered bomber. This idea however was abandoned because of the impracticality of it and the arrival of ICBM's (Inter Continental Ballistic Missiles).

Although the advent of ICBM's negated the need for nuclear powered aircraft, Weinberg's project was continued and in the sixties the first real MSR was built at Oak Ridge National Laboratory, it ran successfully for five years and withstood all practical tests. The reactor is still there and the working salts are safely sequestered in dump tanks beneath the reactor. The project was canceled because President Nixon preferred to develop a new kind of reactor called a breeder reactor that he wanted to build in his home state of California. That project was subsequently canceled due to cost overruns and technical difficulties.

So what have we learned? We had the technology back in the sixties, but it got stifled due to political errors. Weinberg, who designed the first nuclear reactors, was convinced that the Molten Salt Reactor was by far the best means to create nuclear energy, but it didn't happen, and now we have to catch up for fifty years of stagnation. In this case I would have been an advocate of trying to keep as many possible lanes of development open. Shutting down the MSRE was a critical error.

The nuclear stigma

One of the difficulties for nuclear fission in the context of a molten salt reactor is the material where the reactor will be made off has to withstand a steady bombardment of neutrons and fission products. The material itself is being warped on an atomic level, meaning that you have to account for "wear and tear", basically meaning that you will have to make the reactor-vessel thick enough, and decommission it after an X amount of time.

In nuclear fusion constant neutron flux is the issue. Neutrons will be flying around all the time during the fusion process, meaning that they will impact on the materials the reactor is made off, causing Embrittlement and other issues. These are the challenges we need to solve amongst other things.

Do we have to hide nuclear "waste" in mountains? Do we want to shove it down long pipes in the earth? Do we want to store it on the moon or set it off into space? Humanity is faced with the "*problem*" of "*nuclear waste*", we have no idea how to handle it. At least it looks like it and it is still an issue that keeps raising its head. Last year's headlines included Yucca Mountain, and several other possible places to store nuclear waste. Humanity is played with the notion that nuclear waste is a problem. As mentioned earlier, nuclear waste is not a problem, as a matter of fact it is a golden opportunity waiting to be grasped.

Nuclear waste and spent fuel still have large amount of energy content. Just look at Einstein's principle of Mass-Energy Equivalence or $E=MC^2$, where C^2 equals to 8.9875 x 10^{16} meters per second! Which means that if there's fissionable material in nuclear "*spent*" fuel, or nuclear waste each gram of it contains 89,87 × 10^{12} joules of energy, which equates to the energy of roughly 15.000 barrels of crude oil, which in term equates to 7.995 million kWh's. Circling back, you can fulfill the energy needs of hundreds of average American Households, for a year, on one gram of fissile material.

Highway to Dystopia

I honestly have to pass the buck on to the experts here, I don't know if above math is absolutely true or not. I don't know precisely how much energy you could get from a gram of fissionable material. But the general idea is clear. Thanks to mass-energy equivalence we can deduce that using nuclear fission is to tap into bizarre amounts of energy using miniscule amounts of fuel.

It is estimated that there's enough energy in our nuclear waste to power all the energy needs of the world for 60 to 70 years, and this factors in population growth and an increase in energy demand. In addition, if we move ahead with MSR technologies, that use Thorium or Uranium, we will have enough fuel for thousands of years, well enough time to go look for these energy sources elsewhere in the universe. Without there being any carbon emissions during energy generation anymore. And also giving us the time to possibly crack the issue of nuclear fusion.

A couple of bright and young nuclear physicists from the Massachusetts Institute of Technology have designed a nuclear reactor that will be able to tap into the energy contained in the nuclear waste. This new type of reactor is called a WAMSR or Waste Annihilating Molten Salt Reactor. What this nuclear reactor basically does is turn nuclear waste into megawatts. They've started a company called Transatomic Power, I really suggest you look them up if you are interested in this marvelous prospective piece of technology.

The MSR can work on the principle of transmutation, this means that you hit an atom with a neutron, which then gets absorbed turning this atom into another type of atom, for instance fertile Thorium 232 absorbs a neutron and transforms into protactinium 233 which then decays in 27 days and becomes a fissile Uranium 233 atom.

A possible boon provided by the transmutation process and the WAMSR is the propensity to turn Megatons into Megawatts. We're talking about turning weapons grade Uranium and Plutonium into energy. Our planet is still being captured in fear by the tens of thousands of nuclear warheads that could be used to end human civilization and destroy many parts of the world. This reactor could actually "eat" nuclear weapons! It can also use "spent fuel" from other contemporary nuclear reactors to generate energy, thus greatly reducing the existing waste issues.

The WAMSR could be an incredible force for peace in the world. The energy needs of humanity are growing exponentially. 4 Billion people in the developing countries will be in need of energy to fuel their progress into prosperity. What do we want to them to get? Coal or gas fired power plants? I know many people are scared of the prospect of hillbillies getting their hands on nuclear technology, yet it is going to be necessary to provide these emerging peoples with emission free energy, and we will figure out how to do it safely.

Some of the focal points of these new designs are an immense reduction in water use, a vastly improved fuel efficiency, significantly reducing nuclear waste, Increased and passive safety features, reduced proliferation issues, and the great propensity for the desalination of water, which will become an absolute necessity in the near future.

The advantages of MSR's over traditional reactors summed up:

The fuel is dissolved in a molten salt, which allows you to reach up to 97% fuel efficiency in contrast to 3-4% of conventional reactors.

The reactor runs at atmospheric pressure, meaning that controlling the pressure isn't necessary and a "blow-out" is impossible

The reactor is what they call "walk-away" safe, meaning that if there is an accident no humans are required to keep a cooling process running, because the molten salt automatically gets dumped into sub-critical dump/storage tanks where the heat will dissipate gradually and the liquid will solidify, the fission process will grind to a halt and the working materials plus the radioactive elements are safely stored in these tanks, without any risk of a meltdown or other calamity.

The MSR doesn't require vast amounts of water for cooling in contrast to pressurized/light water reactors, it can also be cooled passively, just by air.

Terrestrial Energy (another MSR company) uses a slightly different passive safety feature, the molten salt remains in the reactor in case of a shutdown, a blanket of salt around the reactor vessel functions as a buffer, helping to absorb the remaining decay heat assuring that the process can be fired up again easily after a shutdown.

There are also dual fluid designs, pebble bed designs and other forms of either MSR's or Generation IV reactors that show promise.

Among the major contenders in the MSR field are: Terrestrial Energy, Thorcon Power, Flibe Energy, and Transatomic Energy. Each of these companies approach the MSR design philosophy from a slightly different angle, I think all of their designs are promising and we should give them the opportunity to set things in motion, to go and build test reactors, involve institutes of safety and learning in the process and increase our knowledge along the way.

Bill Gates, is also invested in nuclear energy. He is working with a company called Terrapower to create a waste-recycling nuclear reactor. First it seemed that they were going for a "Travelling Wave Reactor" but it now seems that they are changing course. In the meanwhile Terrapower has been given access to China in order to make practical headway in their developments. Bill Gates says that energy is the most important metric for the success of civilization, and he is absolutely right, energy is the most important subject of our age (is directly tied to our survival). We are in dire need of an "energy miracle", which is why I endorse MSRs and other developments like those of terrapower.

If we want to start building test reactors, we need to start removing uncertainty and opening up pathways through test licensing, investments, and research.

These Molten Salt Reactors are excellent at desalinating brackish or salt water. Since humanity is putting increased strain on water resources, this is an excellent feature attached to this energy generating capacity. I would advocate that instead of building huge columns to support thousands of windmills, we could use the steel to create pipelines to transport desalinated water from energy producing and desalination plants to area's where water supplies are under tremendous strain. This would be far more valuable than for instance a gas or oil pipeline. Fresh and potable water are far more valuable than crude oil or any other fossil resource and MSR's can deliver.

We could then use the water in an agricultural sense, or for human use i.e. drink water, water for the dishes and water to use in the shower. But the thing that excites me even more is that if we could desalinate water on a large scale, we could actually use it to recharge aquifers. Imagine the tremendous propensity this technology has in terms of re-humidifying the soil. Making sure life sustaining plants and trees can remain growing, seriously mitigate wildfires, making sure our carbon and hydrological cycles become healthy again. This of course will take decades to be effective, however, I think we should start doing it because it will significantly improve our biosphere. Imagine not having to worry about severe droughts and massive forest fires any more.

The most important point about nuclear energy is that it is clean-air-energy. It doesn't emit any harmful elements during operation.

Highway to Dystopia

Life cycle emissions of nuclear energy are better than those of practically all the renewable energies. What makes the life cycle emissions of renewables higher than Nuclear energy? It is the necessity to have fossil fuel backup, not even Tesla's much-hyped home battery will change that. I love Tesla, but its home battery isn't going to solve grand scale problems, at all.

Compared to nuclear, gas and coal and other fossil fueled energy sources are off the charts, releasing between 30 and 60 times more green house gasses throughout their life cycles.

The question is: "What stands in the way?"

We can sum it up quite easily: Public acceptance, politics, money, *and* the current reactors are so successful and safe that it's just too easy to keep doing the same thing..

We have to address this question from a financial and regulatory viewpoint. To get one of these prototypes going is to engage in a lengthy timeline with high costs: regulatory pathways, regulatory approval, and licensing a prototype facility. Investors have to be confident that the design will deliver on its promise. The problem is that it takes too long and some of the elements of the pathways are not transparent in terms of costs and time to complete, these form barriers to investments. In order to get investors on board demonstrations are needed, a better regulatory and licensing pathway needs to be made to make these advancements in nuclear energy possible. Currently, licensing costs are estimated to be anywhere from 100 million to 600 million dollars.

A possible solution to ease up the process could be that the licensing and regulatory agencies could embed observers into the companies building these prototypes in order to obtain real-time knowledge and to get the investment costs down by streamlining communication between the developing company and the regulating agency. In the meanwhile these regulatory agencies could build up expertise on the type of technology which is being developed and the developers could showroom their practical progress to potential investors, a win-win situation.

Unfortunately, we are still ensnarled in regulatory pathways, non-transparent licensing costs and unrealized paper designs. Who will invest in that? Looking at it from a capitalist short term gain perspective, as discussed earlier, these designs do not satiate an immediate thirst for wealth. One has to become committed and place a bet on developing something which might take five to ten years to come to fruition, and stick with it.

Big international projects like ITER and LHC get billions of capital decades ahead, because they are non-commercial, so perhaps we would make more progress if we used government funds just as we did to send men to the moon or to pay for Grand Coulee Dam or Boulder Dam - later renamed Hoover dam. This might provide some straws in the wind.

Commercialization of something that is beyond current licensing and regulatory pathways means that you'll be stuck within the confines of a rigid framework, until someone alters it, people will be unwilling to take the risk from a capitalistic viewpoint.

Like I said repeatedly in previous chapters: there is no free lunch in energy. From my point of view this is the list of energy generation possibilities going from best to worse: providence & conservation, nuclear Fusion, nuclear fission generation IV, nuclear fission as is, geothermal, wave energy, wind, solar, natural gas, petroleum, coal and finally the worst of the worst lignite. Let's face it, we're still in the dark segment: Lignite, coal, petroleum and gas are still completely dominant in the world of energy with a share larger than ninety percent.

Also consider that without nuclear energy we wouldn't have any rovers elsewhere in space, no deep space probes, we would have no

X-ray machines, no MRI's, no organ function scans, no cancer research, no possibility of treatment of certain diseases, we would have no smoke detectors, no luminescent dials on watches, etc.. The list is endless. Nuclear energy might seem ominous to many, but it could also be the silver bullet we need to solve several pressing matters that couldn't be solved otherwise.

A stigma is instilled by fear, mostly by misunderstanding or a significant lack of knowledge. Nothing in life is to be feared only understood as Marie Curie told us. We can do better, we have to find out better ways of doing things. Remain skeptical and inquisitive, look at the evidence and if there is none suspend your judgment but don't let your opinions be clouded by fear!

I am convinced that MSR technology can provide a huge contribution to our energy needs, simultaneously creating large volumes of de-salinated water, which climate change has already begun to make a necessity.

Nuclear energy will help create a cleaner atmosphere and a healthier biosphere due to near nil pollution and significantly less carbon dioxide emissions, compared to any other resource out there, even wind and solar...

Energy decision making

The sustainability of a growing civilization trembles under the great stress of the availability of water and energy. As mentioned before, the diminishing of fresh water supplies, the heating of our atmosphere and its effects on life on earth are factors that have to be put into perspective. Our energy consumption is one of the defining factors because its emissions are a cause for the terrible things that are about to happen, and have happened in a climato-logical and ecological sense.

Something has to change, we have to become smarter. The growing need for more fresh water, food, and services, will require more energy than ever before.

Providence will only work if we exactly know who is producing what, which kinds of materials are used, what emissions are being made. Closely monitoring the earth's resources and the way we use them is paramount. Knowledge through making observations is essential in this process. We need to keep track of our emissions, our manufacturing and mining efforts and have to scale them against reasonable conservation and recovery efforts. This is the first and most important part of creating a sustainable future.

The question shouldn't be "how do we go all renewable?" The question should be: "how do we phase out _all_ of the coal-fired energy plants and eventually also the gas- and diesel-powered energy plants?" Why? Because they produce at least 90% of all the electrical energy in the world, while creating huge amounts of emissions that lead to early deaths and disabilities – and accelerate Climate change. This is our ultimate challenge: ending the use of fossil fuels for energy production and transportation.

Try to create steel, aluminum, concrete, solar panels, windmills without fossil fuels. Not a single manufacturer does this, and some of these processes are presently impossible without coal, diesel or gas.

We have to face the fact that renewable energy sources cannot be expanded fast enough to meet all the world's energy demands while at the same time defeating carbon-fueled energy production. It is not going to happen. If you ask climate science experts, the vast majority would agree.

The capricious nature of solar and wind power must be addressed. For example, windmills rated at one megawatt will generate that amount only during ideal conditions, which are rare. As it turns out, windmills only generate about one fourth of their maximum output over the long run, so they have a Capacity Factor of 25%, which means that they are highly inefficient.

Solar power is only available during the day and also depends on factors like cloud cover, dust and the intensity of the sun. Photo voltaic cells also degrade over time, making them increasingly inefficient.

Because both solar and wind are intermittent, they need constantly running backup generators that are usually powered by coal or natural gas. Alternatively, some plans call for storing electricity via batteries or water pumped into reservoirs that can theoretically supply the needed power whenever wind or solar can't fill the bill.

In addition, wind and solar have small energy densities, which means that they can only provide base load power for millions of people if they are implemented in great numbers – in other words, overbuilt. We are talking about millions of wind mills and trillions of PV panels.

Thirdly, consider energy storage. How will we do it? There are some hydro pumps around the world that are used to store energy by pumping water to basins at higher elevation at times when there is surplus energy. When the demand rises the potential energy from the water in the basins gets turned into kinetic energy which drives generators in order to create extra electricity. "What a wonderful idea!" one might say. That's true, were it not that the amount of energy stored in these basins is marginal and hardly enough to satiate the energy needs of millions of people for a prolonged period of time.

A second possibility for storing energy is by converting electricity into methane gas, which in times of need can be used in a gas turbine to generate electricity. This also poses a number of problems. First of all, the conversion steps are highly inefficient:

Loss 1 - Electricity gets turned into hydrogen

Gain 1 - An exothermic process is used to turn the hydrogen into methane and water by combining it with carbon dioxide

Loss 2 - liquefaction or compaction of the methane gas

Loss 3 - It gets stored in vast containers that have to be airtight, one small leak and you'll lose precious energy

Loss 4 - Starting up these generators

Loss 5 - The methane gas has to be turned into energy again using a gas turbine power plant.

With this chain of inefficiency, you supposedly start with 100KWh and end up with about 25KWh.

Highway to Dystopia

A horrendously inefficient process. We can do it, there is no question about that. Lets accept that this requires a vast infrastructure in order to produce several megawatts and only when needed. You would have a big industrial sized energy conversion and storage plant that just sits there, doing nothing most of the time. Hardly an exciting idea – especially if one takes into account the amount of material, construction and maintenance required to build this storage network and get it running. No energy company would invest in this solution, at least not from a commercial viewpoint unless there are lucrative incentives from the government, which is the case with wind and solar energy.

It also possible that some kind of battery technology will be developed to store this energy. However, these batteries must remain as efficient as they are in the beginning and for as long as possible. If they degrade we will have produced a vast process of manufacturing, maintaining, decommissioning and recycling batteries for yet another industry. And if the number of electrically powered cars increases as much as is expected, the battery industry would be hard-pressed to satisfy the need. And let's remember that we live on a world of finite resources.

Are we really going to look for the "holy grail" of renewable energy? The pinnacle of inefficiency? While there are greater problems still? Especially the water problem which simply cannot be overlooked!

What I would suggest is this, use renewable energies at remote places in an off-grid context. There is a role to play for solar energy and wind energy. Build nuclear reactors to provide base load and in order to get rid of coal fired energy plants, make limited use of gas-fired power stations to quickly bridge any loss of capacity, and only use gas temporarily.

I suspect that once the viability and safety of MSR technology gets accepted by the people, that there will be a mass implementation of this technology – and also consider the fact that we have enough uranium and thorium to power them for 10.000 years. This operation will be nigh insurmountable since we're talking about thousands of nuclear reactors. It might sound daunting? It is... But then again, there is no free lunch and I believe it to be the only way, without the possibility of human regression.

What would you rather have? A thousand lignite- or coal-fired energy plants that make more CO_2 and kill millions, or a thousand, safe molten salt reactors that have zero emissions? Some people would say neither, but I question if they've thought it through well enough.

I am a great advocate of solar heat systems because they can be built from completely ubiquitous materials that are already being used in construction and would be an excellent means to diminish the use for fossil fuels in heating houses.

Instead of building vast arrays of solar panels and windmills that cover large pieces of land, we would have relatively small buildings across the country, that work at high efficiencies, and are far better for human health than coal and gas fired power plants because they, MSR's, do not emit any greenhouse gases or other harmful elements detrimental to our health and our atmosphere. We would also be much more provident with our resources, using the highest energy density currently available while we wait for the most brilliant and bright minds of our kind to come up with newer and even better alternatives to provide more electricity and fresh water for humanity.

I think it would be much more elegant if we would have highly efficient energy plants providing base load, exceeding demand at all times. Solar energy could be used as a surplus for the desalination of water thus remediating the strain on fresh water supplies. We can build a self balancing energy system in which nuclear provides base load, and all the excess energy gets used for desalination. How would this work? People generating their own energy would get rewards for it from the government, why? Because they help balance out the anthropogenic water cycle with the natural hydrological cycle. This would diminish the need for grid energy storage. Instead of turning acres of land into solar farms or wind farms we could use that money to create water pipelines running from the seas and the oceans to the great plains and other distant parts that require water for agricultural and human use. A leak in one of these pipes would have no negative environmental impacts whatsoever and could easily be fixed without any cleanup issues afterwards.

Since I've already claimed that fresh water will become more valuable than oil or gold, I would find it a far better practice to use all the spare energy to convert brackish or salt water into potable water rather than storing energy in batteries or electricity to gas systems. One could also use the excess energy for drawing water from the air through thermoelectric water generators in locations too remote to reach with a pipeline.

I would like to make a passionate case for nuclear going hand in hand with localized and small scale solar (heat) as the two prime sources for energy on our world. To use Geothermal in places where it can be used, to lessen the amount of hydro power, since it has a detrimental effect on aquifers and poses a threat to people living downstream. And to use Wind Power only in an off grid capacity where there is plenty of wind to begin with. This approach alleviates the need to produce large quantities of Windmills and Solar Panels. Instead we can take a more gradual approach, keep developing these technologies and keep improvement and inno-vation going on. The implementation of contemporary nuclear reactors and MSR technology shall provide a steeper curve in energy generation growth, which is essentially required to defeat fossil fuel energy generation.

Another thing that could help us in many ways is green roofs. What does this do for our energy problems one would ask? For one it is an excellent insulator, keeping your house cool in the summer and warm in the winter. Secondly it helps increase biodiversity of cities and towns. Instead of having bare concrete or shingled roofs, we would have grass and plants on roofs. I'm pretty sure it would provide a more healthy environment to live in. And finally I'd like to think that green roofs would alleviate the "urban heat island" effect, through increased reflectivity and through the absorption of energy through photosynthesis.

We are still burning coal and lignite to get energy, we are far from optimum efficiency in capturing solar and wind power, we still have not figured out how to store energy in large quantities effectively, We don't know how to build a battery that can store the energy for a car to let it drive a thousand miles which can be charged in fifteen minutes, we haven't built new test MSR's yet, we are still trying to make different kinds of fusion work and we are still innovating solar panel technology.

That's why we need inquisitive and intelligent and skilled people who want to engage in science and innovation and we have to keep investing in individuals who want to contribute to this noble quest.

Let's do some simple math. The figures I use come from the "Renewables 2015 Global Status Report" from REN21/Renewable Energy Policy Network for the 21st century.

I'll promise you it'll be over quite soon, but these numbers have to be in here because they provide a clear explanation for my controversial stance on energy.

Highway to Dystopia

We are faced by a very big challenge, consider the following figures:

The Energy Information Administration estimates that we currently consume about 550 Quadrillion BTu of energy, converted to electricity this is 160.000 TWh.

Current worldwide wind capacity is 370 Gigawatt, and this means that you could expect an annual production of about 1000 TWh from wind. The current worldwide solar capacity is 182 Gigawatt, and this means that you could expect an annual production of 320 TWh from solar. Combined wind and solar currently account for an annual production of 1320 TWh or 0.825% of the total worldwide energy consumption.

Current nuclear capacity is 380 Gigawatt, and we may expect it to produce about 3000 TWh annually which is 1.9% of all energy consumption, about double from wind and solar combined.

The rest of the non fossil energy generation capacity is 1160 GW which amounts to 5 to 6000 TWh or 3.8% of all energy consumption. Combined Non-Fossil capacity is 2092 GW and about 10.420 TWh of annual generation, or 6.5% of world energy consumption.

These numbers have forced me to re-examine my reasoning, even though the growth ratios in these industries are quite impressive, sum total progress is very marginal on a global and total energy scale. The daunting conclusion we have to make is that we have to decarbonize *more than ninety percent* of all energy.

Wind Turbines and Solar Panels are mature technologies, given the fact that they are heavily subsidized it's very disappointing to see them struggle to add any significant figures to the mix. In the most optimal scenario about 50 Gigawatt of wind capacity is added annually, This is about 20.000 2,5 Megawatt Wind Turbines world-

221

wide or an expected 130TWh. Solar energy comes out even worse with an annual growth of about 40 Gigawatt, somewhere between 160 and 400 million panels or 70 TWh. We're in dire need of thousands of Terawatt hours added each year to compete with fossil fuels.

There are hard material caps on solar and wind because they depend on resources like silver, titanium, neodymium, indium, gallium, copper, and more... Also consider that Silica refinement is a high-energy, carbon-dioxide emitting process, either through burning coal or by using an electrical arch-furnace with introduced carbon to remove the oxygen atoms from the $SiO2$ and $SiO4$ molecules in order to produce the pure crystalline silicon structure that is required for silicon wafers.

The limiting materials aren't as ubiquitous as the materials required to build for instance a conventional nuclear reactor, this is also the reason why adding more coal- and gas-burning capacity is such a trivial matter, these do not have material caps imposed on them. Also consider the question how much denuding is required to get the materials required for all these devices?

On my blog, I've published an article in which I compare the material requirements per terawatt hour of generation capacity. I used the September 2015 issue of the Quadrennial Technology Review from the Department of Energy of the United States.

The outcome wasn't that surprising but I have to share them with you to make you understand what I'm talking about when I speak about material requirements, otherwise, it wouldn't make any sense.

Suppose we need 10.000 TWh of energy annually, what kind of capacity would we require per technology? (note the figure is determined by capacity factor) Solar 5703,9 Gigawatt, Wind 3259,3 Gigawatt, Geothermal 1629,7 Gigawatt and Nuclear 1267,5 Gigawatt. As you can see Solar and Wind require at least two and a half times the amount of capacity to generate the same amount of energy.

How do these technologies stack up against each other if we look at the amount of materials required to produce this 10.000 TWh of annual generation capacity? Solar 164 Billion tons, Wind 102 Billion tons, Geothermal 53 Billion tons and nuclear 9 Billion tons. From these figures we can conclude that we need 18 times more materials for Solar to create this generation capacity and 11 times more materials for wind. And it gets even worse! Nuclear power plants have a durability of at least 50 years while solar and wind only last for 25 years. So we can double the figures for solar (36x) and wind (22x). From this perspective it becomes perfectly clear that nuclear (and geothermal) are the technologies that will be able to compete with coal and gas.

We might also expect hydro to grow as existing hydro-facilities might be adapted in the future to become more efficient and generate even more energy.

Let's extrapolate this to 250.000 TWh: Solar 4,1 Trillion tons, Wind 2.5 Trillion tons, Geothermal 1,3 Trillion tons, Nuclear 0,225 Trillion tons. Given these figures it has to be clear that solar and wind energy fall utterly short if we want to stop denuding the Earth for material extraction.

To give you an idea of the scale involved, we would need to build 35.000 reactors rated at 1000 Megawatt to generate 250.000 TWh, we currently have about 600 reactors in operation.

Suppose we would be able to build 200 Gigawatt worth of nuclear reactors each year or a total expected generation of roughly 1.580 TWh, Even with this figure it would take 100 years to completely decarbonize 550 Quadrillion BTu of annual energy consumption and we also have to recognize that energy demand is going to grow, the Energy Information Administration of the United States estimates that we will consume 850 Quadrillion BTu by the 2040's, this equals 250.000 TWh, 80.000 TWh more than we currently consume in a year.

I am quite certain that solar and wind are now reaching peak production, so there isn't much more scalability in these figures, even if these would double over the next decade it wouldn't make a significant difference. We have seen this in the expansion of biomass and gas-fired power plants. The US for instance is dialing down on coal, but has to increase gas in order to keep up. Solar requires a one-for-one backup generation which basically always means burning natural gas.

How can we increase the production rate of reactors? Thorcon Power, for instance, proposes a standardized and modular and almost production line-like process for building MSR's. It is these kinds of ideas and innovations that will help us overcome the energy crisis in the battle against Anthropogenic Climate Change.

These are key issues that need to be debated... We are in serious trouble and in desperate need of an *"energy miracle"* – Bill Gates

As shown ad nauseam and ad infinitem, we have no other choice but to engage in creating a nuclear future. Whatever the risks and current problems might be, they are all solvable. How did I arrive at this conclusion? By free inquiry, looking at physics and by doing the calculations.

A 250.000 TWh world cannot be sustained by anything other than nuclear energy. It simply cannot be done otherwise. And even worse, it is my contention that fission itself will prove insufficient, we need to get fusion working as well, especially in a context of mass transportation.

Most people tend to focus on Gigawatts or dollars per kilowatt hour, but these figures are irrelevant when you have to supply a demand of 850 Quadrillion BTu. People in the current zeitgeist are still preoccupied with money. Decarbonisation of our energy generation is essential and money is irrelevant, not only because of Climate Change, but also because the World Health Organization estimates that about 7 million die annually from the adverse effects on human health from the combustion economy. Is it moral or wise to perpetuate this specter of death out of [an irrational] fear of nuclear energy, which, ironically, is the safest of all means of power production? Because that's what we're doing when we choose the cul-de-sac, lined exclusively with "Renewables", that leads into oblivion. Renewables are touted as the solution to Climate Change, but I submit to you that they are not.

Many people are being deluded into believing that we can mitigate our use of fossil fuels just by adding enough wind turbines and solar panels, but this is an irrational and unsubstantiated claim, fostered by people who deny science and are apparently too lazy to do the math. Unfortunately, fact avoiders and science deniers have been given thousands of hours of media time and many pages of print, these quacks are playing with the future of my children and yours and this is something that makes me angry, at some times even furious.

While climate change worsens, governments and organizations all over the world are engaged in spending a lot of time, money and resources in a feeble attempt to solve the problem with hopelessly inadequate technologies (wind and solar and "storage"). For the sake of future generations we have to stop this madness as soon as possible and come to our senses.

The new "Global Manhattan Project"

Bear with me, this might sound quite paradoxical but I'm not advocating the development of a new super weapon. I am advocating worldwide collaboration in the advancement of fundamental knowledge and significant technologies.

The antagonistic nature of governments and the ruling classes has been the primary driver behind technological advancements in many fields, but especially in regard to war. For example, consider the development of the jet engine that powered the Messerschmitt 262, the work of rocket pioneers like Werner von Braun and Robert H. Goddard or the Manhattan project that relied on the cooperation of scientists from many facilities and disciplines who came together at locations like Chicago MET lab and Hanford and Oak Ridge National Laboratory and Los Alamos.

Let's take a look at pre-world II America – then only a marginal military power on par with countries like Portugal or Spain. The US wanted to remain neutral in the Second World War. Yet it was provoked to enter by the Japanese empire and Nazi Germany. Their economy was recovering and they had plenty problems of their own. Factories were unprofitable, many people were unemployed and trade was grinding to a halt. Yet once the Americans were drawn into the war, a massive economic and military giant woke up. All the eligible men were drafted into the military and the women had to join the labor force in order to create all the necessary means to go to war and to become a superpower. All this might came forth from sheer determination and the need for all to jump in.

Their economy had grown so much and so fast that factories became profitable again and kept producing many luxury goods after the war. Their defense industries kept working as a reaction to the cold war, and it became the biggest economy in the world. The second world war accidentally set it all in motion, it was not per design. One can only imagine what would have happened if the Americans were never drawn into the war. England would have fallen and Europe would have been lost to the Nazi regime which in term would have to fight against a determined and hardened soviet union.

If for immense proliferation purposes we can bring together the most brilliant minds like Einstein, Bohr, Weinberg, Oppenheimer and hundreds more. It is strange to see that back then an arms race was so important that no amount of expense could keep the United States from pursuing it. But today, it's difficult to persuade politicians and others who form public opinion to develop and fund a comprehensive, practical and efficient plan to combat the most pressing problem we have faced since the dawn of Homo Sapiens. That problem is Climate Change

What the United States did then, the world must do now if we are to reduce the consequences of Climate Change that loom larger every year. We need, in effect a mega-Manhattan project that seeks and acquires the cooperation of the best and brightest from all around the world.

This brings a question to mind: "how do we bridge the gap between countries with different ideologies and geopolitical interests?" This is one of the more difficult problems. As discussed earlier, there are a lot of limiting factors: political and regulatory capture, ideological differences and doctrinal zealotry. The odds might be against us, but we have to try nonetheless, our existence depends on it. Everything has to be set aside in order to pursue a common goal: survival.

I am not saying that we need another Manhattan project to conceive one silver bullet against Anthropogenic Climate Change and the possible mass extinction event that is caused by it. We however do need a Manhattan project to build a comprehensive approach, We basically need five things to happen:

1. We have to lift the population of the world into a more knowledgeable state through the distribution of a neutral and un-censored internet and by emphasizing science in schools and increasing science programming on television;

2. We need to empower the women, especially those in the third world countries, give them control over their own reproductive cycle, engage them into being whatever they want to be;

3. We need to address the growing energy problems, preferably pursuing an energy source, or sources, with high densities, low carbon debts, low feedstock requirements, and low material costs – as articulated earlier this predominantly means nuclear energy;

4. We have to find a way to do mass desalination of water, we simply have to, in order to keep aquifers from running out of water, to get water to the 700+ million people that don't have any, to keep crop and livestock yields at a reasonable and sustainable level, and to stop the lands from drying up. Restoring the hydrological cycle can also be done with massive reforestation efforts. Nuclear energy is essential in the race for desalination. With a sufficient number of power plants we can desalinate enough water to relieve the crippling droughts that are already affecting the American Southwest;

5. Our way of future transportation needs to become smarter and preferably zero emission, beginning with cars and trains. This means investing in battery technology research. The advancement for carbon neutral ways of shipping and flying will be the ultimate challenge in terms of world-wide transportation.

We are able to build a more sustainable and fair society, based on equality, freedom and prosperity for all i.e. the Jean-Luc Picard/Star Trek future, if we embrace those principles. We need to figure out how to help the developing countries gain more energy generation capabilities, to help them build an infrastructure for fresh running water, for sanitation, the availability of food, education, internet and jobs. We need to create a level playing field for humanity. I am not talking about the US, The West, but about the world. We have to do all of this on a global scale.

Some US Senators are urging NASA to look less at the Earth and more at space exploration, but space exploration will be worthless if life on Earth is jeopardized. I believe that agencies like NASA and ESA should use their expertise to analyze the health issues of our space ship, "Earth". The health of the Earth can be assessed with a higher degree of accuracy if we increase our observational capacities. We should be making more observations and measurements, not less. But let's not cut space exploration, because it helps us become more knowledgeable about the cosmos that surrounds us. We need to know a lot more about it.

Not only are we in dire need of a sound technological course away from a fossil fuels, humanity is yet to grasp the harm being done in name of our civilization. We're making a mess of things and it is only getting worse. We need to put our differences aside and acknowledge that this ecosystem, which supports us, is not going to last. Our petty differences are insignificant in the scale of deep time and the cosmos.

The new "Global Manhattan Project"

In just over 150 years – a mere blink of an eye on the cosmic scale – we've changed the face of the Earth completely. waged great wars that killed millions of people and we've developed weapons that are capable of killing millions of people in one detonation, in a matter of microseconds. We also removed mountaintops, and dug deep holes – that are miles across – in our search for fuel and minerals and ores. We've polluted our landscape and much of our precious water reserves and we have destroyed large forested areas for lumber, resources and for farm land.

Even though we have not yet reached the limits of our water resources, these limits certainly loom on the horizon. Many countries are dependent on desalination of brackish and salt water for their supply of potable water. The four billion people living in the developing countries are hungry for water, food and energy. Their energy needs will be growing exponentially within the coming decades, energy consumption is expected to grow fifty percent over the next two-and-a-half decade.

As civilization grows, so will the demand for food and water. roughly fifty percent of all fresh water usage in the world is spent on food production. The diminishing of aquifers and other sources of fresh water will become an ever more pressing matter. The thirst for water, energy and food will be growing exponentially and all of these issues are connected. Humanity could tackle these issues by creating immense world spanning projects in increasing energy production and addressing water usage and working towards solutions that alleviate stress on aquifers and other fresh water sources needed for human activities.

Instead of building pipelines that transport oil, we could build pipelines that transport desalinated water. A much more elegant, safe and worth wile solution to many of our problems. We have the means for creating a future in transportation that is both plentiful and free of emissions, if only we would combine our efforts to actually do it. Restoring the hydrological cycle is tremendously important.

One of the best ideas to combat carbon emissions is called Fee and Dividend, which is supported by James Hansen and groups like the 350 organization and the Citizens Climate Lobby that propose to put a fee on carbon at the mine or the well. The government subsequently distributes these funds on an even basis to its citizens. As the price for carbon-based products rises it will be offset by increased income distributed to the people, who will decide what to do with that money. Some people will start to look for cheaper alternatives, which could encourage the development of non-polluting, energy technologies. Because this carbon fee would also extends to the ports of entry, people importing goods with a high carbon footprint would pay a fee as well, thus creating a cascade effect on a global scale.

Fee and Dividend will be more effective than Cap and Trade. To be quite frank, taxing the well is a far better means of slowing down the consumption of carbon, since the cost of producing carbon-based fuels will become less profitable. It also forces the oil and energy companies to develop new strategies in order for their businesses to remain viable. If they are able to adapt, they deserve to survive.

Seeking new strategies and avenues leading to a sustainable way of energy production has to be one of the major subjects of this new "Global Manhattan Project". The way we produce energy has to change significantly. We have to get rid of Coal, Gas and Petro-leum based power plants if we want the ecosystem to survive. Carbon based energy generation needs to be decreased aggress-ively. In order to achieve this, we have to explore more avenues than just Solar, Wind, Hydro and Geothermal. We need to include the densest possible energy source as well: nuclear.

The new "Global Manhattan Project"

Generation IV nuclear reactors are not being built because they only exist on paper, and the regulations regarding new nuclear reactors are restrictive. We have to clear regulatory pathways and tie the government back into the field as a primary stakeholder for the benefit of the people. There are some brilliant concepts and designs ready to be tested, however these cannot be tested due to the non-transparent and high-cost pathways that lie ahead. Once these hurdles are removed, we can actually build reactors and test them. Then we can get the empirical evidence, the data, knowledge and understanding required to prove the merit of each design.

The MSR, WAMSR and LFTR designs are especially interesting, the propensity to turn nuclear waste into megawatts and megatons into megawatts is something we simply cannot overlook. These two designs could be a boon for humanity. Especially with their intrinsic propensity to desalinate large amounts of brackish and salt water through the use of waste heat. We have to look into these designs and test them in the near future.

The development of thermo nuclear fusion is an ongoing quest to try to harness the power of the stars on Earth. If we succeed at it, we would have unlocked the greatest energy potential yet known to man: nuclear fusion. The problem with this process is that it is really hard to "smash" atoms together because nuclei are repulsive to each other. Just look at the immensity of the LHC, its sole purpose it to make particles collide, the scale of this machine and the amount of people working on it is stupefying. The trick with fusion will be getting more energy out of it, than we need to put into starting up the fusion process. We are trying to prove that it is possible with several projects like ITER or the Wendelstein 7X. If we can harness the power of nuclear fusion, several ways of doing business in the energy sector will become disrupted.

Low Energy Nuclear Reactions (LENR) is another area of a possible [yet questionable] form of energy generation. If it create low-cost energy in an incredibly small footprint. It would be an ideal solution for small sized energy grids and transportation. The problem with it is that the process is not well understood and more research needs to be done before it can be commercialized. If they ever get it to go, because no one actually knows what happens, what the products are, and what kind of reactions occur. It looks like a promising technology, yet we've only seen falsified claims so far. The pioneers in "cold fusion" have been branded snake-oil salesmen, and that's where my skepticism about this technology comes from. We are still waiting for someone to make it happen and to get it tested and reproduced by peers. LENR or "Cold Fusion" will be met with a lot of skepticism, since it's track record has been lousy so far.

There are also companies that are pushing for the realization of small fusion reactors using different principles than the Tokomak design. It is these companies that should get far more credit than they are getting now. Although many people remain skeptical about the possibility of small scale fusion or even fusion at all. Small scale fusion reactors could be used to fuel the energy needs of small communities or to propel ships, trains, airplanes or even spaceships. If one of these companies were to solve the puzzle of small scale fusion, they would be revolutionizing energy production significantly. We would leap forward.

Small Fusion Reactors could be an answer to all our energy problems, reactors the size of cargo containers, or even smaller, could propel humanity into a new age of prosperity and optimism. Nuclear Fusion has the propensity to diminish the need for Renewables and fossil fuels entirely. It is in nuclear energy all together that our future lies. We have a two tiered step up away from Renewables and fossil fuels. The first tier is embracing new nuclear and particularly MSR technology and the second tier is making sustained nuclear fusion possible and subsequently downsizing it. In effect nuclear fission processes would be the technology required to bridge the gap to a completely clean energy future.

Even though I believe that Nuclear energy will become the dominant technology in the future, renewables still have a marginal role to play in a remote or rural off-grid context.

The dark side of renewable energy is that all over the world governments are heavily investing in the application of renewable energy sources. These endeavors into the world of renewable energies have consequences for energy grids, energy prices, stability and the production of electrical and chemical waste. Also renewable growth, even though large in volume is very marginal when faced with the total sum consumption of the human species and civilization. We're talking about energy from renewable sources which is less than two percent of the total sum energy production on the world, despite years of heavy investments and subsidies.

Energy storage is considered to be the holy grail needed to set off the renewable revolution. The problem with Renewable energies, at this point, is that they aren't generating power all the time. And the issue about energy storage is that we will be engaging in a new chain of inefficiency, if this is necessary to create an energy future depending on Renewables, its disruptive nature does not have the desired effect. We have to acknowledge the fact that mass scale energy storage is improbable, wasteful and still far ahead in time. In order to combat the capricious nature of renewable energy sources, we need backup, this backup will be gas and coal. Instead of creating a more sustainable future, we would again have built a future of mass consumption of materials and waste production. We would have shifted the problem from the waste products of fossil fuels to waste products of energy capturing technologies like solar panels and windmills.

Unfortunately, wind and solar have become sacrosanct for many environmentalists who, also unfortunately, fear nuclear power. It is unpopular to question renewable technologies within the community that is fighting Anthropogenic Climate Change, many people have branded me a "renewable hater" for this. However, I do not hate renewable energy.

I question whether environmentalists like Naomi Klein or Helen Caldicott have examined the physics and have done the math. I've tried to envision a 100% renewable future, yet fail every time. Not because my calculations are incorrect, but because the demand, physics, materials, production capabilities, and calculations involved do not support the 100% renewable future hypotheses, not even by a long shot. These people are peddling non-solutions.

Energy storage has to be "relegated" to the area of transportation or small and off-grid situations.

New nuclear reactors (Generation III & IV) that can provide safe, efficient, emission-free power are often vehemently opposed by most "greens" despite their many advantages. In addition, the proponents of new designs are sometimes opposed by corporations that are content to continue to profit from making conventional nuclear plants with only minor improvements that do not equal the advantages of Generations III and IV designs. If the human race is to maintain any semblance of the civilization that the developed nations enjoy we will need an abundance nuclear energy in the struggle against climate change.

Molten Salt Reactor technology is so vastly different from what we use to create nuclear energy today, that we may call it a disruptive technology, it is revolutionary. It changes several paradigms in terms of nuclear energy production. MSR technology has passive safety features, smaller feedstock requirements, higher fuel efficiencies and ancillary benefits such as desalination and the possibility of synthetic fuel creation and that's why I would make

MSR research and development and deployment a priority in the "global Manhattan Project".

We do not know for sure, but I think there are still a lot of undiscovered scientific principles that could change our ways of doing things. Who knows what will happen if we further our understanding of quantum physics, dark energy or dark matter. There might be some fundamental answers lurking somewhere in the dark where have not yet looked. The search for new scientific understanding could unlock secrets in energy production or faster than light travel for instance. We won't know of them if we do not engage in the quest for new knowledge. Knowledge comes from jumping into the deep and the unknown. The development for new nuclear reactors for instance could be a boon for the world of chemists, material researchers and engineers. Who knows what they will come up with within the next couple of decades. We will never know if we keep stifling them and their progress, if we keep the pool of knowledge stagnant, no real progress is to be made.

Consider all of the money involved in renewable energy research and production. The Netherlands (my country) alone has invested 61 billion euro's in renewable energy over the last twenty years, and despite all this money being thrown at it, renewable energy doesn't produce more than two percent of the energy used in the Netherlands. What a waste! If we had invested the same amount of money in nuclear energy, we could have had multiple designs built and tested. Building just one reactor would easily outstrip the amount of renewable energy capacity built so far.

If we want the "*Star Trek future*" to become a reality, the one in which traveling to distant solar systems becomes a trivial matter, we are going to need nuclear energy. There's no alternative in high density energy, perhaps somewhere in the distant future we could build some sort of anti-matter or dark-matter reactor, but there's a lot of questions that need to be answered before we get to that point. In the meanwhile I will stick with the power of the strong force, the nuclear force.

Once we've solved the energy problem, we can attack our water issues more effectively. Starting with desalination efforts, water capture from air, and water transport. A network of water metering and smart water distribution could be build up to combat droughts and keep agriculture viable, helping our global civilization remain sustainable.

Simultaneously with solving the energy and water issues of our world, we need to engage more people and resources into conservation efforts. The pursuit of the highest possible energy density has yet another reason, we need to stop growing crops for energy. Areas of land currently used for the cultivation of corn, sugar cane, rapeseed, palm oil, jatropha, soy, wheat and switch grass can be given back to nature. Especially the large areas of land in the tropics used for the cultivation of biofuels should be given back to nature. We could simply leave these places alone and let nature grab it back or we could help nature a little by planting seedlings.

Forests play an incredibly important role in the hydrological cycle, something often overlooked. Therefore I suggest that we start to engage in global reforestation efforts. I think this would create just as many jobs and would mitigate manufacturing pollution and subsequently give us far more positive tradeoffs like clean air, a healthy hydrological cycle, habitats for wild animals, better agricultural practices and a healthier world all together. Mind you, being outdoors is good for you, at least that's what people always tell me when I am feeling depressed. With an increase in forests we are going to need a lot of foresters and caretakers.

It might not seem important in the context of providing energy and food, but trees are an absolutely essential part of our biosphere. Without a healthy biosphere, our civilization is unsustainable.

The new "Global Manhattan Project"

Building a civilization, more in tune with nature would be a good start. To teach children how nature works, to show them how trees grow and to engage them in a curiousness and love for nature would be a good thing. The destruction of nature and the many species has to stop and this should be an integral part of the "Global Manhattan Project".

We also have to take a look at the way we construct buildings. We are in need of new Building Principles. The materials we use, the quantities we use have a direct consequence on the Earth. We are using too much concrete and steel, and too little "renewable" wood. We are also being to wasteful with the space required for buildings. We could for instance make every roof a living roof. Instead of building roofs out of tiles or shingles, we could create roofs where plants grow, increasing the biodiversity of cities and towns and making sure that these homes are better insulated against heat or cold. Also using building living roofs would reduce the urban heat-island-effect as these roofs absorb more energy, which then gets turned into biomass, rather than infrared radiation.

We could cultivate bamboo as a building material for instance. It has a high growth rate, captures a lot of CO_2 and can be used to create construction beams, wall panels, and window frames. We could also use other organic materials to reinforce a more sustainable way of building new homes, shops and office buildings. We can easily create buildings that use far less energy to keep warm or cool and are more in tune with the natural surroundings.

All human beings have equal value regardless of creed or color. The notion that one's destiny is determined by the tribe in which you were born is detestable. Instead, let's adopt what we call the empathic principles and compassion principles. I'm not advocating that one should love his neighbor as is being told in the doctrines of Christ, I am not in favor of compulsory love (in line with Christopher Hitchens). However our governments should engage in these principles. They should be empathic and compassionate to their people. They should take care of everyone.

Governments should be in the business of giving everyone the chance to build a meaningful existence based on personal development, and should give aid whenever necessary.

An essential part in this new project to save civilization is tailor made education for everyone. Education should be free at all levels. And entering education should be unbarred. It does not matter if you are interested in science or the arts or the humanities or languages. Education on all levels should be available for all people. Access to solid and tailor made education will raise human potential. Attaining a form of excellence could spur people on to new heights. Among the educators should be coaches, people who understand how to nourish the capacity for understanding and skepticism and how to seed an appetite for wonder in the minds of the students.

Instead of only treating the sick, we could also take care of each other's health. Sports facilities, Periodic checkups, genetic analysis to look for possible ailments that can be prevented, true health care instead of sick care. Current health care, not the one I mean, is a giant costs and profit machine. Many countries have health systems in which expensive treatments are only available to those who can pay for it. This notion nauseates me. People have to pay for health care insurance and still have to pay part of their treatment. In some countries health care is outdated or extremely plain and rudimentary. Yet it is my contention that every human being deserves the same high standard in medical care, regardless of wealth, position, creed or color.

Wouldn't it be amazing if top class health care was available for everyone, with routine checkups, no bounds in medical insights, full medical innovation and progress, the search for medicine not based on the highest profitability, but to find cures for all kinds of sicknesses and ailments, even the ones that are less profitable. This new health care system would not be limited to just countries but would span the entire world. If one were to become sick, and needed to go to an specialist in South Africa or Venezuela, no problem. One would be put on a carbon neutral plane, visit the specialist, enjoy a brief vacation and afterwards return home. People from all over the world would work together in joined efforts to find new cures, to become more knowledgeable about the human species and all its intricacies.

In Japan, some people are working on robots because there could be a shortage of people to take care of the sick and the elderly. However, the elderly often yearn for human interaction. In the Netherlands, many budgets for the care of the elderly have been cut, resulting in fewer nurses and less human interaction. Personally, I would advocate human to human interaction, not robotics. Why build thousands of robots when thousands of people from all around the world want to do meaningful things for other humans?

We must take care of each other, and we must reject Darwinist capitalism – "*the survival of the fittest*". The struggle to keep up with the ever growing stresses of monetary squabbles and debts. Many of us are living with debt, debt collection is a vicious business, keeping people subdued and in trouble. Many people cannot cope and eventually become homeless. Many people are homeless to begin with, due to their unfortunate lot in life, it was determined for them by birth. Where's the morality in that?

It isn't right or proper that people with problems are not being cared for. Whether it be people with mental illnesses, or people having trouble with keeping jobs, it does not matter. In order to maximize the human potential, we have to acknowledge that no one can be left behind (not to be confused with the school-program). There are always possibilities for these people to become happy again, and we need to provide these possibilities. We can help anyone if we chose to, we simply do not do it in the current context. It is a rat race, either you keep up, or you get squashed. This grinding people into a pulp has to change.

In order to change these paradigms we have to start thinking about things that are now considered to be controversial. Imagine capping everyone's income at $300,000 - still a staggering sum of money. Each dollar above 300.000 would go to a fund that would be distributed to those in the lowest income brackets all the people or even better, to provide everyone with a job with decent wages, far above levels of subsistence. This is hypothetical, but wouldn't it be better than the way that wealth is being distributed today.

People work for companies and make sure that these companies succeed, part of the profit is distributed to the shareholders, another part goes to the corporate executives and the rest goes into a bank account. The people don't benefit from the profit, the only thing they get in return is a job. In many companies jobs (people) are sacrificed at the expense of making more profit. Either their jobs are being off-shored to countries that allow employers to pay extremely low wages, or these jobs completely terminated. This isn't fair, nor proper.

Instead of subsidizing big corporations, we should tax them, especially the ones that pollute our climate and the ones that only reward their shareholders and executives.

Instead of making big corporations being run by corporate executive officers, we could democratize these big companies. Using referendums among the workers in order to find out what the best course for the company would be. Making it a fairer enterprise, looking out for its workers rather than using them. Perhaps we should subsidize the creation of corporations that pay their employees in part with company stock, or worker/customer-owned companies, commonly known as co-ops.

A person would really get a sense of belonging and would be highly motivated to work for this company, since its success will be also his or her success! "*Democratize the enterprise*" – Richard Wolff

This course would also mean that we need to start changing the stock markets. It would become a new form of economy in which the people are the beneficiaries of the success of companies, no longer the venture capitalistic risk takers that could doom the future of a company and all its employees out of greed. Instead newly styled companies would be build up with an idea that a community has to benefit from it, rather than a couple of rich people. I would also love the idea of companies being in existence not to tailor mass consumption, but to innovate and create wonderful and durable and new technologies.

It is safe to assert that water, food, forests and copious amounts of energy are the most important metrics for the survival and well being of the human species.

I am aware that it costs a lot of money to embark on these scientific adventures, but economics really are too bothersome to address and to be quite frank, I think economics, ideological and doctrinal issues *do not matter* in the struggle for survival and progress.

The Chinese expect to be building modular nuclear reactors for 2 billion each, which is peanuts compared to many of the programs, including military, that have little or nothing to do with the survival of our species.

If we can do the *"stuff"* we do with the LHC or with ITER or in places like Oak Ridge National Laboratories, why can't we truly progress? We should! Regardless of the money involved... The quest for truth, knowledge and understanding are more important than the mundane monetary squabbles of our insignificant civilization in light of the cosmic scale, not only because of its practical value, but because it is the one thing that truly unlocks the human capacity for understanding the fundamental questions. I think that scientific progress, whatever field it is in, is far more enthralling than the insignificant and stupid drudgeries of economics and geopolitics.

We have done it before, look for instance at the International Space Station. It might not be the best or cheapest way to do science in space, but bear with me. The ISS has been put together and is constantly being used by astronauts from many different countries. Countries that are antagonists and enemies on Earth, are united in a space endeavor. We have to use Russian Soyuz rockets launched from Kazakhstan to get there. Soyuz carries people, experiments, new equipment and supplies from the space agencies NASA, ESA, JAXA, Roscosmos and CSA to the ISS. The ISS is the showpiece of the future. It shows us that we can unite despite our petty terrestrial differences, we can set our differences aside and work together to achieve a common goal. There is no strife or war in the International Space Station which is orbiting Earth, scientists from all over the world work together for the acquisition of knowledge and the betterment of life on our planet. This is what I take away from the ISS, other than the pictures and the videos, if it can be done out there in space, it can be done down here on Earth.

Retrospect & conclusions

You've reached the final chapter of my first book, and I thank you for hanging in there. I won't pretend that it has been exciting to read, I hope others will judge it as being interesting and engaging. I've presented you with my opinions and thoughts, which are based on evidence with an occasional sprinkling of intuition. However, because I hate taking things on faith, I always try to find out what others have discovered. If the evidence doesn't support my premise, I check my reasoning.

Because I don't want you to take what I've written at face value, I have written an extensive appendix that contains some reading, listening and viewing recommendations. I hope you will make use of them. There is an enormous wealth of information out there that is freely available to you, go out there and get it! I would like you to make up your own mind, use your critical faculties. Look at the evidence presented to you by people and organizations in various fields of science.

Sometimes I can't stop being depressed; the specter of despair is always present. But that isn't that strange because I have been treated for clinical depression for fourteen years, so writing about the future stirs a dystopian cloud in my head. I realized that there are many reasons to be hopeful about the future and I hope we can reason ourselves out of the mess we've created. There is hope because there are many people who are inquisitive, compassionate and driven. We can leave this place better than we found it, and I hope to help make that happen with my own small contributions.

I'm no authority on the topics I've covered, nor will I ever claim to be, but I care deeply about humanity and our world. I love the notion that we are explorers – not destructors – who can venture into unknown territories and discover new wonders. My journey has led me to some depressing conclusions, but also to some optimistic ones. Nevertheless, dystopia is coming if we don't address our shortcomings and keep riding the chariot of greed. We need to become far more skeptical about the claims that people make and look with a keen eye at the processes around us.

Some people think that Climate Change or Anthropogenic Climate Change is "not that big of a deal". Emitting green house gasses through anthropogenic processes has upset the carbon cycle, and this means that we have increased concentrations of important, heat trapping, gases like carbon dioxide and methane. As a result, we can now deduce scientifically that dangerous effects have been put into the pipeline. When these effects precisely will occur is not known, but we can assert with a reasonable degree of certainty that they will occur before this century is over.

We have learned that some disastrous effects might occur that have been caused by ACC, the most dire of which being Ocean Acidification and the impending demise of almost all ocean life, not to mention increased wildfires and famine, decreased fresh water availability, sea-level rise and the implosion of a society due to shortages, mass migrations and political instability.

It has also become clear that we can expect the biosphere to implode, the possible extinction of aforementioned photosynthetic life forms will have a cascading effect on life in the oceans and on the land. The Permian Extinction, which occurred 250 million years ago, exemplifies this and serves as a reminder.

In the meantime, we're hunting precious animals to the brink of extinction and are destroying others' habitats. Hundreds of thousands of square kilometers of oxygen-producing and carbon-capturing forests are being clear-cut just to make a buck.

The denudation of our world has to be curbed down tremendously. We're headed for a giant crash, as soon as commodities run low, prices go up. Many don't realize that oil, for instance, has been a commodity over which to start wars. I'm going to take it one step further, water is going to be a commodity that is going to fall into the hands of regimes and criminal elements and will only be available to those fortunate enough to either have enough money or to have been born on the right side. These abhorrent things are already becoming a reality in countries like Pakistan, India and Bangladesh.

Consider Saudi Arabia, it is headed for a big crunch because they have usurped natural resources and made a big living out of it, but their wells will run dry, also remember that their oil reserves have been prospected and it is well known that they will only last for a couple of decades. What is their exit-strategy? Will they be able to keep their populace at rest as soon as the wells run dry and their country goes bankrupt? And how are they going to manage this?

As we run out of energy sources like gas and oil, we're nearing a new resource crash. In the meanwhile, the developing countries are building new power plants, particularly gas- and coal-fired. On the other side of the spectrum, environmentalists are vouching for a 100 percent "*renewable energy future*", which I will classify as an unreachable utopia, for which the push came far too late.

As our water resources are becoming increasingly stressed, energy and water are going to be intertwined more than ever. The diminishing of our water supplies will force us to invest more time and attention to water management, water consumption and the desalination of water. This is going to require vast amounts of energy, just as it is going to cost us a lot of energy to get carbon sequestered again, as Alex Cannara proposes (see appendix).

Efficiency is the specter that haunts the renewable technologies. As I did the math, I concluded that renewables will not be able to satiate a world energy demand equivalent to 250.000 TWh, not by a long-shot. It's obvious that the government authorities who decided to push these "solutions" never understood their downsides and never "ran their numbers".

By investing a lot of time and money in renewable energy, people are being misled in thinking that we can build a renewable future, which I submit to you is not possible given the constraints physics and the Earth have put on us.

Even worse, this all-in renewable course will cost us too much money, materials, and effort while not it has no chance of eliminating fossil fuels, which by the way is more than 90% of the total energy consumption in the world.

Nuclear energy, on the other hand, has been proven to be very safe and reliable. Its dark sides are completely overshadowed by stupid habits from human beings themselves: drinking, smoking, driving around i.e. *burning stuff...* These three combined trump nuclear energy by a million times, *each year*, and this juxtaposition is justified as nuclear energy is being haunted by a stigma, an irrational and unjustified cloud of fear and hatred. The people that are fighting nuclear energy are welcome to contact me and get a firm brush-up of the real numbers and "*death-prints*" in the world, nuclear is somewhere at the bottom.

Although I've been skeptical about nuclear power, I did a 180 after reading about its many proven advantages and it's excellent safety record, of which there is abundant evidence.

Not long ago I was investigating ways to create a completely green and "off-grid" home, and after a few months of exhaustive research, I figured that that feat alone is quite difficult to achieve if you want to maintain a comfortable standard of living. But when you elevate this practice from the home-scale to the city-scale, the scale of a country or even the world you start to recognize that our energy problems are far bigger than you might initially have thought.

The main issue is that more than ninety percent of our energy consumption is fossil fueled and that renewables (not counting hydro) is less than a percent, and even though solar is growing with 40 to 50 GW per annum and wind is growing with equal figures, these figures are insignificant on a global scale, translated into percentages these are tenths of a percent, and this despite all the subsidies, a multi-billion dollar trade, worth nothing.

Only nuclear energy can displace coal and gas. Given its efficiency, safety, and reliability, it is madness to avoid expanding this potent technology. In America, just their four newest reactors generate more energy than the entire fleet of solar installations, and unlike wind and solar, they do it 24/7. In addition, companies in China will soon be building new, super-efficient, reactors like the MSR that ran successfully in the US for 22,000 hours in the 60s.

The ability to help with our water troubles, the alleviation of impending the commodity crashes, the catalyst for cancer research and medical applications and a vital piece in the quest for space exploration is still being mucked down, this has to stop.

We must also improve the essential arteries through which the life-juice of civilization runs: Transportation, which is fueled almost exclusively by the combustion economy. Huge volumes of gas and oil are being produced and transported to keep our civilization going while we conveniently ignore the fact that we are flooding the air with greenhouse gases and harmful particulates. We must convert these carbon-burners into the vehicle that only relies on electricity. With new battery and nuclear technologies, we can make a significant step toward drastically reducing the emissions created by all modes of transportation.

BEV manufacturers like Tesla, BMW, and Nissan are already pioneering into the world of electrical transportation. Also the Airbus E-fan is a testament for the idea that we need to "*decarbonize*".

I also examined the idea of the "*Hydrogen-Economy*" and I submit to you that this is not going to work either. Not because the technology doesn't exist, but because it will require vastly more energy than we would need by "*simply*" electrifying our future. The amount of conversion steps required to make the hydrogen economy make it too inefficient and not interesting enough if saving humanity is required. The sum-total energy required to create the hydrogen-economy is too big.

In terms of energy consumption hydrogen will always cause demand to double or triple, simply because of its inherent inefficiency and that's why this ludicrous idea needs to be abandoned for the sake of solving the emissions problem as quickly as possible.

If we do not change our ways, if we keep burning and consuming, we will end up in a situation in which the dystopia will become complete. Before our civilization collapses in its entirety, there will be much strife and instability, people who usurp all power, fascistic movements that can claim power. The instability will lead to refugee crises of unimaginable proportions like the one we are currently seeing in Europe. No one will stay put if no water, food or medical services are available anymore. We all want to live in stability, and I won't blame anyone for seeking it.

Retrospect & conclusions

Xenophobia is one of the most primordial causes of antagonism and violence. Perhaps it is hardwired into our brains: Fear of the unknown. These modes have given rise to religions and nationalisms and in term evolved into ideological antagonisms of any kind. It has been the catalyst behind movements like the NSDAP, the KKK, and ISIS. Reactionary forces fueled by ideological absolutist interpretations, set out to gain dominion over others, in order to "*protect*" their own tribe and create "*stability*".

And it gets even more complex as many other factors come into view (I'm now taking it through from a reviewing stance). Religious belief in this regard is a catalyst and mostly a source of much hardship and instability. Of course, other factors can lead to suffering, but they are almost always amplified if religion is the motivating factor, as with the Arabic Spring, the war in Syria and Iraq, and terrorist actions all over the world. Unquestionable belief and faith are pathways to the dark side of human nature.

"*Many of these people really believe what they say they believe*" – Sam Harris

"*Those who can make you believe absurdities can make you commit atrocities*" – Voltaire

Because of the religious abuse of children and the terroristic attacks generated by malignant faiths, I've become an outspoken anti-theist. Consider the attack on Charly Hebdo and the November 13, 2015, bombings in Paris, and the many deaths precipitated by religious zealots in many other countries. The writings and words of the late Christopher Hitchens have persuaded me to adopt this stance.

Although I will work hard to eliminate religious dogma, I know I won't live long enough to see my efforts bear fruit. This goal can be best achieved by the rapid expansion of knowledge-sharing, and by urging people to require evidence for every claim regardless of its source, including religion.

Consider the beautiful views astronauts get, the amazing vistas of our little blue orb, the pale blue dot, no borders are visible from up there, our non-significance on a cosmic scale makes all this religious hoopla and terror ridiculous.

I'm confident that Daniel Dennett's proposal of teaching comparative religion [and religious history in context] will be an excellent start to erode the base of religion, the base being future generations of children. Children are skeptics... They will be able to figure it out on their own if we present them with evidence.

In my opinion, religions are evil ideologies that promote obedience, self-denial, non-thinking and encourage xenophobia, which is often used to justify the committing of repugnant acts and atrocities.

In contrast, to engage in science is to engage in a thoughtful, inspiring adventure. In science, we formulate a theory and then test it with other scientists to see if the theory is confirmed by all or rejected by evidence. Reproducibility means that other scientists must be able to get the same result repeatedly in order for a theory to be accepted.

We have been given a treasure, a great vault of discoveries undiscovered: the stupefying beauty of our Earth in terms of physics, chemistry, geology and biology. We can enjoy it for many generations to come, and make more sense of it. If we can survive our follies, the age of discovery will never be over. We are part of a universe too beautiful to be ignored, and we must try to make sense of the time machine that envelops our tiny bubble of existence.

As a scientist, you could be traveling around the world to look at a great variety of things, but one could also be engaged in the small, looking tirelessly into a microscope all day. One could also engage in other inspiring endeavors like looking for life in outer space at institutes like SETI and NASA, or looking upwards to the skies for new discoveries in the universe, but also going down into deep oceans in order to look for undiscovered life or other possible interesting finds. To look at life, the elements, our world, the seas and the skies, to look beyond the horizon into space, to see the galaxies, the nebulas and the supernovae, to see the awe-inspiring majesty all around us, to go look for it... that is to be engaged in science and discovery, that is to extend your horizon, that is to push into the boundaries of the unknown, to discover new vistas. Without science it would be impossible, without it wonder would have far less meaning, science is amazing, science is inspiring!

Technological progress is ongoing. The technologies that we are developing today are a hundred fold better than they were decades ago. Look at Airplanes, TV's, Computers, World Wide Networks, refrigerators, 3D printers, Medicine, etc. Yet we have also stunted some important technologies, like BEV's and new Nuclear technologies. We need to restart these technological advances, the BEV's are already progressing into the future, thanks to Tesla, Nissan and BMW and a couple of other manufacturers like Sakti3 for instance, the battery "guys". Nuclear, however, is set to go ahead, yet many political hurdles need to be taken before we can build these new forms of energy generation, possible technological solutions to many of our problems.

The renewed treks into space will show the full measure of our technical prowess and fortitude. When we abandon our carbon-based economy and switch to nuclear power, we will be able to push for the moon and mars and the planets beyond and this is to show promise and seed a sense of optimism in humanity. Leaving our solar system and reaching another will mark the coming of age of human civilization. This is the ultimate challenge for humanity.

Highway to Dystopia

Do I mean to say everyone should engage in science? I do not, I want you to make up your own mind. One can and should be able to shape one's own destiny, there are enough pleasurable and meaningful things to do. The arts, the humanities, languages and the Alpha studies all have equal value since they address a multitude of human capacities that can make this place more beautiful and worthwhile. To create art or to take care of other people or animals or nature is a beautiful calling as well and we are in need of all sorts of people engaging in a multitude of different activities to make this world a better place.

It has become clear that on the crossroads of Science, Religion, Politics, and Technology, we've taken the expressway, the "Highway to Dystopia". We're on a steady course to oblivion. It has become apparent that the mentioned subjects have strong correlations with each other. Religion and Politics are closely intertwined, even in countries that claim to be secular, religion grossly abuses vast amounts of people and regulations. Corporations do the same, malign ideologies do the same. Technology and science and Faith are constantly at odds with each other as Religious people seek new *hidey-hole* for their deities to hide in while Science keeps expanding the realms of knowledge. Technology has given us the opportunity to become more advanced and to start tapping into untold resources and, therefore, has become a force for evil as well, the driving force behind a possible impending extinction. It is in human nature that the answers to our problems can be found, the erosion of greed and antagonism and xenophobia are necessary for us to survive.

Technology can also save us, but it requires an overhaul of all subjects mentioned before. Not because they (Politics, Religion, Science, and Technology) have to change, but because people have to change. Instead of taking everything on faith, or let the "*market decide*", we have to learn how to be doubtful and be skeptical and to use our critical faculties in order to find a course that is more in tune with reality and provides long-term stability.

I started this book by telling you that one of my creeds is: "It is up to you to educate yourself." I want to add two more: "Always require evidence" (thank you Richard Dawkins) & "Never refrain from calling bullshit, bullshit".

It might sound arrogant or even aggressive but I stand by it, and this is essential because there are a lot of people who either want to lie to/and mislead other people for their own gain, or those who want to curb free-speech because they think it hurts other people's feelings or might illicit an unfavorable or even deadly response.

Just as we make our own meaning in life, we make our own meaning as a civilization. Will it be the meaning of compassion and empathy, of technological progress, of discovery, of using logic and our critical faculties to do what is right? Or will we continue on this course of attrition, subjugation, and destruction?

Unless we change our ways, our attitudes and our priorities, we will be in deep trouble long before the Sun writes an end to life on earth. In a sense, the sun is involved with our current state of affairs. As the Earth's mechanisms for capturing and radiating the sun's heat are at an imbalance, the sun keeps warming up our Earth. Without green house gasses, our Earth would be a very cold place. Atmospheric carbon dioxide levels have been stable at around 280 ppm for 7000 years, but our carbon-hungry society, which has been nurtured by the Industrial Revolution, has caused the carbon dioxide levels to rise. By 1950, the concentration had increased to 320 ppm, but since then, it has rocketed up to 400, and 450 ppm is widely acknowledged to result in an absolute disaster. We are already out of bounds by 50 parts per million of CO_2 in the atmosphere and the debt will be paid in a couple of decades or maybe even years: increased heat and acidity in the oceans, droughts, fires, famine, civil strife, extinction...

Highway to Dystopia

Will we be able to avert this? Will we be able to achieve a higher sense of civilization, one that takes care of everyone, regardless of the costs in financial terms? Addressing the issues of humanity and the health of the earth needs to be a holistic and comprehensive approach. We cannot expect everything to fall into place by just introducing one silver bullet to our problems and then keep a steady course, keep consuming and keep antagonizing. We need to change several paradigms. Human civilization and the health of the world's ecosystems are directly tied to each other.

We are the most destructive species ever to have lived on the face of the earth and it is deeply worrying. Why are we mortgaging our children's future? I find this utterly detestable and feel responsible for it.

As noted before, only international cooperation and a massive effort to replace the burning of fossil fuels with nuclear power that is allied with education, conservation, and government support will give us a chance. Moving quickly and wisely must become worldwide priorities. To delay while we argue about costs will be tantamount to suicide. And if we fall back on inefficient "solutions" like those that Germany adopted, we will crush our hopes for the future.

Free speech and freedom of thought are paramount and un-touchable, no idea is above ridicule, especially those that aren't true.

Everybody has to be given access to the internet, unrestricted. The internet will help connect people from all over the world, helps to share ideas, helps to propagate knowledge and I am confident that it helps with the accelerated reduction of religiosity.

It is to become more knowledgeable, intelligent and provident about our (food) consumption because we are reaching the limits of our water resources and these resources are vital to the production of food and the sustainability of our civilization.

I can't fathom how a technologically advanced country like Germany has fooled itself into believing that it would be able to sustainably provide energy to a country of tens of millions on renewable energy alone. Get the data, check the physics and do the math and conclude that it is impossible.

It is to acknowledge the need to minimize the use of fossil fuels and to mitigate the use of them aggressively in order for the biosphere to be able to become healthy again.

It is to help the reforestation efforts and stop the destruction of nature, give back areas of land for the development of forests and involve people in this process in a working capacity.

It is to stop using crops for energy i.e. to turn them into carbohydrates to burn in engines.

It is to acknowledge that nuclear energy is a clean and safe force for good in this world by providing energy for humanity, by delivering us isotopes for a wide variety of uses, by becoming a massive contributor of the creation of potable water and by providing a solution for aquifer replenishment and carbon sequestration.

It is to supercharge innovation in transportation since it is a major source for emissions. The future belongs to electrical vehicles in the water, on the land, and in the air. Globalization will increase and so will transportation.

It is stop dividing people, especially in terms of religious or ethnic division. Also diminish the blaming for non-issues such as the amount of melanin in one's skin and/or one's sexual preferences. Humanity in the cosmological context is totally insignificant in order for these mundane, and often idiotic, squabbles to have any weight, at all...

In the 21st century, our news is still being dominated by suicide attacks, refugees, disputed lands and building walls. And this is incredibly frustrating.

It is to stop the nonsensical conflicts and unite in order to reach for the stars and planets beyond our horizon. Because there is where our future lies, perhaps not for you and me but certainly for future generations. If we are to become a civilization which lasts peacefully and harmoniously for a very long time, it is up we must go.

These are arbitrary and subjective statements, it is up to you to agree with them or not. As a matter of fact, I do not expect everyone to agree with me nor do I want them to. To those who disagree with me, I beg you to examine your beliefs and see what evidence, if any, supports them. Free inquiry, evidence-based thinking, rationalism, and science are the only way to save the Earth and our Biosphere from being destroyed [by humanity].

Economics are giant wheels of Greed, these wheels turn because there's consumption. Consumption is the base for all monetary exchanges on this world. As we see less regulation in the marketplace of trade, we see the disparity between haves and have-nots grow. Not only in the third world, but also in the developed countries. Wages are a burden that could be cut or outsourced, all these things happen to maximize efficiency and profit. Greed will be the driving force for much hardship and the un-fulfillment of lives. Politics in this regard doesn't help either, because in times of recession most of these choose the path of austerity, by this they increase the pressure on the commoner. I am a proponent of Keynesianism because it doesn't hurt people like you and me. It might make life for the government a little more difficult, but they are there to help the people, right?

Retrospect & conclusions

I would love to see a reversal of the privatization of essential industries and energy companies and healthcare. To get these out of the clutches of the greedy and to make them for the common good again. Let's put an end to the "*monstrum*" that has become the "*market*" where profit is the goal, regardless of the social cost. The same can be said for the revival of labor-unions. Moving the power back from the market-place to the election boot.

The reality we face is more severe than any problem humans have encountered since we stopped walking like apes and stood tall upon our feet. It is time to let go of ideology. Extinction is creeping closer every day while we fail to change our ways.

The rich History of our world also provides ample reason to be Optimistic, consider all the amazing and often enthralling discoveries made in Biology, Cosmology, Physics, and Chemistry. The contribution of technological advances, to peer into space, to make sense of the basic elements of our universe, the list is endless. It makes me optimistic, it tells me that we have crafted tools by which we can find and share new knowledge.

In conclusion, as an avid proponent of Egalitarianism and Humanism, I believe that all humans have equal value, all humans are equal. I think it is justified to keep working towards a more prosperous society for all humans on Earth with equal chances for everyone, no matter where they are born, what their sexuality is, no matter the amount of melanin in their skin.

I hope that this book will be read by people who are inquisitive and who like to make up their own minds and apply their critical faculties. Not only has this book been written to inspire them to engage in science, but also to inspire them to support the scientific endeavor and to remain curious and to go and look at nature and to visit museums and to watch science-related programs and to keep reading about it and finally and most importantly to keep sharing ideas! We are all torch carriers for science and reason.

Change won't bring about a utopia, that will never happen, but we can make things better if we stay committed to it.

"For goodness sake" – Daniel Dennett

Free your mind. Get serious. The end is almost in sight.

Appendix I

Reading, listening, and viewing recommendations

Anthropogenic Climate Change and *Education* and *Secularism* and *Anti-Theism* and *Science* are the main subjects of this book. They are connected to each other through overlaps in culture, politics, and economics. I want you to become a skeptic and immerse yourself in the realm of free inquiry and to join us in the world of reason!

In this appendix you will find a couple of reading, listening and viewing recommendations concerning all these subjects. Most of the people and organizations listed in this appendix have a profound influence in my writing and some even greatly inspired me to engage in this endeavor, although they might not know it, nor ever will.

You might like or dislike some of the people that I've listed here, for any reason. I do not care because it is a subjective list, it is a case of taste or some might say a lack thereof. I am in no way affiliated to any of them, none of them have paid me to get in here, I've constructed this appendix on my own merit, by my own taste.

If you want to know how I build my cases and are interested in my own continued literary adventures you can drop by at:

thecloudedhead.blogspot.com

Facebook: thies.beckers

Twitter: @thiesbeckers

The list on the following pages is build up in random order, however some individuals have deserved their top spot. If this book has in some way inspired you to embark or continue on a pursuit of knowledge, please take a look at the people mentioned below. They are far more fascinating, clear, inquisitive, knowledgeable and eloquent than I am.

These people deserve all the attention they can get, why? Because they matter!

Expect many more great and inspiring individuals in the appendix of my next book... This song isn't over!

Christopher Hitchens was, in my opinion, the best orator of my time. He was a brilliant writer, journalist and debater. He could debate multiple opponents simultaneously and win. His discourse was near perfect and he was one of the greatest influences in my writing. I fall utterly short at his knowledge, his style, eloquence and command of the English language. His brilliant books are available in fine bookstores everywhere. I admit, I sometimes HAVE TO watch his debates and interviews to get my own prosaic writing engine going, I certainly hope it shows and does something to honor his greatness.

"Hitch 22", "God is not great", "Letters to a young contrarian"

Watch this video on YouTube, it enthralls me every time I watch it ""If you want to be awe inspired.." (Christopher Hitchens)"

Raif Badawi for his hardship in the face of tyranny, a very brave man, set out to improve the world for his fellow human beings, he is currently being corporally punished by religious zealots for being an advocate of secularism and blogging about it.

www.amnesty.org.uk/tags/raif-badawi

Carl Sagan the world-renowned cosmologist and critical thinker. Read and watch anything made by him. He was a great champion for reason. Cosmos is one of the greatest science documentaries ever on TV.

Richard Dawkins (one of my personal favorites) is an evolutionary biologist and professor emeritus at Oxford University in England. He has authored several bestselling books. And is an avid advocate for using science and reason. Please take a look at the website of the Richard Dawkins Foundation for Science and Reason. Also watch "The Unbelievers", an amazing film about his and Lawrence Krauss's efforts to advocate science and reason all across the world.

www.richarddawkins.net
www.ted.com/spealers/richard_dawkins

He also has a YouTube Channel called "Richard Dawkins Foundation for Reason & Science". Most interesting are his video's on evolution, I highly recommend them.

"The selfish gene", "An appetite for wonder", "The blind watchmaker", "The god delusion"

George Orwell "The animal farm", "1984"

Stephen Hawking: GENIUS "A brief history of time"

Neil DeGrasse Tyson is an Astrophysicist and Cosmologist. He is also the director of the Hayden Planetarium in New York and another champion for science. "NDT" is one of the most eloquent science communicators in the world. A couple of excellent video's featuring him are "the storytelling of science" with a panel of scientists and science-related people and "The poetry of science" with Richard Dawkins. He has also presented the television documentary "Cosmos: A Spacetime Odyssey" and beautifully presented the wonders of our solar system in "The inexplicable universe – Unsolved mysteries".

Lawrence Krauss is an astrophysicist, a teacher, and a brilliant speaker. He has authored several bestselling books and occasionally engages in debates and discussions about a variety of subjects including science and religion.

https://origins.asu.edu/
http://krauss.faculty.asu.edu/

"The physics of Star Trek", "A universe from nothing"

Ayaan Hirsi Ali Ik had je graag als buurvrouw gehad, een brainiac next door. She's a real hero, a champion!

Founder of the AHA Foundation.

"Infidel", "Nomad", "Heretic"

Daniel Dennett is a great contemporary philosopher whose countenance would fit right in with the great philosophers of old. A kind looking bespectacled man featuring a magnificent father Christmas beard, a man whose ideas, reasoning and kindness are a gift to mankind.

Dennett has a founded a great organization that helps people from "the cloth" to find help coping with their growing unbelief. Yes, there are preacher men and women who start to question their own faith, start to disbelief or do not believe in god anymore.

"TCP was established in 2011 to provide a safe haven of protected, anonymous online community for former and active religious professionals who no longer hold to supernatural beliefs."

If you are one of them, please visit:

clergyproject.org

Highway to Dystopia

Sam Harris is someone who is often mischaracterized. I think his views are incredibly important, he dares to challenge ideas that are considered taboo. He discusses hefty and worrisome and controversial topics. He is a neuroscientist a philosopher and an author. He has founded the Project Reason foundation: "a nonprofit foundation devoted to spreading scientific knowledge and secular values in society."

www.project-reason.org
www.samharris.org

 "Letter to a Christian nation", "The end of faith"

George Erikson is a friend and a fellow activist for humanism, for secular values and smart decisions in terms of energy. He – as I – acknowledges that anthropogenic climate change poses a serious threat to the future of our world. We share the view that nuclear energy is an absolute necessity in the struggle against climate change.

He is the former Vice President of the American Humanist Association and has written several books.

http://energyrealityproject.com/nuclear-power-climate-change-warrior-for-the-21st-century/

"Time Traveling with Science and the Saints"

Alex Cannara (also a very good friend of mine) is a kind guy that can also become quite terse and strident if people spout pseudo-scientific nonsense, mostly about energy and climate change. He is a prolific nuclear proponent and is pushing for a practical solution to solve the disastrous issue of Ocean Acidification.

https://www.youtube.com/watch?v=rzoW_cVg2hE

Stephen Fry is one of my favorite actors, he has made several interesting and fascinating documentaries, one of which concerns coping with manic depression. He also authored several books and is featured in many [block busting] films.

www.stephenfry.com

Bill Nye the science guy! An engineer engaged in teaching science to the general public, he debates journalists and other public figures particularly on matters of climate change. President of the planetary society and an avid supporter of space exploration.

www.billnye.com

"Undeniable, evolution and the science of creation"

Phil Mason aka Thunderf00t is a chemist and nuclear physicist who is very active in the world of egalitarianism. He is an opponent of the new feminism movement. More importantly, though, he shares a lot of funny and interesting scientific videos on his YouTube and Patreon Channel.

J.R.R. Tolkien If you want to read amazing works of fiction, I would advise you to read the works of this grand master.

"The Hobbit", "The Lord of the Rings".

Henry Rollins for inspiring me to get the fuck going. This life isn't a smooth plane ride.

AronRa aka the Ace of Clades is Texas state director of American Atheists and a biologist. He has a YouTube channel. He travels the world speaking about biology, giving his opinion on religious matters. He also debates creationists and debunks their false claims.

http://freethoughtblogs.com/aronra/

Bill Maher For his outspokenness, he comments everything worth commenting: religion, politics, secular values, liberalism, freedom of speech, freedom of assembly, equality for women, etc., etc. He helps us keep our wits sharp.

"Dearly beloved, we are gathered here today in the presence of math, gravity, evolution and electricity, to honor brother Edward and to send the powers of Seal Team 666 to rescue him from Planet Kolob so that he can spend eternity with the kind of freethinkers he tried to hang out with on earth... So by the power granted to me by the Blair Witch, Schlemiel, Schlimazel, e pluribus mumbo jumbo, expecto patronum, su su sudio, yo mamma, I call upon the Mormon spirits to leave your body the fuck alone." – Bill Maher

Dave Rubin has a new YouTube show called ***"The Rubin Report"***. Dave receives well-known guests and has very interesting and open conversations with them. His show is particularly interesting for people who are interested in daily in-depth commentary, and open and free discussion. Do subscribe to his show, it's excellent!

"Believe in free speech? Tired of political correctness? Like discussions about big ideas? Welcome to The Rubin Report."

Richard Wolff is an emeritus economics professor who addresses economic injustices and promotes a more social economic system. I think his ideas are a first step to the "star trek" future I'm promoting.

http://www.rdwolff.org/
http://www.democracyatwork.info/

Appendix I

James Hansen is a former NASA researcher, a man who started researching the planetary science of Venus. He became, however, more interested in the planetary science of Earth and has studied it closely. He has become an activist against the factors that lead into Anthropogenic Climate Change. His activism is being fueled by the love for his grandchildren and the notion that it is morally reprehensible not to act. He's given several talks and keeps a really interesting journal online.

www.columbia.edu/~jeh1
www.ted.com/speakers/james_hansen

You can also use Google and YouTube in order to find some of the talks he has given. The one titled "James Hansen explains Climate Change and the Solution" is particularly interesting.

Michael Shermer Look up his baloney detection kit video! He also runs a magazine and website dedicated to science and skepticism:

http://www.skeptic.com

Hemant Mehta to me is "the friendly atheist" on YouTube, he comments on religious items and is a really friendly guy, he has a blog at Patheos:

http://www.patheos.com/blogs/friendlyatheist/

George Takei is an avid and outspoken champion for the LGBT community. The actor portraying the awesome Mr. Sulu is also a great and inspiring man in real life.

http://www.georgetakei.com/

Kyle Kulinski has a YouTube channel called "Secular Talk", he criticizes daily political and societal matters from a secular viewpoint. This is my daily portion of [mainly] political news. I don't read any papers nor watch much television anymore, so Kyle is basically my outlook on the world of [American] politics.

The amazing James Randi is a freethinker a skeptic and a magician. James Randi has been a skeptic of supernatural claims and has debunked a lot of them. He has a great foundation which concentrates on exposing paranormal and pseudoscientific frauds and helping educators inspiring young people to be skeptical, inquisitive and investigative.

web.randi.org

Ben Heard gave me the final push to start writing. He is a climate consultant and a nuclear energy advocate.

http://www.thinkclimateconsulting.com.au/

Tasso Azevedo is a proponent for forestation efforts and forest conservancy in Brazil. Tasso has also given an interesting talk at TED.

www.ted.com/speakers/tasso_azevedo

Patrick Stewart is an amazing individual. He played Jean-Luc Picard in Star Trek, a formative fictional character of my youth and adolescence. Later he played Charles Xavier in X-men.

What made me an even bigger fan was the episode of "Who do you think you are" in which he delved into the history of his family and discovered that his father probably and most unfortunately suffered from shellshock (now known as PTSD) and his mother had a very hard time as a result of it. I was moved to tears by his story.

He's a patron of "Refugee", a charity that takes care of women who've suffered domestic violence. He also is a supporter of "Combat Stress", a charity that takes care of ex–Soldiers suffering from PTSD and other disorders.

Harrison Ford Sure he is the awe-inspiring embodiment of Han Solo, Indiana Jones, Blade Runner, Richard Kimble and Jack Ryan *but* he is also the epic sounding voice of "THE OCEAN" and cares deeply for the environment. I played "him" countless of times, he was the face of the great heroes in my youth, and now continues to inspire people in other more pressing fields. He is not last for being the least noteworthy man in this list of inspiring fellows, he's last because this part of the book has to end with a fifty gun salute and a big bang.

http://natureisspeaking.org/theocean.html

Also participated in: "Years of living dangerously"

And upcoming in: "Star Wars Episode VII: The Force Awakens"

Appendix II

Organizations

Amnesty International does not really need an introduction. It is these non–religious organizations that are indispensable. They take care of people regardless of their respective backgrounds. Amnesty International is a human rights movement. They campaign for a world where **human rights are enjoyed by all**. They have an active contingent of approximately 7 million activists, members, and supporters all over the globe.

www.amnesty.org

Women for Women is an organization which helps women who are facing violence, marginalization, and poverty as a result of war. They help these women by empowering them and spur them on to being self–determined.

www.womenforwomen.org

Medecins sans frontieres/Doctors without borders are true hero's of humanity, they go headfirst and stand vast into areas where people are in dire need of medical attention. These people are to be applauded for their employed courage to save fellow human beings, whatever the circumstances may be!

www.doctorswithoutborders.org/

350 is a grass roots movement across the world dedicating their time to creating solutions which ensure that CO_2 levels will drop below 350 PPM.

www.350.org

Oxfam delivers emergency aid to people who have become victims of war or natural disasters.

www.oxfam.org.uk

Weforest Is an organization that tries to counter the heavy deforestation which is going on in the world. They are trying to give the reforestation movement more body.

www.weforest.org

The Planetary Society their mission statement: *"Empower the world's citizens to advance space science and exploration."* Says it all! A fantastic group of people that is sponsoring space technology projects and projects helps incubate a love for space science and exploration in children. They are the people working hard to achieve my dream of the "star trek" and "star wars" future.

www.planetary.org

WWF a great organization that works fervently for the protection of nature and to make sure that there will be a sustainable future where humans live in harmony with nature.

www.wwf.org

SETI the search for extraterrestrial intelligence. A fantastic human endeavor in space exploration, technological advancement, and science. You can actually help them by lending them the processing power of your personal computer. SETI is amazing and SETI is inspiring, they are always pushing the boundaries, trying to develop better means of looking for signs of intelligent life in outer space.

www.seti.org

Appendix III

References & Backgrounds

Most of the assertions I've made have been the culmination of years of personal research. Most of which is unscientific. As said earlier, I'm a science voyeur, I love to peek over scientist' shoulders while they are working and sharing their work. Trying to make sense of the world, I read avidly, especially on the Internet, scientifically aligned websites in particular. This list is far from complete. Take nothing at face value, investigate for yourself. This appendix will continuously be extended on my blog...

Scientific publications from NASA regarding climate change
Climate.nasa.gov
Climate.nasa.gov/faq/

Scientific journals regarding climate change
http://www.technologyreview.com/
http://www.phys.org
http://www.skepticalscience.com
http://www.aip.org
http://www.climateplace.com
http://sciencedaly.com

Cosmology
http://apod.nasa.gov/apod/

Ice sheet developments in the Arctic, Antarctic and Greenland
http://climate.nasa.gov/news/2254/
http://www.nature.com/ngeo/journal/vaop/ncurrent/full/ngeo2388.h
tml
http://www.antarctica.gov.au/about-us/publications/australian–
antarctic–magazine/2011-2015/issue–21–2011/antarctic-
science/model-simulations-investigate-totten-thinning
http://onlinelibrary.wiley.com/enhanced/doi/10.1002/2014GL0619
40/

Ogallala Aquifer depletion
http://www.meteor.iastate.edu/gccourse/issues/society/ogallala/ogal
lala.html
http://en.wikipedia.org/wiki/Ogallala_Aquifer
http://www.washingtonpost.com/blogs/wonkblog/wp/2013/09/12/h
ow-long-before-the-midwest-runs-out-of-water/

Nuclear development & information
http://hyperphysics.phy–astr.gsu.edu/hbase/hph.html
http://hyperphysics.phy–astr.gsu.edu/hbase/nucene/fusion.html
http://www.fusenet.eu
http://www.thoriumenergyreport.org/
http://fusion4freedom.us/development-of-practical-fusion-power-
plasma-jet-driven-magneto-inertial-fusion/

Nuclear issues
http://climate.nasa.gov/news/903/
http://thebreakthrough.org/index.php/issues/nuclear/nopetheres-no-
thyroid-cancer-epidemic-in-fukushima
http://unclear2nuclear.com/
http://energyrealityproject.com/letter-to-the-california-energy-
commission/
http://www.who.int/ionizing_radiation/about/what_is_ir/en/index2.
html
http://www.cfact.org/2015/02/16/the-lesson-of-fukushima-is-that-

nuclear-energy-is-safe/
http://www.ncbi.nlm.nih.gov/pmc/articles/PMC2663584/
http://www.hiroshimasyndrome.com/fukushima-accident-updates.html
http://deepseanews.com/2014/01/all-the-best-scientifically-verified-information-on-fukushima-impacts/
http://www.japantimes.co.jp/news/2014/07/31/national/science-health/experts-question-fukushima-thyroid-screening/#.VQknuOHLjA7

Possible nuclear benefits
http://energyrealityproject.com/californias-water-emergency–a-solution-worth-considering/
http://www.nei.org/Master-Document-Folder/Backgrounders/Fact-Sheets/Water-Use-and-Nuclear-Power-Plants
http://jmkorhonen.net/2013/11/29/graphic-of-the-week-the-hidden-fuels-of-renewable-energy/

Refutations of the claims: "Nuclear is not low-carbon"
http://energyrealityproject.com/point-refuted-a-thousand-times-nuclear-is-not-low-carbon/

Fossil Fuel issues
http://ocean.si.edu/gulf-oil-spill
http://en.wikipedia.org/wiki/List_of_oil_spills
http://en.wikipedia.org/wiki/Fly_ash
http://en.wikipedia.org/wiki/Ash_pond
http://en.wikipedia.org/wiki/List_of_oil_spills
http://en.wikipedia.org/wiki/Deepwater_Horizon_oil_spill
http://www.desmogblog.com/2014/10/17/nasa-confirms-2500-square-mile-cloud-methane-floating-over-american-southwest

Energy production & usage
http://www.iea.org/publications/freepublications/publication/keywo

rld2014.pdf
http://www.eia.gov/

CO2   emissions

http://www.iea.org/statistics/
http://cdiac.ornl.gov/
http://www.eia.gov/
http://www.carbonindependent.org/sources_car.htm

Water   issues

http://www.worldwatercouncil.org/
http://www.thestar.com/news/world/2015/06/19/depletion-of-worlds-underground-aquifers-raises-alarms.html
http://www.globalchange.umich.edu/globalchange2/current/lectures/freshwater_supply/freshwater.html
http://www.whoi.edu/science/B/people/kamaral/plasticsarticle.html
http://www.water.ca.gov/
http://www1.american.edu/ted/baikal.htm

http://wwf.panda.org/what_we_do/where_we_work/lake_baikal/

http://rt.com/news/186088-lake-baikal-pollution-swamp/
http://www.irkutsk.org/baikal/ecology.htm
http://www.bww.irk.ru/baikalwater/pollution.html
http://earthsky.org/earth/how-is-pollution-changing-lake-baikal

http://www.theguardian.com/environment/2014/sep/15/drought-bites-as-amazons-flying-rivers-dry-up

EPA Website

http://www.epa.gov/cleanenergy/energy-resources/refs.html

Food production

http://www.fao.org/wairdocs/lead/x6116e/x6116e02.htm

Forestation issues

http://afforestt.com/index.html

http://www.treesforthefuture.org

http://www.conservation.org/what/Pages/forests.aspx

http://wwf.panda.org/about_our_earth/about_forests/forest_conserv ation/

Technology & science blogs and websites

http://nextbigfuture.com/

http://www.technologyreview.com

http://www.worldometers.info/

http://www.newscientist.com/

http://www.madehow.com/

http://solarimpulse.com/

http://www.seia.org/research-resources/solar-industry-data

http://www.solarindustrymag.com/issues/SI1309/FEAT_05_Hazar dous_Materials_Used_In_Silicon_PV_Cell_Production_A_Primer. html

BEV & Battery developments

http://www.nature.com/nclimate/journal/v5/n4/full/nclimate2564.ht ml

http://www.greencarreports.com/

http://www.tesla.com

http://www.sakti3.com

World Stability & Safety

https://www.gov.uk/foreign–travel–advice

https://freedomhouse.org/

http://www.vox.com/2015/8/17/9164499/el-nino-2015

Bees

http://thoughtscapism.com/2015/10/14/if–you–care–about–bees– look–past–neonicotinoids/

http://journals.plos.org/plosone/article?id=10.1371%2Fjournal.pon e.0070182#abstract0

https://en.wikipedia.org/wiki/Colony_collapse_disorder
http://www.ted.com/talks/marla_spivak_why_bees_are_disappearin
g?language=en
http://journals.plos.org/plosone/article?id=10.1371%2Fjournal.pon
e.0059589
http://phys.org/news/2015-02-neonicotinoid-insecticides-impair-
bee-brains.html

Nature & Biology
http://news.nationalgeographic.com
http://en.wikipedia.org/wiki/Extinction_event
http://www.bbc.com/earth/uk
http://rt.com/news/242441-earth-facing-human-extinction/
http://en.wikipedia.org/wiki/Bonobo
http://en.wikipedia.org/wiki/Orangutan

http://animals.nationalgeographic.com/animals/mammals/oranguta
n/

http://en.wikipedia.org/wiki/Whale_shark
http://orma.com/sea-life/plankton-facts/
http://en.wikipedia.org/wiki/Monarch_butterfly
http://www.globalresearch.ca/death-and-extinction-of-the-
bees/5375684

http://en.wikipedia.org/wiki/Dodo
http://www.tigersincrisis.com/the_tigers.htm
http://ocean.si.edu/ocean-acidification
http://www.marinebio.net/marinescience/03ecology/mlplankton.ht
m

http://www.pewtrusts.org/en/about/news-
room/news/2015/03/06/bad-news-on-the-west-coast-pacific-
sardines-are-collapsing

http://elementalescapes.com/knoweverything/Coral_Reef_Extinctio
n.pdf

http://www.sciencemag.org/content/301/5635/955.short
http://www.worldwatch.org/node/5960
http://www.nhm.ac.uk/nature–online/environmental-
change/climate-impacts/coral-extinction/
http://www.cbsnews.com/news/coral-reefs-face-extinction-within-
century/

https://www.worldwildlife.org/species/whale
http://www.seethewild.org/whale–threats/
http://seaworld.org/animal-info/animal-
bytes/mammals/endangered%20whales/
http://www.worldwildlife.org/species/rhino
http://www.savetherhino.org/rhino_info/species_of_rhino

THE LETTER...

http://www.nytimes.com/interactive/2015/03/09/world/middleeast/
document-the-letter-senate-republicans-addressed-to-the-leaders-
of-iran.html